THOMSON
─────
URSE TECHNOLOGY

fessional ▪ Technical ▪ Reference

BEGINNING

C++ GAME
PROGRAMMING

MICHAEL DAWSON

INCLUDES CD-ROM

ISBN-13: 978-1-59200-205-4
ISBN-10: 1-59200-205-6
Library of Congress Catalog Card Number: 2004105652
Printed in Canada
07 08 WC 10 9 8

SVP, Thomson Course Technology PTR:
Andy Shafran

Publisher:
Stacy L. Hiquet

Senior Marketing Manager:
Sarah O'Donnell

Marketing Manager:
Heather Hurley

Manager of Editorial Services:
Heather Talbot

Acquisitions Editor:
Mitzi Koontz

Associate Marketing Managers:
Kristin Eisenzopf and Sarah Dubois

Project Editor/Copy Editor:
Cathleen D. Snyder

Technical Reviewer:
Shawn Holmes

Thomson Course Technology PTR Market Coordinator:
Amanda Weaver

Interior Layout Tech:
Susan Honeywell

Cover Designer:
Steve Deschene

CD-ROM Producer:
Arlie Hartman

Indexer:
Katherine Stimson

Proofreader:
Gene Redding

THOMSON

COURSE TECHNOLOGY

Professional ■ Technical ■ Reference

Thomson Course Technology PTR, a division of
Thomson Course Technology
25 Thomson Place
Boston, MA 02210
http://www.courseptr.com

*To my sweet, tough cookie—for all of the help,
support, understanding (and distractions) you offered.
I love you, Keren.*

ACKNOWLEDGMENTS

Every book you've ever read perpetuates a big fat lie. And I'm here to out the publishing industry's dirty little secret—books are not "by" only one person. Yes, you see only one name on book covers (including this one), but it takes a team of dedicated people to pull off the final product. Authors could not do it alone; I certainly could not have done it alone. So I want to thank all those who helped make this book a reality.

Thanks to Cathleen Snyder for her dual role as Project Editor and Copy Editor. Cathleen kept things moving along. She knew when to nudge and when to lay back. On top of coordinating everything, she looked at the book from a reader's point of view, always striving to be sure things were clear.

Thanks to Shawn Holmes, my Technical Editor. Shawn kept me honest and made sure my programs worked the way I said they did.

Thanks to Sue Honeywell, my Layout Tech, and Gene Redding, my Proofreader. Their work makes the book look good—literally.

I also want to thank Mitzi Koontz, my Acquisitions Editor, for seeing the need for this book and having the will to move it forward when there was nothing out there quite like it.

Finally, I want to thank all of the game programmers who created the games I played while growing up. They inspired me to work in the industry and create games of my own. I hope I can inspire a few readers to do the same.

ABOUT THE AUTHOR

MICHAEL DAWSON has worked as both a programmer and a computer game designer and producer. In addition to real-world game industry experience, Mike earned his bachelor's degree in Computer Science from the University of Southern California. Mike currently teaches game programming and design to students of all ages through UCLA Extension courses and private lessons. Visit his website at http://www.programgames.com to learn more or to get support for any of his books.

CONTENTS

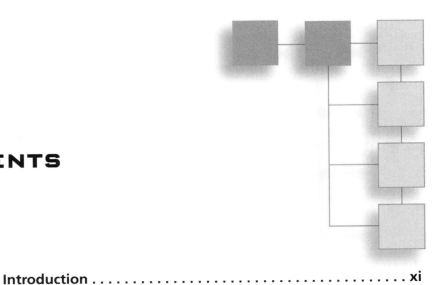

INTRODUCTION

Cutting-edge computer games rival the best that Hollywood has to offer in visual effects, musical score, and pure adrenaline rush. But games are a form of entertainment unlike any other; they can keep players glued to their monitors for hours on end. What sets games apart and makes them so engrossing is interactivity. In a computer game, you don't simply sit back and watch a hero fighting against all odds, you *become* the hero.

The key to achieving this interactivity is programming. It's programming that allows an alien creature, an attack squadron, or an entire army to react differently to a player in different situations. Through programming, a game's story can unfold in new ways. In fact, as the result of programming, a game can respond to a player in ways that the game creators might never have imagined.

Although there are literally thousands of computer programming languages, C++ is the game industry standard. If you were to wander the PC game section of your favorite store and grab a title at random, the odds are overwhelming that the game in your hand would be written largely or exclusively in C++. The bottom line is this: If you want to program computer games professionally, you must know C++.

The goal of this book is to introduce you to the C++ language from a game programming perspective. Although no single book can make you the master of two deep topics such as C++ and game programming, this book will start you on your journey.

Who This Book Is For

This book is for anyone who wants to program games. It's aimed at the total beginner and assumes no previous programming experience. If you're comfortable using your computer, then you can start your game programming odyssey right here. But just because this book is written for the beginner, that doesn't mean learning C++ and game programming will be easy. You'll have to read, work, and experiment. By the end of this book, you'll have a solid foundation in the game programming language of the professionals.

How This Book Is Organized

I start at the very beginning of C++ and game programming, assuming no experience in either. As the chapters progress, I cover more advanced topics, building on previous material.

In each chapter, I cover one or several related topics. I move through concepts one step at a time by writing bite-sized, game-related programs to demonstrate each idea. At the end of each chapter, I combine some of the most important concepts in a single game. The last chapter of the book ends with the most ambitious project—one that harnesses all of the major concepts presented throughout the book.

In addition to learning about C++ and game programming, you'll also learn how to organize your work, break down problems into manageable chunks, and refine your code. You'll be challenged at times, but never overwhelmed. Most of all, you'll have fun while learning. In the process, you'll create some cool computer games and gain insight into the craft of game programming.

Chapter 1: Types, Variables, and Standard I/O: Lost Fortune. You'll be introduced to the fundamentals of C++, the standard language of the game industry. You'll learn to display output in a console window, perform arithmetic computations, use variables, and get player input from the keyboard.

Chapter 2: Truth, Branching, and the Game Loop: Guess My Number. You'll create more interesting games by writing programs that execute, skip, or repeat sections of code based on some condition. You'll learn how to generate random numbers to add some unpredictability to your games. And you'll learn about the game loop—a fundamental way to organize your games to keep the action going.

Chapter 3: For Loops, Strings, and Arrays: Word Jumble. You'll learn about sequences and work with strings—sequences of characters that are perfect for word games. You also learn about software objects—entities that can be used to represent objects in your games, such as alien spacecrafts, healing potions, or even the player himself.

Chapter 4: The Standard Template Library: Hangman. You'll be introduced to a powerful library—a toolbox that game programmers (and even non-game programmers) rely on to hold collections of things, such as items in a player's inventory. You'll also learn about techniques that can help you plan larger game programs.

Chapter 5: Functions: Mad-Lib. You'll learn to break up your game programs into smaller, more manageable chunks of code. You'll accomplish this by discovering functions, the fundamental units of logic in your game programs.

Chapter 6: References: Tic-Tac-Toe. You'll learn how to share information with different parts of your programs in an efficient and clear manner. You'll also see a brief example of AI (*artificial intelligence*) and you'll learn how to give a computer opponent a little bit of personality.

Chapter 7: Pointers: Tic-Tac-Toe 2.0. You'll begin to discover some of the most low-level and powerful features of C++, such as how to directly address and manipulate your computer's memory.

Chapter 8: Classes: Critter Caretaker. You'll learn how to create your own kinds of objects and define the ways they'll interact with each other through object-oriented programming. In the process, you'll create your very own critter to care for.

Chapter 9: Advanced Classes and Dynamic Memory: Game Lobby. You'll expand on your direct connection with the computer and learn to acquire and free memory as your game programs require. You'll also see the pitfalls of using this "dynamic" memory and how to avoid them.

Chapter 10: Inheritance and Polymorphism: Blackjack. You'll learn how to define objects in terms of other objects. Then you'll pull everything you've learned together into one big final game. You'll see how a sizeable project is designed and implemented by creating a multiple player version of the classic casino game of Blackjack (tacky green felt not included).

Conventions Used in This Book

Throughout the book, I'll throw in a few other tidbits. For example, I italicize any *new term* and explain what it means. I also use a number of special elements, including the following:

hint
_____
These are good ideas that will help you become a better game programmer.

trap

These point out areas where it's easy to make a mistake.

trick

These suggest techniques and shortcuts that will make your life as a game programmer easier.

in the real world

These are facts about the real world of game programming.

The CD-ROM

The CD-ROM that comes with this book includes the following:

- All of the source code for the programs and games presented in the book
- The Bloodshed Dev-C++ IDE, which uses the MinGW port of GCC as its compiler
- A walkthrough of how to use the Dev-C++ IDE to create your first program
- SGI's Standard Template Library Programmer's Guide
- Useful links for C++, game programming, and industry news and information

A Word about Compilers

I might be getting a little ahead of myself here by talking about compilers, but the issue is important because a *compiler* is what translates the source code you write into a program that your computer can run. I strongly recommend that you use the Dev-C++ IDE that's on the CD-ROM that came with this book. It's easy to use, includes a modern C++ compiler, and best of all, it's free! I feel so strongly about this that I've included a walkthrough on the CD-ROM (Appendix A, "Creating Your First C++ Program") that explains how to compile your first C++ program using Dev-C++. So, what are you waiting for? Grab that CD-ROM, install Dev-C++, and check out the walkthrough.

trap

I hate to pick on any particular compiler or software company, but I have to say that I cannot recommend Microsoft Visual C++ 6.0. Its compiler fails to correctly implement C++ in some important ways. As a result, a few of the programs in this book will not compile under Visual C++ 6.0. I do my best to point out the issues when they arise in the programs in the book. If you want to go with Microsoft, I recommend their current line of Visual Studio .NET products, which implement the C++ standard quite faithfully.

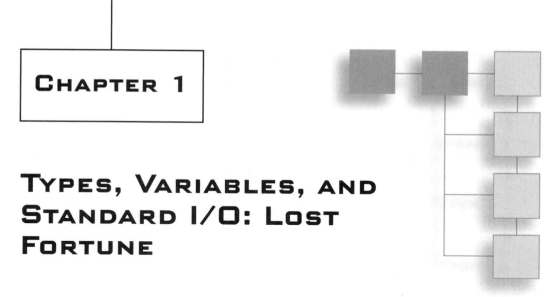

CHAPTER 1

TYPES, VARIABLES, AND STANDARD I/O: LOST FORTUNE

G ame programming is demanding. It pushes both programmer and hardware to their limits. But it can also be extremely satisfying. In this chapter, you'll be introduced to the fundamentals of C++, the standard game industry language. Specifically, you'll learn to:

- Display output in a console window
- Perform arithmetic computations
- Use variables to store, manipulate, and retrieve data
- Get user input
- Work with constants and enumerations

Introducing C++

C++ is a modern, high-level programming language leveraged by millions of programmers around the world. It's one of the most popular languages for writing computer applications—and *the* most popular language for writing computer games.

Created by Bjarne Stroustrup, C++ is a direct descendant of the C language. In fact, C++ retains almost all of C as a subset. However, C++ offers better ways to do things and some brand-new capabilities, too.

Using C++ for Games

C++ is the language of choice among game programmers. Almost every published computer game is written using C++. There is a variety of reasons why game programmers choose the language. Here are a few:

- **It's fast.** Well-written C++ programs can be blazingly fast. One of C++'s design goals is performance. And if you need to squeeze out even more performance from your programs, C++ allows you to use *assembly language*—the lowest-level human-readable programming language—to communicate directly with the computer's hardware.

- **It's flexible.** C++ is a multi-paradigm language that supports different styles of programming, including *object-oriented programming*. Unlike some other modern languages, though, C++ doesn't force one particular style on a programmer.

- **It's well supported.** Because it is the dominant game programming language, there's a large pool of assets available to the C++ game programmer, including graphics APIs and 2D, 3D, physics, and sound engines—all of which allow a programmer to leverage previous work to greatly speed up the process of writing a new game.

Creating an Executable File

The file that you run to launch a program—whether you're talking about a game or a business application—is an *executable file*. There are several steps to creating an executable file from C++ *source code* (a collection of instructions in the C++ language). The process is illustrated in Figure 1.1.

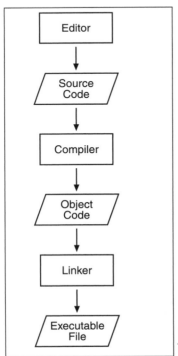

Figure 1.1
The creation of an executable file from C++ source code

1. First, the programmer uses an *editor* to write the C++ source code, a file that usually has the extension .cpp. The editor is like a word processor for programs; it allows a programmer to create, edit, and save source code.

2. After the programmer saves a source file, he invokes a C++ *compiler*—an application that reads source code and translates it into an *object file*. Object files usually have the extension .obj.

3. Next, a linker links the object file to any external files as necessary, and then creates the executable file, which generally ends with the extension .exe. At this point, a user (or gamer) can run the program by launching the executable file.

hint

The process I've described is the simple case. Creating a complex application in C++ often involves multiple source code files written by a programmer (or even a team of programmers).

To help automate this process, it's common for a programmer to use an all-in-one tool for development, called an IDE (*Integrated Development Environment*). An IDE typically combines an editor, a compiler, and a linker, along with other tools. Popular commercial IDEs for Windows include Visual Studio .NET and C++Builder Studio. Dev-C++ is an excellent free and open source IDE for Windows (and just so happens to be included on the CD-ROM that came with this book).

Dealing with Errors

When I described the process for creating an executable from C++ source, I left out one minor detail—errors. If to err is human, then programmers are the most human of us. Even the best programmers write code that generates errors the first (or fifth) time through. Programmers must fix the errors and start the entire process over. Here are the basic types of errors you'll run into as you program in C++:

- **Compile errors.** These occur during code compilation. As a result, an object file is not produced. These errors are often *syntax errors*, meaning that the compiler doesn't understand something. They're often caused by something as simple as a typo. Compilers can issue warnings, too. Although you usually don't have to heed the warnings, you should treat them as errors, fix them, and recompile.

- **Link errors.** These occur during the linking process and may indicate that something the program references externally can't be found. These errors are usually solved by adjusting the offending reference and starting the compile/link process again.

- **Run-time errors.** These occur when the executable is run. If the program does something illegal, it can crash abruptly. But a more subtle form of run-time error, a *logical error*, can make the program simply behave in unintended ways. If you've ever played a game where a character walked on air (that is, a character who shouldn't be able to walk on air), then you've seen a logical error in action.

in the real world

Like other software creators, game companies work hard to produce bug-free products. Their last line of defense is the quality assurance personnel (the game testers). Game testers play games for a living, but their jobs are not as fun as you might think. Testers must play the same parts of a game over and over—perhaps hundreds of times—trying the unexpected and meticulously recording any anomalies. On top of monotonous work, the pay ain't great either. But being a tester is a terrific way to get into a game company on the proverbial bottom rung.

Understanding the ISO Standard

The *ISO standard* for C++ is a definition of C++ that describes exactly how the language should work. It also defines a group of files, called the *standard library*, that contain building blocks for common programming tasks, such as *I/O*—getting input and displaying output. The standard library makes life easier for programmers and provides fundamental code to save them from reinventing the wheel. I'll be using the standard library in all of the programs in this book.

For this book, I used Dev-C++, which is also included on the CD-ROM that came with this book. The compiler that comes with Dev-C++ is quite faithful to the ISO standard, so you should be able to compile, link, and run all of the programs using some other modern Windows compiler. In fact, you should be able to compile, link, and run all of the programs under any operating system as long as you use an ISO-compliant compiler.

hint

The ISO standard is often called the *ANSI standard* or *ANSI/ISO standard*. These different names involve the acronyms of the various committees that have reviewed and established the standard. The most common way to refer to C++ code that conforms to the ISO standard is simply *Standard C++*.

Writing Your First C++ Program

Okay, enough theory. It's time to get down to the nitty-gritty and write your first C++ program. Although it is simple, the following program shows you the basic anatomy of a program. It also demonstrates how to display text in a console window.

Introducing the Game Over Program

The classic first task a programmer tackles in a new language is the Hello World program, which displays Hello World on the screen. The Game Over program puts a gaming twist on the classic and displays Game Over! instead. Figure 1.2 shows the program in action.

Figure 1.2
Your first C++ program displays the two most infamous words in computer gaming.

You can type the code in yourself, but I've also provided the source code for all of the programs on the CD-ROM that came with this book. The code for this program is in the Chapter 1 folder on the CD-ROM; the file name is game_over.cpp.

```cpp
// Game Over
// A first C++ program

#include <iostream>

int main()
{
    std::cout << "Game Over!" << std::endl;
    return 0;
}
```

hint

For step-by-step instructions on how to create, save, compile, and run the Game Over program using Dev-C++, check out Appendix A, "Creating Your First C++ Program," on the CD-ROM that came with this book. If you're using another compiler or IDE, check its documentation.

Commenting Code

The first two lines of the program are comments.

```cpp
// Game Over
// A first C++ program
```

Comments are completely ignored by the compiler; they're meant for humans. They can help other programmers understand your intentions. But comments can also help you. They can remind you how you accomplished something that might not be clear at first glance.

You can create a comment using two forward slashes in a row (//). Anything after this on the rest of the physical line is considered part of the comment. This means you can also include a comment after a piece of C++ code, on the same line.

hint

> You can also use what are called *C-style comments*, which can span multiple lines. All you have to do is start the comment with /* and end it with */. Everything in between the two markers is part of the comment.

Using Whitespace

The next line in the program is technically a blank line. The compiler ignores blank lines. In fact, compilers ignore just about all *whitespace*—spaces, tabs, and newlines. Like comments, whitespace is just for us humans.

Judicious use of whitespace helps make programs clearer. For example, you can use blank lines to separate sections of code that belong together. I also use whitespace (a tab, to be precise) at the beginning of the two lines between the curly braces to set them off.

Including Other Files

The next line in the program is a preprocessor directive. You know this because the line begins with the # symbol.

```
#include <iostream>
```

The *preprocessor* runs before the compiler does its thing and substitutes text based on various directives. In this case, the line involves the #include directive, which tells the preprocessor to include the contents of another file.

I include the file iostream, which is part of the standard library, because it contains code to help me display output. I surround the filename with less than (<) and greater than (>) characters to tell the compiler to find the file where it keeps all the files that came with the compiler. A file that you include in your programs like this is called a *header file*.

Defining the main() Function

The next non-blank line is the header of a function called main().

```
int main()
```

A *function* is a group of programming code that can do some work and return a value. In this case, int indicates that the function will return an integer value. All function headers have a pair of parentheses after the function name.

All C++ programs must have a function called main(), which is the starting point of the program. The real action begins here.

The next line marks the beginning of the function.

```
{
```

And the very last line of the program marks the end of the function.

```
}
```

All functions are delimited by a pair of curly braces, and everything between them is part of the function. Code between two curly braces is called a *block* and is usually indented to show that it forms a unit. The block of code that makes up an entire function is called the *body* of the function.

Displaying Text through the Standard Output

The first line in the body of main() displays Game Over!, followed by a newline, in the console window.

```
std::cout << "Game Over!" << std::endl;
```

"Game Over!" is a *string*—a series of printable characters. Technically, it's a *string literal*, meaning it's literally the characters between the quotes.

cout is an object, defined in the file iostream, that's used to send data to the standard output stream. In most programs (including this one), the standard output stream simply means the console window on the computer screen.

I use the *output operator* (<<) to send the string to cout. You can think of the output operator as a funnel; it takes whatever's on the open side and funnels it to the pointy side. So the string is funneled to the standard output—the screen.

I use std to prefix cout to tell the compiler that I mean cout from the standard library. std is a *namespace*. You can think of a namespace as an area code—it identifies the group to which something belongs. You prefix a namespace using the *scope resolution operator* (::).

Finally, I send std::endl to the standard output. endl is defined in iostream and is also an object in the std namespace. Sending endl to the standard output acts like pressing the Enter key in the console window. In fact, if I were to send another string to the console window, it would appear on the next line.

I understand this might be a lot to take in, so check out Figure 1.3 for a visual representation of the relationship between all of the elements I've just described.

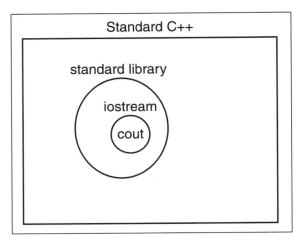

Figure 1.3
An implementation of Standard C++ includes a set of files called the standard library, which includes the file iostream, which defines various things, including the object cout.

Terminating Statements

You'll notice that the first line of the function ends with a semicolon (;). That's because the line is a *statement*—the basic unit controlling the execution flow. All of your statements must end with a semicolon—otherwise, your compiler will complain with an error message and your program won't compile.

Returning a Value from main()

The last statement in the function returns 0 to the operating system.

```
return 0;
```

Returning 0 from main() is a way to indicate that the program ended without a problem. The operating system doesn't have to do anything with the return value, but the C++ standard requires that you return an integer from main(). In general, you can simply return 0 like I did here.

trick

When you run the Game Over program, you might only see a console window appear and disappear just as quickly. That's because C++ is so fast that it opens a console window, displays Game

Over!, and closes the window all in a split second. If you have this problem, just insert the following lines before the `return 0;` in `main()` in this program.

```
std::cout << "Press the enter key to exit";
std::cin.ignore(std::cin.rdbuf()->in_avail() + 1);
```

These new lines wait for the user to press the Enter key. You can use this technique for the other programs in this book as well.

Working with the std Namespace

Because it's so common to use elements from the `std` namespace, I'll show you two different methods for directly accessing these elements. This will save you the effort of using the `std::` prefix all the time, plus it will make your code a bit cleaner.

Introducing the Game Over 2.0 Program

The Game Over 2.0 program produces the exact results of the original Game Over program, illustrated in Figure 1.2. But there's a difference in the way elements from the `std` namespace are accessed. The code for the program is in the Chapter 1 folder on the CD-ROM that came with this book; the file name is game_over2.cpp.

```
// Game Over 2.0
// Demonstrates a using directive

#include <iostream>
using namespace std;

int main()
{
    cout << "Game Over!" << endl;
    return 0;
}
```

Employing a using Directive

The program starts in the same way. I use two opening comments and then include `iostream` for output. But next, I employ a new type of statement.

```
using namespace std;
```

This `using` directive gives me direct access to elements of the `std` namespace. Again, if a namespace is like an area code, then this line says that all of the elements in the `std` namespace should be like local phone numbers to me now. That is, I don't have to use their area code (the `std::` prefix) to access them.

I can use cout and endl, without any kind of prefix. This might not seem like a big deal to you now, but when you have dozens or even hundreds of references to these objects, you'll thank me.

Introducing the Game Over 3.0 Program

Okay, there's another way to accomplish the same thing, and that's exactly what I'm going to show you in the Game Over 3.0 program, which displays the same text as its predecessors. The code for the program is in the Chapter 1 folder on the CD-ROM that came with this book; the file name is game_over3.cpp.

```
// Game Over 3.0
// Demonstrates using declarations

#include <iostream>
using std::cout;
using std::endl;

int main()
{
    cout << "Game Over!" << endl;
    return 0;
}
```

Employing using Declarations

In this version, I write two using declarations.

```
using std::cout;
using std::endl;
```

By declaring exactly which elements from the std namespace I want local to my program, I'm able to access them directly, just as in Game Over 2.0. Although it requires more typing than a using directive, the advantage to this technique is that it clearly spells out which elements I plan to use. Plus, it doesn't make local a bunch of elements that I have no intention of using.

Understanding When to Employ using

Okay, you've seen two ways to make elements from a namespace local to your program. But which is the best technique?

A language purist would say you shouldn't employ either version of using and that you should always prefix each and every element from a namespace with its identifier. In my opinion, that's like calling your best friend by his first and last name all the time. It just seems a little too formal.

If you hate typing, you can employ the using directive. A decent compromise is to employ using declarations. In this book, I'll employ the using directive most of the time for brevity's sake.

in the real world

I've laid out a few different options for working with namespaces. I've also tried to explain the advantages of each so you can decide which way to go in your own programs. Ultimately, though, the decision may be out of your hands. When you're working on a project, whether it's in the classroom or in the professional world, you'll probably receive coding standards created by the person in charge. Regardless of your personal tastes, it's always best to listen to those who hand out grades or paychecks.

Using Arithmetic Operators

Whether you're tallying up the number of enemies killed or decreasing a player's health level, you need your programs to do some math. As with other languages, C++ has built-in arithmetic operators.

Introducing the Expensive Calculator Program

Most serious computer gamers invest heavily in a bleeding-edge, high-powered gaming rig. This next program, Expensive Calculator, can turn that monster of a machine into a simple calculator. The program demonstrates built-in arithmetic operators. Figure 1.4 shows off the results.

Figure 1.4
C++ can add, subtract, multiply, divide, and even calculate a remainder.

The code for the program is in the Chapter 1 folder on the CD-ROM that came with this book; the file name is expensive_calculator.cpp.

```cpp
// Expensive Calculator
// Demonstrates built-in arithmetic operators

#include <iostream>
using namespace std;

int main()
{
    cout << "7 + 3 = " << 7 + 3 << endl;
    cout << "7 - 3 = " << 7 - 3 << endl;
    cout << "7 * 3 = " << 7 * 3 << endl;

    cout << "7 / 3 = " << 7 / 3 << endl;
    cout << "7.0 / 3.0 = " << 7.0 / 3.0 << endl;

    cout << "7 % 3 = " << 7 % 3 << endl;

    cout << "7 + 3 * 5 = " << 7 + 3 * 5 << endl;
    cout << "(7 + 3) * 5 = " << (7 + 3) * 5 << endl;

    return 0;
}
```

Adding, Subtracting, and Multiplying

I use the built-in arithmetic operators for addition (the plus sign, +), subtraction (the minus sign, -), and multiplication (an asterisk, *). The results depicted in Figure 1.4 are just what you'd expect.

Each arithmetic operator is part of an *expression*—something that evaluates to a single value. So, for example, the expression 7 + 3 evaluates to 10, and that's what gets sent to cout.

Understanding Integer and Floating Point Division

The symbol for division is the forward slash (/), so that's what I use in the next line of code. However, the output might surprise you. According to C++ (and that expensive gaming rig), 7 divided by 3 is 2. What's going on? Well, the result of any arithmetic calculation involving only *integers* (numbers without fractional parts) is always another integer. And since 7 and 3 are both integers, the result must be an integer. The fractional part of the result is thrown away.

To get a result that includes a fractional part, at least one of the values needs to be a *floating point* (a number with a fractional part). I demonstrate this in the next line with the expression 7.0 / 3.0. This time the result is a more accurate 2.33333.

trap

You might notice that while the result of 7.0 / 3.0 (2.33333) includes a fractional part, it is still truncated. (The true result would stretch out threes after the decimal point forever.) It's important to know that computers store only a limited number of significant digits for floating point numbers. However, C++ offers categories of floating point numbers to meet the most demanding needs—even those of computationally intensive 3D games.

Using the Modulus Operator

In the next statement, I use an operator you might not be familiar with—the modulus operator (%). The modulus operator returns the remainder of integer division. In this case, 7 % 3 produces the remainder of 7 / 3, which is 1.

Understanding Order of Operations

Just as in algebra, arithmetic expressions in C++ are evaluated from left to right. But some operators have a higher precedence than others and are evaluated first, regardless of position. Multiplication, division, and modulus have equal precedence, which is higher than the precedence level that addition and subtraction share.

The next line of code provides an example to help drive this home. Because multiplication has higher precedence than addition, you calculate the results of the multiplication first. So the expression 7 + 3 * 5 is equivalent to 7 + 15, which evaluates to 22.

If you want an operation with lower precedence to occur first, you can use parentheses, which have higher precedence than any arithmetic operator. So in the next statement, the expression (7 + 3) * 5 is equivalent to 10 * 5, which evaluates to 50.

hint

For a list of C++ operators and their precedence levels, see Appendix B, "Operator Precedence," on the CD-ROM that came with this book.

Declaring and Initializing Variables

A *variable* represents a particular piece of your computer's memory that has been set aside for you to use to store, retrieve, and manipulate data. So if you wanted to keep track of a player's score, you could create a variable for it, and then you could retrieve the score to display it. You could also update the score when the player blasts an alien enemy from the sky.

Introducing the Game Stats Program

The Game Stats program displays information that you might want to keep track of in a space shooter game, such as a player's score, the number of enemies the player has destroyed, and whether the player has his shields up. The program uses a group of variables to accomplish all of this. Figure 1.5 illustrates the program.

Figure 1.5
Each game stat is stored in a variable.

The code for the program is in the Chapter 1 folder on the CD-ROM that came with this book; the file name is game_stats.cpp.

```cpp
// Game Stats
// Demonstrates declaring and initializing variables

#include <iostream>
using namespace std;

int main()
{
    int score;
    double distance;
    char playAgain;
    bool shieldsUp;

    short lives, aliensKilled;

    score = 0;
    distance = 1200.76;
    playAgain = 'y';
    shieldsUp = true;
    lives = 3;
```

```
aliensKilled = 10;

double engineTemp = 6572.89;

cout << "\nscore: "          << score << endl;
cout << "distance: "      << distance << endl;
cout << "playAgain: "     << playAgain << endl;
//skipping shieldsUp since you don't generally print Boolean values
cout << "lives: "           << lives << endl;
cout << "aliensKilled: "<< aliensKilled << endl;
cout << "engineTemp: "      << engineTemp << endl;

int fuel;
cout << "\nHow much fuel? ";
cin >> fuel;
cout << "fuel: " << fuel << endl;

typedef unsigned short int ushort;
ushort bonus = 10;
cout << "\nbonus: " << bonus << endl;

return 0;
}
```

Understanding Fundamental Types

Every variable you create has a *type*, which represents the kind of information you can store in the variable. It tells your compiler how much memory to set aside for the variable and it defines exactly what you can legally do with the variable.

Fundamental types include bool for Boolean values (true or false), char for single character values, int for integers, float for single-precision floating point numbers, and double for double-precision floating point numbers.

Understanding Type Modifiers

You can use modifiers to alter a type. short is a modifier that can reduce the total number of values a variable can hold. long is a modifier that can increase the total number of values a variable can hold. short may decrease the storage space required for a variable while long may increase it. short and long can modify int. long can also modify double.

signed and unsigned are modifiers that work only with integer types. signed means that a variable can store both positive and negative values, while unsigned means that a variable can store only positive values. Neither signed nor unsigned changes the total number of values a variable can hold; they only change the range of values. signed is the default for integer types.

Okay, confused with all of your type options? Well, don't be. Table 1.1 summarizes commonly used types with some modifiers thrown in. The table also provides a range of values for each.

Table 1.1 Commonly Used Types

Type	Values
short int	−32,768 to 32,767
unsigned short int	0 to 65,535
int	−2,147,483,648 to 2,147,483,647
unsigned int	0 to 4,294,967,295
long int	−2,147,483,648 to 2,147,483,647
unsigned long int	0 to 4,294,967,295
float	3.4E +/− 38 (seven significant digits)
double	1.7E +/− 308 (15 significant digits)
long double	1.2E +/− 4932 (19 significant digits)
char	256 character values
bool	true or false

trap

The range of values listed in Table 1.1 is based on my compiler. Yours might be different. Check your compiler's documentation.

hint

For brevity's sake, short int can be written as just short and long int can be written as just long.

Declaring Variables

All right, now that you've got a basic understanding of types, it's time to get back to the program. One of the first things I do is declare a variable in the line:

```
int score;
```

With this code, I declare a variable of type int, which I name score. You use a variable name to access the variable.

From this line, you can see that to declare a variable you specify its type followed by a name of your choosing. Because the declaration is a statement, it must end with a semicolon.

I declare three more variables of yet three more types in the next three lines. `distance` is a variable of type `double`. `playAgain` is a variable of type `char`. And `shieldsUp` is a variable of type `bool`.

Games (and all major applications) require many variables. Fortunately, C++ allows you to declare multiple variables of the same type in a single statement. That's just what I do next in the following line.

```
short lives, aliensKilled;
```

This line establishes two `short` variables—`lives` and `aliensKilled`.

Even though I've defined a bunch of variables at the top of my `main()` function, you don't have to declare all of your variables in one place. As you'll see later in the program, I define a new variable just before I use it.

Naming Variables

To declare a variable, you must provide a name, known as an *identifier*. There are only a few rules you have to follow to create a legal identifier.

- An identifier can contain only numbers, letters, and underscores.
- An identifier can't start with a number.
- An identifier can't be a C++ keyword.

A *keyword* is a special word that C++ reserves for its own use. There aren't many, but to see a full list, check out Appendix C, "Keywords," on the CD-ROM that came with this book.

In addition to the rules for creating *legal* variable names, following are some guidelines for creating *good* variable names.

- **Choose descriptive names.** Variable names should be clear to another programmer. For example, use `score` instead of `s`. (One exception to this rule involves variables used for a brief period. In that case, single-letter variable names, such as `x`, are fine.)
- **Be consistent.** There are different schools of thought about how to write multi-word variable names. Is it `high_score` or `highScore`? In this book, I use the second style, where the initial letter of the second word (and any other words) is capitalized. But as long as you're consistent, it's not important which method you use.
- **Follow the traditions of the language.** Some naming conventions are just traditions. For example, in most languages (C++ included) variable names start with a lowercase letter. Another tradition is to avoid using an underscore as the first character of your variable names. Names that begin with an underscore have a special meaning.

- **Keep the length in check.** Even though `playerTwoBonusForRoundOne` is descriptive, it can make code hard to read. Plus, long names increase the risk of a typo. As a guideline, try to limit your variable names to fewer than 15 characters. Ultimately, though, your compiler sets an actual upper limit.

trick

Self-documenting code is written in such a way that it's easy to understand what is happening in the program independent of any comments. Choosing good variable names is an excellent step toward this kind of code.

Assigning Values to Variables

In the next group of statements, I assign values to the six variables I declared. I'll go through a few assignments and talk a little about each variable type.

Assigning Values to Integer Variables

In the following assignment statement I assign the value of 0 to `score`.

```
score = 0;
```

Now `score` stores 0.

You assign a value to a variable by writing the variable name followed by the assignment operator (=) followed by an expression. (Yes, technically 0 is an expression, which evaluates to, well, 0.)

Assigning Values to Floating Point Variables

In this statement I assign `distance` the value 1200.76.

```
distance = 1200.76;
```

Because `distance` is of type `double`, I can use it to store a number with a fractional part, which is just what I do.

Assigning Values to Character Variables

In the following statement I assign `playAgain` the single-character value 'y'.

```
playAgain = 'y';
```

As I did here, you can assign a character to a variable of type `char` by surrounding the character with single quotes.

Variables of type `char` can store the 128 ASCII character values (assuming that your system uses the ASCII character set, which most do). *ASCII,* short for *American Standard*

Code for Information Interchange, is a code for representing characters. To see a complete ASCII listing, check out Appendix D, "ASCII Chart," on the CD-ROM that came with this book.

Assigning Values to Boolean Variables

In the following statement I assign `shieldsUp` the value `true`.

```
shieldsUp = true;
```

In my program, this means that the player's shields are up.

`shieldsUp` is a `bool` variable, which means it's a Boolean variable. As such, it can represent either `true` or `false`. Although this is intriguing, you'll have to wait until Chapter 2, "Truth, Branching, and the Game Loop: Guess My Number," to learn more about this kind of variable.

Initializing Variables

You can both declare and assign a value to variables in a single initialization statement. That's exactly what I do next.

```
double engineTemp = 6572.89;
```

This line creates a variable of type `double` named `engineTemp`, which stores the value `6572.89`.

Just as you can declare multiple variables in one statement, you can initialize more than one variable in a statement. You can even declare and initialize different variables in a single statement. Mix and match as you choose!

---

hint

Although you can declare a variable without assigning it a value, it's best to initialize a new variable with a starting value whenever you can. This makes your code clearer, plus it eliminates the chance of accessing an uninitialized variable, which may contain any value.

Displaying Variable Values

To display the value of a variable of one of the fundamental types, just send it to `cout`. That's what I do next in the program. Note that I don't try to display `shieldsUp` because you don't normally display `bool` values.

---

trick

In the first statement of this section I use what's called an *escape sequence*—a pair of characters that begins with a backslash (\), which represents special printable characters.

```
cout << "\nscore: "          << score << endl;
```

The escape sequence I used is \n, which represents a newline. When sent to cout as part of a string, it's like pressing the Enter key in the console window. Another useful escape sequence is \t, which acts as a tab.

There are other escape sequences at your disposal. For a list of escape sequences, see Appendix E on the CD-ROM that came with this book.

Getting User Input

Another way to assign a value to a variable is through user input. So next, I assign the value of a new variable, fuel, based on what the user enters. To do so I use the following line:

```
cin >> fuel;
```

Just like cout, cin is an object defined in iostream which lives in the std namespace. To store a value in the variable, I use cin followed by >> (the extraction operator), followed by the variable name. You can follow this usage pattern with cin and the extraction operator to get user input into variables of other fundamental types, too. To prove that everything works, I display fuel to the user.

Defining New Names for Types

You can define a new name for an existing type. In fact, that's what I do next in the line:

```
typedef unsigned short int ushort;
```

This code defines the identifier ushort as another name for the type unsigned short int. To define new names for existing types, use typedef followed by the current type, followed by the new name. typedef is often used to create shorter names for types with long names.

You can use your new type name just like the original type. I initialize a ushort variable (which is really just an unsigned short int) named bonus and display its value.

Understanding Which Types to Use

You have many choices when it comes to the fundamental types. So how do you know which type to use? Well, if you need an integer type, you're probably best off using int. That's because int is generally implemented so that it occupies an amount of memory that is most efficiently handled by the computer. If you need to represent integer values greater than the maximum int or values that will never be negative, feel free to use an unsigned int.

If you're tight on memory, you can use a type that requires less storage. However, on most computers, memory shouldn't be much of an issue. (Programming on game consoles is another story.)

Finally, if you need a floating point number, you're probably best off using `float`, which again is likely to be implemented so that it occupies an amount of memory that is most efficiently handled by the computer.

Performing Arithmetic Operations with Variables

Once you have variables with values, you'll want to change them during the course of your game. You might want to add a bonus to a player's score for defeating a boss. Or you might want to decrease the oxygen level in an airlock. By using operators you've already met (along with some new ones), you can accomplish all of this.

Introducing the Game Stats 2.0 Program

The Game Stats 2.0 program manipulates variables that represent game stats and displays the results. Figure 1.6 shows the program in action.

Figure 1.6
Each variable is altered in a different way.

The code for the program is in the Chapter 1 folder on the CD-ROM that came with this book; the file name is game_stats2.cpp.

```cpp
// Game Stats 2.0
// Demonstrates arithmetic operations with variables

#include <iostream>
using namespace std;

int main()
{
    unsigned int score = 5000;
    cout << "score: " << score << endl;
```

```
//altering the value of a variable
score = score + 100;
cout << "score: " << score << endl;

//combined assignment operator
score += 100;
cout << "score: " << score << endl;

//increment operators
int lives = 3;
++lives;
cout << "lives: "   << lives << endl;

lives = 3;
lives++;
cout << "lives: "   << lives << endl;

lives = 3;
int bonus = ++lives * 10;
cout << "lives, bonus = " << lives << ", " << bonus << endl;

lives = 3;
bonus = lives++ * 10;
cout << "lives, bonus = " << lives << ", " << bonus << endl;

//integer wrap around
score = 4294967295;
cout << "\nscore: " << score << endl;
++score;
cout << "score: "   << score << endl;

return 0;
}
```

Altering the Value of a Variable

After I create a variable to hold the player's score and display it, I alter the score by increasing it by 100.

```
score = score + 100;
```

This assignment statement says to take the current value of score, add 100, and assign the result back to score. In effect, the line increases the value of score by 100.

Using Combined Assignment Operators

There's an even shorter version of the preceding line, which I use next.

```
score += 100;
```

This statement produces the same results as score = score + 100;. The += operator is called a *combined assignment operator* because it combines an arithmetic operation (addition, in this case) with assignment. This operator is shorthand for saying "add whatever's on the right to what's on the left and assign the result back to what's on the left."

There are versions of the combined assignment operator for all of the arithmetic operators you've met. To see a list, check out Table 1.2.

Table 1.2 Combined Assignment Operators

Operator	Example	Equivalent To
+=	x += 5;	x = x + 5;
-=	x -= 5;	x = x - 5;
*=	x *= 5;	x = x * 5;
/=	x /= 5;	x = x / 5;
%=	x %= 5;	x = x % 5;

Using Increment and Decrement Operators

Next I use the *increment operator* (++), which increases the value of a variable by one. I use the operator to increase the value of lives twice. First I use it in the following line:

```
++lives;
```

Then I use it again in the following line:

```
lives++;
```

Each line has the same net effect; it increments lives from 3 to 4.

As you can see, you can place the operator before or after the variable you're incrementing. When you place the operator before the variable, the operator is called the *prefix increment operator*; when you place it after the variable, it's called the *postfix increment operator*.

At this point, you might be thinking that there's no difference between the postfix and prefix versions, but you'd be wrong. In a situation where you only increment a single variable (as you just saw), both operators produce the same final result. But in a more complex expression, the results can be different.

To demonstrate this important difference, I perform a calculation that would be appropriate for the end of a game level. I calculate a bonus based on the number of lives a player has, and I also increment the number of lives. However, I perform this calculation in two different ways. The first time, I use the prefix increment operator.

```
int bonus = ++lives * 10;
```

The prefix increment operator increments a variable *before* the evaluation of a larger expression involving the variable. ++lives * 10 is evaluated by first incrementing lives, and then multiplying that result by 10. Therefore, the code is equivalent to 4 * 10, which is 40, of course. This means that now lives is 4 and bonus is 40.

After setting lives back to 3, I calculate bonus again, this time using the postfix increment operator.

```
bonus = lives++ * 10;
```

The postfix increment operator increments a variable *after* the evaluation of a larger expression involving the variable. lives++ * 10 is evaluated by multiplying the current value of lives by 10. Therefore, the code is equivalent to 3 * 10, which is 30, of course. Then, after this calculation, lives is incremented. After the line is executed, lives is 4 and bonus is 30.

C++ also defines the *decrement operator* (--). It works just like the increment operator, except it decrements a variable. It comes in the two flavors (prefix and postfix) as well.

Dealing with Integer Wrap Around

What happens when you increase an integer variable beyond its maximum value? It turns out you don't generate an error. Instead, the value "wraps around" to the type's minimum value. Next up, I demonstrate this phenomenon. First I assign score the largest value it can hold.

```
score = 4294967295;
```

Then I increment the variable.

```
++score;
```

As a result, score becomes 0 because the value wrapped around, much like a car odometer does when it goes beyond its maximum value (see Figure 1.7).

Figure 1.7
A way to visualize an unsigned int variable "wrapping around" from its maximum value to its minimum

Decrementing an integer variable beyond its minimum value "wraps it around" to its maximum.

hint

Make sure to pick an integer type that has a large enough range for its intended use.

Working with Constants

A *constant* is an unchangeable value that you name. Constants are useful if you have an unchanging value that comes up frequently in your program. For example, if you were writing a space shooter in which each alien blasted out of the sky is worth 150 points, you could define a constant named ALIEN_POINTS that is equal to 150. Then, any time you need the value of an alien, you could use ALIEN_POINTS instead of the literal 150.

Constants provide two important benefits. First, they make programs clearer. As soon as you see ALIEN_POINTS, you know what it means. If you were to look at some code and see 150, you might not know what the value represents. Second, constants make changes easy. For example, suppose you do some playtesting with your game and you decide that each alien should really be worth 250 points. With constants, all you'd have to do is change the initialization of ALIEN_POINTS in your program. Without constants, you'd have to hunt down every occurrence of 150 and change it to 250.

Introducing the Game Stats 3.0 Program

The Game Stats 3.0 program uses constants to represent values. First the program calculates a player's score, and then it calculates the upgrade cost of a unit in a strategy game. Figure 1.8 shows the results.

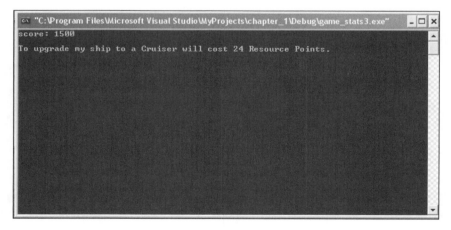

Figure 1.8
Each calculation involves a constant, making the code behind the scenes clearer.

The code for the program is in the Chapter 1 folder on the CD-ROM that came with this book; the file name is game_stats3.cpp.

```cpp
// Game Stats 3.0
// Demonstrates constants

#include <iostream>
using namespace std;

int main()
{
    const int ALIEN_POINTS = 150;
    int aliensKilled = 10;
    int score = aliensKilled * ALIEN_POINTS;
    cout << "score: " << score << endl;

    enum difficulty {NOVICE, EASY, NORMAL, HARD, UNBEATABLE};
    difficulty myDifficulty = EASY;

    enum ship {FIGHTER = 25, BOMBER, CRUISER = 50, DESTROYER = 100};
    ship myShip = BOMBER;
    cout << "\nTo upgrade my ship to a Cruiser will cost "
         << (CRUISER - myShip) << " Resource Points.\n";
    return 0;
}
```

Using Constants

I define a constant, ALIEN_POINTS, to represent the point value of an alien.

```cpp
    const int ALIEN_POINTS = 150;
```

I simply use the keyword const to modify the definition. Now I can use ALIEN_POINTS just like any integer literal. Also, notice that the name I chose for the constant is in all capital letters. This is just a convention, but it's a common one. An identifier in all caps tells a programmer that it represents a constant value.

Next I put the constant to use in the following line:

```cpp
    int score = aliensKilled * ALIEN_POINTS;
```

I calculate a player's score by multiplying the number of aliens killed by the point value of an alien. Using a constant here makes the line of code quite clear.

trap

You can't assign a new value to a constant. If you try, you'll generate a compile error.

Using Enumerations

An *enumeration* is a set of `unsigned int` constants, called *enumerators*. Usually the enumerators are related and have a particular order. Here's an example of an enumeration:

```
enum difficulty {NOVICE, EASY, NORMAL, HARD, UNBEATABLE};
```

This defines an enumeration named `difficulty`. By default, the value of enumerators begins at zero and increases by one. So `NOVICE` is 0, `EASY` is 1, `NORMAL` is 2, `HARD` is 3, and `UNBEATABLE` is 4. To define an enumeration of your own, use the keyword `enum` followed by an identifier, followed by a list of enumerators between curly braces.

Next I create a variable of this new enumeration type.

```
difficulty myDifficulty = EASY;
```

The variable `myDifficulty` is set to `EASY` (which is equal to 1). `myDifficulty` is of type `difficulty`, so it can only hold one of the values defined in the enumeration. That means `myDifficulty` can only be assigned `NOVICE`, `EASY`, `NORMAL`, `HARD`, `UNBEATABLE`, 0, 1, 2, 3, or 4.

Next I define another enumeration.

```
enum ship {FIGHTER = 25, BOMBER, CRUISER = 50, DESTROYER = 100};
```

This line of code defines the enumeration `ship`, which represents four kinds of ships in a strategy game. In it, I assign specific integer values to some of the enumerators. The numbers represent the Resource Point value of each ship. You can assign values to the enumerators if you want. Any enumerators that are not assigned values get the value of the previous enumerator plus one. Because I didn't assign a value to `BOMBER`, it's initialized to 26.

Next I define a variable of this new enumeration type.

```
ship myShip = BOMBER;
```

Then I demonstrate how you can use enumerators in arithmetic calculations.

```
(CRUISER - myShip)
```

This piece of code calculates the cost of upgrading a `BOMBER` to a `CRUISER`. The calculation is the same as 50 - 26, which evaluates to 24.

Introducing Lost Fortune

The final project for this chapter, Lost Fortune, is a personalized adventure game in which the player enters a few pieces of information (including his last name), which the computer uses to enhance a basic adventure story. Figure 1.9 shows a sample run.

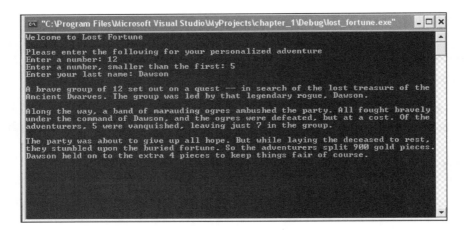

Figure 1.9
The story incorporates details provided by the player.

Instead of presenting all the code at once, I'll go through it one section at a time. The code for the program is in the Chapter 1 folder on the CD-ROM that came with this book; the file name is lost_fortune.cpp.

Setting Up the Program

First I create some initial comments, include two necessary files, and write a few using directives.

```
// Lost Fortune
// A personalized adventure

#include <iostream>
#include <string>

using std::cout;
using std::cin;
using std::endl;
using std::string;
```

I include the file string, part of the standard library, so I can use a string object to access a string through a variable. There's a lot more to string objects, but I'm going to keep you in suspense. You'll learn more about them in Chapter 3, "For Loops, Strings, and Arrays: Word Jumble."

Also, I employ using directives to spell out the objects in the std namespace that I plan to access. As a result, you can clearly see that string is in namespace std.

Getting Information from the Player

Next I get some information from the player.

```
int main()
{
    const int GOLD_PIECES = 900;
    int adventurers, killed, survivors;
    string leader;

    //get the information
    cout << "Welcome to Lost Fortune\n\n";
    cout << "Please enter the following for your personalized adventure\n";

    cout << "Enter a number: ";
    cin >> adventurers;

    cout << "Enter a number, smaller than the first: ";
    cin >> killed;

    survivors = adventurers - killed;

    cout << "Enter your last name: ";
    cin >> leader;
```

GOLD_PIECES is a constant that stores the number of gold pieces in the fortune the adventurers seek. adventurers stores the number of adventurers on the quest. killed stores the number that are killed in the journey. I calculate survivors for the number of adventurers that remain. Finally, I get the player's last name, which I'll be able to access through leader.

trap

This simple use of cin to get a string from the user only works with strings that have no whitespace in them (such as tabs or spaces). There are ways to compensate for this, but that really requires a discussion of something called *streams*, which is beyond the scope of this chapter. So, use cin in this way, but be aware of its limitations.

Telling the Story

Next I use the variables to tell the story.

```
    //tell the story
    cout << "\nA brave group of " << adventurers << " set out on a quest ";
    cout << "-- in search of the lost treasure of the Ancient Dwarves. ";
    cout << "The group was led by that legendary rogue, " << leader << ".\n";

    cout << "\nAlong the way, a band of marauding ogres ambushed the party. ";
    cout << "All fought bravely under the command of " << leader;
    cout << ", and the ogres were defeated, but at a cost. ";
```

```
    cout << "Of the adventurers, " << killed << " were vanquished, ";
    cout << "leaving just " << survivors << " in the group.\n";

    cout << "\nThe party was about to give up all hope. ";
    cout << "But while laying the deceased to rest, ";
    cout << "they stumbled upon the buried fortune. ";
    cout << "So the adventurers split " << GOLD_PIECES << " gold pieces.";
    cout << leader << " held on to the extra " << (GOLD_PIECES % survivors);
    cout << " pieces to keep things fair of course.\n";

    return 0;
}
```

The code and thrilling narrative are pretty clear. I will point out one thing, though. To calculate the number of gold pieces that the leader keeps, I use the modulus operator in the expression GOLD_PIECES % survivors. The expression evaluates to the remainder of GOLD_PIECES / survivors, which is the number of gold pieces that would be left after evenly dividing the stash among all of the surviving adventurers.

Summary

In this chapter, you should have learned the following concepts:

- C++ is a fast, high-level language that is the game industry standard.
- A program is a series of C++ statements.
- The basic lifecycle of a C++ program is idea, plan, source code, object file, executable.
- Programming errors tend to fall into three categories—compile errors, link errors, and run-time errors.
- The #include directive tells the preprocessor to include another file in the current one.
- The standard library is a set of files that you can include in your program files to handle basic functions.
- A function is a group of programming code that can do some work and return a value.
- Every program must contain a main() function, which is the starting point of the program.
- iostream, which is part of the standard library, is a file that contains code to help with standard input and output.
- The std namespace includes facilities from the standard library. To access an element from the namespace, you need to prefix the element with std:: or employ using.

- cout is an object, defined in the file iostream, that's used to send data to the standard output stream (generally the computer screen).
- cin is an object, defined in the file iostream, that's used to get data from the standard input stream (generally the keyboard).
- C++ has built-in arithmetic operators, such as the familiar addition, subtraction, multiplication, and division—and even the unfamiliar modulus.
- C++ defines fundamental types for Boolean, single-character, integer, and floating point values.
- The C++ standard library provides a type of object (string) for strings.
- You can use typedef to create a new name for an existing type.
- A constant is a name for an unchangeable value.
- An enumeration is a sequence of unsigned int constants.

Questions and Answers

Q: Why do game companies use C++?

A: C++ combines speed, low-level hardware access, and high-level constructs better than just about any other language. In addition, most game companies have a lot invested in C++ resources (both in reusable code and programmer experience).

Q: How is C++ different than C?

A: C++ is the next iteration of the C programming language. To gain acceptance, C++ essentially retained all of C. However, C++ defines new ways to do things that can replace some of the traditional C mechanisms. In addition, C++ adds the ability to write object-oriented programs.

Q: How should I use comments?

A: To explain code that is unusual or unclear. You should not comment the obvious.

Q: What's a programming block?

A: One or more statements surrounded by curly braces that form a single unit.

Q: What's a compiler warning?

A: A message from your compiler stating a potential problem. A warning will not stop the compilation process.

Q: Can I ignore compiler warnings?

A: You can, but you shouldn't. You should address the warning and fix the offending code.

Q: What is whitespace?

A: A set of non-printing characters that creates space in your source files, including tabs, spaces, and newlines.

Q: Why does the `main()` function of a program return an `int`?

A: Because that's what the ISO standard says it should do. Actually, you can return a value other than 0 to indicate an abnormal program exit, but this is rarely done in practice.

Q: What are literals?

A: Elements that represent explicit values. `"Game Over!"` is a string literal, while `32` and `98.6` are numeric literals.

Q: Why should I always try to initialize a new variable with a value?

A: Because the contents of an uninitialized variable could be any value—even one that is legal but doesn't make sense for your program.

Q: Why do programmers sometimes use variable names such as `myInt` or `myFloat`?

A: To clearly spell out a variable's type. This convention is used frequently in programming instruction.

Q: What are variables of type `bool` for?

A: They can represent a condition that is true or false, such as whether a chest is locked or a playing card is face up.

Q: How did the `bool` type get its name?

A: The type is named in honor of the English mathematician George Boole.

Q: Must the names of constants be in uppercase letters?

A: No. Using uppercase is just an accepted practice—but one you should use because it's what other programmers expect.

Q: How can I store more than one character with a single variable?

A: Using a `string` object.

Discussion Questions

1. How does having a widely adopted C++ standard help game programmers?
2. What are the advantages and disadvantages of employing the `using` directive?
3. Why might you define a new name for an existing type?
4. Why are there two versions of the increment operator? What's the difference between them?
5. How can you use constants to improve your code?

Exercises

1. Create a list of six legal variable names—three good and three bad choices. Explain why each name falls into the good or bad category.

2. What's displayed by each line in the following code snippet? Explain each result.
```
cout << "Seven divided by three is " << cout 7 / 3 << endl;
cout << "Seven divided by three is " << cout 7.0 / 3 << endl;
cout << "Seven divided by three is " << cout 7.0 / 3.0 << endl;
```

3. Write a program that gets three game scores from the user and displays the average.

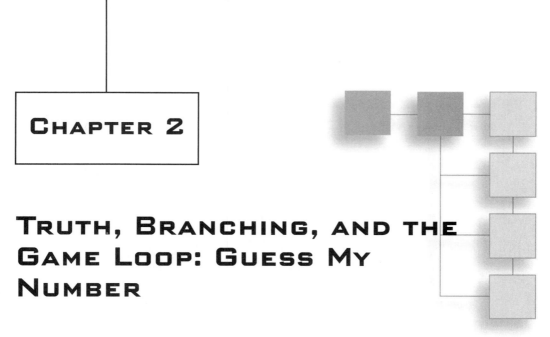

CHAPTER 2

TRUTH, BRANCHING, AND THE GAME LOOP: GUESS MY NUMBER

So far, the programs you've seen have been linear—each statement executes in order, from top to bottom. However, to create interesting games, you need to write programs that execute (or skip) sections of code based on some condition. That's the main topic of this chapter. Specifically, you'll learn to:

- Understand truth (as C++ defines it)
- Use `if` statements to branch to sections of code
- Use `switch` statements to select a section of code to execute
- Use `while` and `do` loops to repeat sections of code
- Generate random numbers

Understanding Truth

Truth is black and white, at least as far as C++ is concerned. You can represent true and false with their corresponding keywords, `true` and `false`. You can store such a Boolean value with a `bool` variable, as you saw in Chapter 1. Here's a quick refresher:

```
bool fact = true, fiction = false;
```

This code creates two `bool` variables, `fact` and `fiction`. `fact` is `true` and `fiction` is `false`. Although the keywords `true` and `false` are handy, any expression or value can be interpreted as `true` or `false`, too. Any non-zero value can be interpreted as `true`, while 0 can be interpreted as `false`.

A common kind of expression interpreted as `true` or `false` involves comparing things. Comparisons are often made by using built-in relational operators. Table 2.1 lists the operators and a few sample expressions.

Table 2.1 Relational Operators

Operator	Meaning	Sample Expression	Evaluates To
==	equal to	5 == 5	true
		5 == 8	false
!=	not equal to	5 != 8	true
		5 != 5	false
>	greater than	8 > 5	true
		5 > 8	false
<	less than	5 < 8	true
		8 < 5	false
>=	greater than or equal to	8 >= 5	true
		5 >= 8	false
<=	less than or equal to	5 <= 8	true
		8 <= 5	false

Using the if Statement

Okay, it's time to put the concepts of true and false to work. You can use an `if` statement to test an expression for truth and execute some code based on it. Here's a simple form of the `if` statement:

```
if (expression)
    statement;
```

If *expression* is true, then *statement* is executed. Otherwise, *statement* is skipped and the program branches to the statement after the `if` suite.

hint

Whenever you see a generic *statement* like in the preceding code example, you can replace it with a single statement or a block of statements because a block is treated as a single unit.

Introducing the Score Rater Program

The Score Rater program comments on a player's score using an `if` statement. Figure 2.1 shows the program in action.

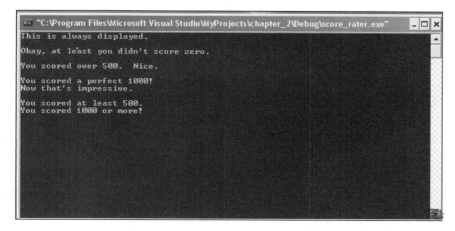

Figure 2.1
Messages are displayed (or not displayed) based on different if statements.

The code for the program is in the Chapter 2 folder on the CD-ROM that came with this book; the file name is score_rater.cpp.

```cpp
// Score Rater
// Demonstrates the if statement

#include <iostream>

using namespace std;

int main()
{
    if (true)
        cout << "This is always displayed.\n\n";

    if (false)
        cout << "This is never displayed.\n\n";

    int score = 1000;

    if (score)
        cout << "Okay, at least you didn't score zero.\n\n";

    if (score > 500)
        cout << "You scored over 500. Nice.\n\n";

    if (score == 1000)
    {
        cout << "You scored a perfect 1000!\n";
        cout << "Now that's impressive.\n";
    }
```

```
    if (score > 500)
    {
        cout << "You scored at least 500.\n";
        if (score >= 1000)
            cout << "You scored 1000 or more!\n";
    }

    return 0;
}
```

Testing true and false

In the first if statement I test true. Because true is, well, true, the program displays the message, This is always displayed.

```
    if (true)
        cout << "This is always displayed.\n\n";
```

In the next if statement I test false. Because false isn't true, the program doesn't display the message, This is never displayed.

```
    if (false)
        cout << "This is never displayed.\n\n";
```

trap

Notice that you don't use a semicolon after the closing parenthesis of the expression you test in an if statement. If you were to do this, you'd create an empty statement that would be paired with the if statement, essentially rendering the if statement useless. Here's an example:

```
if (false);
    cout << "This is never displayed.\n\n";
```

By adding the semicolon after (false), I create an empty statement that's associated with the if statement. The preceding code is equivalent to:

```
if (false)
        ; // an empty statement, which does nothing
cout << "This is never displayed.\n\n";
```

All I've done is play with the whitespace, which doesn't change the meaning of the code. Now the problem should be clear. The if statement sees the false value and skips the next statement (the empty statement). Then the program goes on its merry way to the statement after the if statement, which displays the message, This is never displayed.

Be on guard for this error. It's an easy one to make and because it's not illegal, it won't produce a compile error.

Interpreting a Value as true or false

You can interpret any value as true or false. Any non-zero value can be interpreted as true, while 0 can be interpreted as false. I put this to the test in the next if statement:

```
if (score)
    cout << "Okay, at least you didn't score zero.\n\n";
```

score is 1000, so it's non-zero and interpreted as true. As a result, the message, Okay, at least you didn't score zero, is displayed.

Using Relational Operators

Probably the most common expression you'll use with if statements involves comparing values using the relational operators. That's just what I'll demonstrate next. First, I test to see whether the score is more than 500.

```
if (score > 500)
    cout << "You scored over 500. Nice.\n\n";
```

Because score is greater than 500, the program displays the message, You scored over 500. Nice.

Next, I test to see whether the score is equal to 1000.

```
if (score == 1000)
{
    cout << "You scored a perfect 1000!\n";
    cout << "Now that's impressive.\n";
}
```

Because score is 1000, the block of statements is executed and both strings are displayed. If score hadn't been 1000, neither string would have been displayed, and the program would have continued with the statement following the block.

trap

The equal to relational operator is == (two equal signs in a row). Don't confuse it with = (one equal sign), which is the assignment operator.

While it's not illegal to use the assignment operator instead of the equal to relational operator, the results might not be what you expect. Take a look at this code:

```
int score = 500;
if (score = 1000)
    cout << "You scored a perfect 1000!\n";
```

As a result of this code, score is set to 1000 and the message, You scored a perfect 1000! is displayed. Here's what happens: Although score is 500 before the if statement, that changes. When the expression of the if statement, (score = 1000), is evaluated, score is assigned 1000. The assignment statement evaluates to 1000, and because that's a non-zero value, the expression is interpreted as true. As a result, the string is displayed.

Be on guard for this type of mistake. It's easy to make and in some cases (like this one), it won't cause a compile error.

Nesting if Statements

An if statement can cause a program to execute a statement or block of statements, including other if statements. When you write one if statement inside another, it's called *nesting*. In the following code, the if statement that begins if (score >= 1000) is nested inside the if statement that begins if (score > 500).

```
if (score > 500)
{
    cout << "You scored at least 500.\n";
    if (score >= 1000)
        cout << "You scored 1000 or more!\n";
}
```

Because score is greater than 500, the program enters the statement block and displays the message, You scored at least 500. Then, in the inner if statement, the program compares score to1000. Because score is greater than or equal to 1000, the program displays the message, You scored 1000 or more! Then the program continues to the statement after the block.

hint

You can nest as many levels as you want. However, if you nest code too deeply, it gets hard to read. In general, you should try to limit your nesting to a few levels at most.

Using the else Clause

You can add an else clause to an if statement to provide code that will only be executed if the tested expression is false. Here's the form of an if statement that includes an else clause:

```
if (expression)
    statement1;

else
    statement2;
```

If *expression* is true, *statement1* is executed. Then the program skips *statement2* and executes the statement following the if suite. If *expression* is false, *statement1* is skipped and *statement2* is executed. After *statement2* completes, the program executes the statement following the if suite.

Introducing the Score Rater 2.0 Program

The Score Rater 2.0 program also rates a score, which the user enters. But this time, the program uses an if statement with an else clause. Figures 2.2 and 2.3 show the two different messages that the program can display based on the score the user enters.

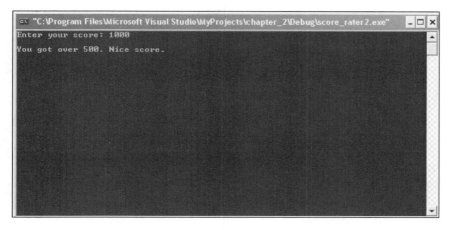

Figure 2.2
If the user enters a score that's more than 500, he is congratulated.

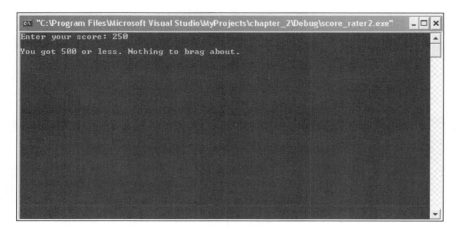

Figure 2.3
If the user enters a score that's 500 or less, he is told he does not have bragging rights.

The code for the program is in the Chapter 2 folder on the CD-ROM that came with this book; the file name is score_rater2.cpp.

```
// Score Rater 2.0
// Demonstrates the else clause

#include <iostream>

using namespace std;

int main()
{
    int score;
    cout << "Enter your score: ";
    cin >> score;

    if (score > 500)
        cout << "\nYou got over 500. Nice score.\n";
    else
        cout << "\nYou got 500 or less. Nothing to brag about.\n";

    return 0;
}
```

Creating Two Ways to Branch

You've seen the first part of the if statement already, and it works just as it did before. If score is greater than 500, the message, You got over 500. Nice score, is displayed.

```
if (score > 500)
    cout << "\nYou got over 500. Nice score.\n";
```

Here's the twist. The else clause provides a statement for the program to branch to if the condition is false. So if (score > 500) is false, then the program skips the first message and instead displays the message, You got 500 or less. Nothing to brag about.

```
else
    cout << "\nYou got 500 or less. Nothing to brag about.\n";
```

Pairing an else Clause with the Correct if Statement

Watch out, because an else clause associates with its nearest preceding if. This can lead to logical errors and unintended results if you're not careful. Here's a bit of new code (not part of the Score Rater program) to show you what I mean:

```
if (false)
    if (true)
        cout << "This will never be displayed.";
else
    cout << "This will always be displayed.";
```

At first glance, you might think that the message, `This will always be displayed`, will, always be displayed. But in fact the code displays nothing because the `else` clause is not associated with `if (false)`; it is associated with `if (true)`. By adding a little whitespace, you can see how the code really works.

```
if (false)
    if (true)
        cout << "This will never be displayed.";
    else
        cout << "This will always be displayed.";
```

I haven't changed the meaning of the code (remember, whitespace is just a convenience for us humans), but I've made the meaning clearer. Because the outer `if` statement never executes its body, no message is ever displayed.

However, I can solve the problem with a pair of curly braces.

```
if (false)
{
    if (true)
        cout << "This will never be displayed.";
}
else
    cout << "This will always be displayed.";
```

As a result, the inner `if` statement is set off in its own little world (called a *scope*) inside the block, and the `else` clause associates with `if (false)`. Now the code will always display the message, `This will always be displayed`.

hint

The concept of scopes is important, but I'll hold off on all of the juicy details until Chapter 5, "Functions: Mad Lib." Right now, just think of scopes as little self-contained worlds.

Using the switch Statement

You can use a `switch` statement to create multiple branching points in your code. Here's a generic form of the `switch` statement:

```
switch (choice)
{
case value1:    statement1;
                break;
case value2:    statement2;
                break;
```

```
case value3:      statement3;
                    break;
                 .
                 .
                 .
case valueN:      statementN;
                    break;
default:          statementN + 1;
}
```

The statement tests *choice* against the possible values—*value1*, *value2*, and *value3*—in order. If *choice* is equal to a value, then the program executes the corresponding *statement*. When the program hits a `break` statement, it exits the `switch` structure. If *choice* doesn't match any value, then the statement associated with `default` is executed.

The use of `break` and `default` is optional. If you leave out a `break`, however, the program will continue through the remaining statements until it hits a `break` or a `default` or until the `switch` statement ends. Usually you want one `break` statement to end each `case`. And although a `default` case isn't required, it's usually a good idea to have one as a catchall.

Here's an example to cement the ideas. Suppose *choice* is equal to *value2*. The program will first test *choice* against *value1*. Because they're not equal, the program will continue. Next, the program will test *choice* against *value2*. Because they are equal, the program will execute *statement2*. Then the program will hit the `break` statement and exit the `switch` structure.

trap

> You can use the `switch` statement only to test an `int` (or a value that can be treated as an `int`, such as a `char` or an `enumerator`). A `switch` statement won't work with any other type.

Introducing the Menu Chooser Program

The Menu Chooser program presents the user with a menu that lists three difficulty levels and asks him to make a choice. If the user enters a number that corresponds to a listed choice, then he is shown a message confirming the choice. If the user makes some other choice, he is told that the choice is invalid. Figure 2.4 shows the program in action.

Figure 2.4
Looks like I took the easy way out.

The code for the program is in the Chapter 2 folder on the CD-ROM that came with this book; the file name is menu_chooser.cpp.

```cpp
// Menu Chooser
// Demonstrates the switch statement

#include <iostream>

using namespace std;

int main()
{
    cout << "Difficulty Levels\n\n";
    cout << "1 - Easy\n";
    cout << "2 - Normal\n";
    cout << "3 - Hard\n\n";

    int choice;
    cout << "Choice: ";
    cin >> choice;

    switch (choice)
    {
    case 1:
            cout << "You picked Easy.\n";
            break;
    case 2:
            cout << "You picked Normal.\n";
            break;
    case 3:
```

```
            cout << "You picked Hard.\n";
            break;
    default:
            cout << "You made an illegal choice.\n";
    }

    return 0;
}
```

Creating Multiple Ways to Branch

The switch statement creates four possible branching points. If the user enters 1, then code associated with case 1 is executed and You picked Easy is displayed. If the user enters 2, then code associated with case 2 is executed and You picked Normal is displayed. If the user enters 3, then code associated with case 3 is executed and You picked Hard is displayed. If the user enters any other value, then default kicks in and You made an illegal choice is displayed.

trap

You'll almost always want to end each case with a break statement. Don't forget them; otherwise, your code might do things you never intended.

Using while Loops

while loops let you repeat sections of code as long as an expression is true. Here's a generic form of the while loop:

```
while (expression)
    statement;
```

If expression is false, the program moves on to the statement after the loop. If expression is true, the program executes statement and loops back to test expression again. This cycle repeats until expression tests false, at which point the loop ends.

Introducing the Play Again Program

The Play Again program simulates the play of an exciting game. (Okay, by "simulates the play of an exciting game," I mean the program displays the message **Played an exciting game**.) Then the program asks the user if he wants to play again. The user continues to play as long as he enters y. The program accomplishes this repetition using a while loop. Figure 2.5 shows the program in action.

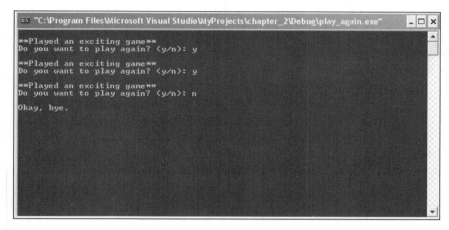

Figure 2.5
The repetition is accomplished using a while loop.

The code for the program is in the Chapter 2 folder on the CD-ROM that came with this book; the file name is play_again.cpp.

```
// Play Again
// Demonstrates while loops

#include <iostream>
using namespace std;

int main()
{
    char again = 'y';
    while (again == 'y')
    {
        cout << "\n**Played an exciting game**";
        cout << "\nDo you want to play again? (y/n): ";
        cin >> again;
    }

    cout << "\nOkay, bye.";

    return 0;
}
```

Looping with a while Loop

The first thing the program does in the main() function is declare the char variable named again and initialize it to 'y'. Then the program begins the while loop by testing again to see whether it's equal to 'y'. Because it is, the program displays the message **Played an exciting game**, asks the user whether he wants to play again, and stores the reply in again. The loop continues as long as the user enters y.

You'll notice that I had to initialize `again` before the loop because the variable is used in the loop expression. Because a `while` loop evaluates its expressions before its *loop body* (the group of statements that repeat), you have to make sure that any variables in the expression have a value before the loop begins.

Using do Loops

Like `while` loops, `do` loops let you repeat a section of code based on an expression. The difference is that a `do` loop tests its expression after each loop iteration. This means that the loop body is always executed at least once. Here's a generic form of a `do` loop:

```
do
      statement;
while (expression);
```

The program executes *statement* and then, as long as *expression* tests `true`, the loop repeats. Once *expression* tests `false`, the loop ends.

Introducing the Play Again 2.0 Program

The Play Again 2.0 program looks exactly the same to the user as the original Play Again program. Play Again 2.0, like its predecessor, simulates the play of an exciting game by displaying the message `**Played an exciting game**` and asking the user whether he wants to play again. The user continues to play as long as he enters y. This time, though, the program accomplishes the repetition using a `do` loop. Figure 2.6 shows off the program.

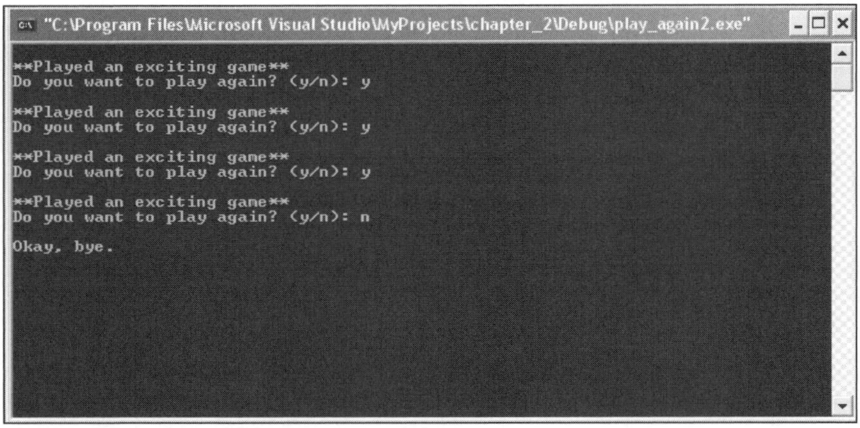

Figure 2.6
Each repetition is accomplished using a `do` loop.

The code for the program is in the Chapter 2 folder on the CD-ROM that came with this book; the file name is play_again2.cpp.

```cpp
// Play Again 2.0
// Demonstrates do loops

#include <iostream>

using namespace std;

int main()
{
    char again;
    do
    {
        cout << "\n**Played an exciting game**";
        cout << "\nDo you want to play again? (y/n): ";
        cin >> again;
    } while (again == 'y');

    cout << "\nOkay, bye.";

    return 0;
}
```

Looping with a do Loop

Before the do loop begins, I declare the character again. However, I don't need to initialize it because it's not tested until after the first iteration of the loop. I get a new value for again from the user in the loop body. Then I test again in the loop expression. If again is equal to 'y', the loop repeats; otherwise, the loop ends.

in the real world

Even though you can use while and do loops pretty interchangeably, most programmers use the while loop. Although a do loop might seem more natural in some cases, the advantage of a while loop is that its expression appears right at the top of the loop; you don't have to go hunting to the bottom of the loop to find it.

trap

If you've ever had a game get stuck in the same endless cycle, you might have experienced an *infinite loop*—a loop without end. Here's a simple example of an infinite loop:

```cpp
int test = 10;
while (test == 10)
    cout << test;
```

In this case, the loop is entered because `test` is 10. But because `test` never changes, the loop will never stop. As a result, the user will have to kill the running program to end it. The moral of this story? Make sure that the expression of a loop can eventually become `false`.

Using break and continue Statements

It's possible to alter the behavior you've seen in loops. You can immediately exit a loop with the `break` statement, and you can jump directly to the top of a loop with a `continue` statement. Although you should use these powers sparingly, they do come in handy sometimes.

Introducing the Finicky Counter Program

The Finicky Counter program counts from 1 to 10 through a `while` loop. It's finicky because it doesn't like the number 5—it skips it. Figure 2.7 shows a run of the program.

Figure 2.7
The number 5 is skipped with a `continue` statement, and the loop ends with a
`break` statement.

The code for the program is in the Chapter 2 folder on the CD-ROM that came with this book; the file name is finicky_counter.cpp.

```cpp
// Finicky Counter
// Demonstrates break and continue statements

#include <iostream>

using namespace std;
```

```
int main()
{
    int count = 0;
    while (true)
    {
        count += 1;

        //end loop if count is greater than 10
        if (count > 10)
            break;

        //skip the number 5
        if (count == 5)
            continue;

        cout << count << endl;
    }

    return 0;
}
```

Creating a while (true) Loop

I set up the loop with the following line:

```
while (true)
```

Technically, this creates an infinite loop. This might seem odd coming so soon after a warning to avoid infinite loops, but this particular loop isn't really infinite because I put an exit condition in the loop body.

hint

Although a while (true) loop sometimes can be clearer than a traditional loop, you should also try to minimize your use of these loops. If a game program does use a while (true) loop, it's often as a main loop around the bulk of the code.

Using the break Statement to Exit a Loop

This is the exit condition I put in the loop:

```
//end loop if count is greater than 10
if (count > 10)
    break;
```

Because count is increased by 1 each time the loop body begins, it will eventually reach 11. When it does, the break statement (which means "break out of the loop") is executed and the loop ends.

Using the continue Statement to Jump Back to the Top of a Loop

Just before count is displayed, I included the lines:

```
//skip the number 5
if (count == 5)
    continue;
```

The continue statement means "jump back to the top of the loop." At the top of the loop, the while condition is tested and the loop is entered again if it's true. So when count is equal to 5, the program does not get to the cout << count << endl; statement. Instead, it goes right back to the top of the loop. As a result, 5 is skipped and never displayed.

Understanding When to Use break and continue

You can use break and continue in any loop you create; they aren't just for while (true) loops. But you should use them sparingly. Both break and continue can make it harder for programmers to see the flow of a loop.

Using Logical Operators

So far you've seen pretty simple expressions evaluated for their truth or falsity. However, you can combine simpler expressions with *logical operators* to create more complex expressions. Table 2.2 lists the logical operators.

Table 2.2 Logical Operators

Operator	Description	Sample Expression
!	Logical NOT	!expression
&&	Logical AND	expression1 && expression2
||	Logical OR	expression1 || expression2

Introducing the Designers Network Program

The Designers Network program simulates a computer network in which only a select group of game designers are members. Like real-world computer systems, each member must enter a username and a password to log in. With a successful login, the member is personally greeted. Also like real-world systems, everyone has a security level. Guests are allowed to log in, too. However, they are given a low security level. To log in as a guest, all a user needs to do is enter guest at either the username or password prompt. Figures 2.8 through 2.10 show the program.

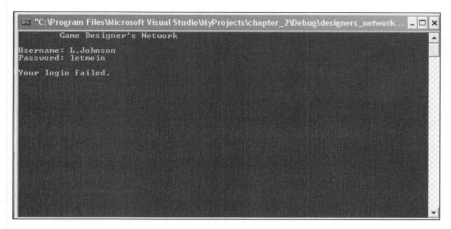

Figure 2.8
If you're not a member or a guest, you can't get in.

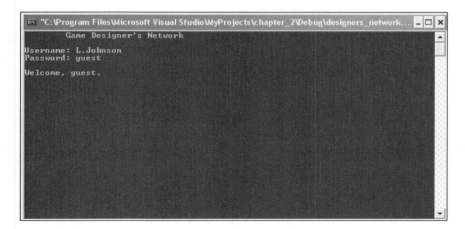

Figure 2.9
If you log in as a guest, your security level is set quite low.

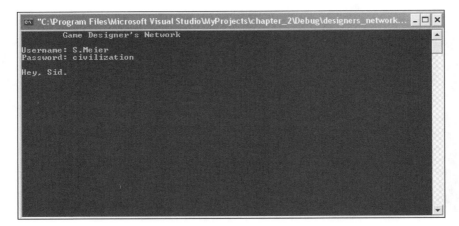

Figure 2.10
Looks like one of the elite logged in today.

The code for the program is in the Chapter 2 folder on the CD-ROM that came with this book; the file name is designers_network.cpp.

```cpp
// Designers Network
// Demonstrates logical operators

#include <iostream>
#include <string>

using namespace std;

int main()
{
    cout << "\tGame Designer's Network\n";
    int security = 0;

    string username;
    cout << "\nUsername: ";
    cin >> username;

    string password;
    cout << "Password: ";
    cin >> password;

    if (username == "S.Meier" && password == "civilization")
    {
        cout << "\nHey, Sid.";
        security = 5;
    }
```

```
if (username == "S.Miyamoto" && password == "mariobros")
{
    cout << "\nWhat's up, Shigeru?";
    security = 5;
}

if (username == "W.Wright" && password == "thesims")
{
    cout << "\nHow goes it, Will?";
    security = 5;
}

if (username == "guest" || password == "guest")
{
    cout << "\nWelcome, guest.";
    security = 1;
}

if (!security)
    cout << "\nYour login failed.";

return 0;
}
```

Using the Logical AND Operator

The logical AND operator, &&, lets you join two expressions to form a larger one, which can be evaluated to true or false. The new expression is true only if the two expressions it joins are true; otherwise, it is false. Just as in English, "and" means both. Both original expressions must be true for the new expression to be true. Here's a concrete example from the Designers Network program:

```
if (username == "S.Meier" && password == "civilization")
```

The expression username == "S.Meier" && password == "civilization" is true only if both username == "S.Meier" and password == "civilization" are true. This works perfectly because I only want to grant Sid access if he enters both his username and his password. Just one or the other won't do.

Another way to understand how && works is to look at all of the possible combinations of truth and falsity (see Table 2.3).

Table 2.3 Possible Login Combinations Using the AND Operator

username == "S.Meier"	password == "civilization"	username == "S.Meier" && password == "civilization"
true	true	true
true	false	false
false	true	false
false	false	false

Of course, the Designers Network program works for other users besides Sid Meier. Through a series of if statements using the && operator, the program checks three different username and password pairs. If a user enters a recognized pair, he is personally greeted and assigned a security level.

Using the Logical OR Operator

The logical OR operator, ||, lets you join two expressions to form a larger one, which can be evaluated to true or false. The new expression is true if the first expression or the second expression is true; otherwise, it is false. Just as in English, "or" means either. If either the first or second expression is true, then the new expression is true. (If both are true, then the larger expression is still true.) Here's a concrete example from the Designers Network program:

```
if (username == "guest" || password == "guest")
```

The expression username == "guest" || password == "guest" is true if username == "guest" is true or if password == "guest" is true. This works perfectly because I want to grant a user access as a guest as long as he enters guest for the username or password. If the user enters guest for both, that's fine too.

Another way to understand how || works is to look at all of the possible combinations of truth and falsity (see Table 2.4).

Table 2.4 Possible Login Combinations Using the OR Operator

username == "guest"	password == "guest"	username == "guest" || password == "guest"
true	true	true
true	false	true
false	true	true
false	false	false

Using the Logical NOT Operator

The logical NOT operator, !, lets you switch the truth or falsity of an expression. The new expression is true if the original is false; the new expression is false if the original is true. Just as in English, "not" means the opposite. The new expression has the opposite value of the original. Here's a concrete example from the Designers Network program:

```
if (!security)
```

The expression !security is true when security is false (or 0). That works perfectly because security is 0 only when there has been a failed login. In this case, I let the user know that the login was unsuccessful.

The expression !security is false when security is true or non-zero. That works perfectly because when security is non-zero, the user has successfully logged in. In this case, I don't want to display the message that the login failed.

Another way to understand how ! works is to look at all of the possible combinations of truth and falsity (see Table 2.5).

Table 2.5 Possible Login Combinations Using the NOT Operator

security	!security
true	false
false	true

Understanding Order of Operations

Just like arithmetic operators, logical operators have precedence levels that affect the order in which an expression is evaluated. Logical NOT, !, has a higher level of precedence than logical AND, &&, which has a higher precedence than logical OR, ||.

Just as with arithmetic operators, if you want an operation with lower precedence to be evaluated first, you can use parentheses. You can create complex expressions that involve arithmetic operators, relational operators, and logical operators. Operator precedence will define the exact order in which elements of the expression are evaluated. However, it's best to try to create expressions that are clear and simple, not ones that require a mastery of the operator precedence list to decipher.

For a list of C++ operators and their precedence levels, see Appendix B, "Operator Precedence," on the CD-ROM that came with this book.

hint

Although you can use parentheses in a larger expression to change the way in which it's evaluated, you can also use *redundant parentheses*—parentheses that don't change the value of the expressions—to make the expression clearer. Let me give you a simple example. Check out the following expression from the Designers Network program:

```
(username == "S.Meier" && password == "civilization")
```

Now, here's the expression with some redundant parentheses:

```
( (username == "S.Meier") && (password == "civilization") )
```

While the extra parentheses don't change the meaning of the expression, they really help the two smaller expressions, joined by the && operator, stand out.

Using redundant parentheses is a bit of an art form. Are they helpful or just plain redundant? That's a call you, as the programmer, have to make.

Generating Random Numbers

A sense of unpredictability can add excitement to a game. Whether it's the sudden change in a computer opponent's strategy in an RTS or an alien creature bursting from an arbitrary door in an FPS, players thrive on a certain level of surprise. Generating random numbers is one way to achieve this kind of surprise.

Introducing the Die Roller Program

The Die Roller program simulates the roll of a six-sided die. The computer calculates the roll by generating a random number. Figure 2.11 shows the results of the program.

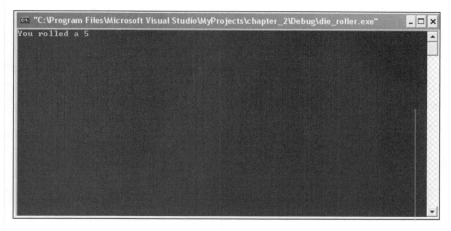

Figure 2.11
The die roll is based on a random number generated by the program.

The code for the program is in the Chapter 2 folder on the CD-ROM that came with this book; the file name is die_roller.cpp.

```cpp
// Die Roller
// Demonstrates generating random numbers

#include <iostream>
#include <cstdlib>
#include <ctime>

using namespace std;

int main()
{
    srand(time(0));   // seed random number generator based on current time

    int randomNumber = rand();   //generate random number

    int die = (randomNumber % 6) + 1;   // get a number between 1 and 6
    cout << "You rolled a " << die << endl;

    return 0;
}
```

Calling the rand() Function

One of the first things I do in the program is include a new file.

```cpp
#include <cstdlib>
```

The file `cstdlib` contains (among other things) functions that deal with generating random numbers. Because I've included the file, I'm free to call the functions it contains, including the function `rand()`, which is exactly what I do in `main()`.

```
int randomNumber = rand();   //generate random number
```

As you learned in Chapter 1, functions are pieces of code that can do some work and return a value. You call or invoke a function by using its name followed by a pair of parentheses. If a function returns a value, you can assign that value to a variable. That's what I do here with my use of the assignment statement. I assign the value returned by `rand()` (a random number) to `randomNumber`.

hint

> The `rand()` function generates a random number between 0 and at least 32,767. The exact upper limit depends on your implementation of C++. The upper limit is stored in the constant `RAND_MAX`, which is defined in `cstdlib`. So if you want to know the maximum random number `rand()` can generate, just send `RAND_MAX` to `cout`.

Functions can also take values to use in their work. You provide these values by placing them between the parentheses after the function name, separated by commas. These values are called *arguments*, and when you provide them, you *pass* them to the function. I didn't pass any values to `rand()` because the function doesn't take any arguments.

Seeding the Random Number Generator

The `rand()` function generates *pseudorandom* numbers—not truly random numbers—based on a formula. One way to think about this is to imagine that `rand()` reads from a huge book of predetermined random numbers. But `rand()` always starts from the beginning of the book when a program begins. This means that `rand()` will always produce the same series of numbers each time the program is run.

However, you can alter the place where `rand()` starts in its book by *seeding* the random number generator with a number using the `srand()` function (also defined in `cstdlib`). To be of any value, the number you use as a seed should be different each time the program begins. A good way to get such a number is to use the function `time()` (defined in the file `ctime`), which returns a number based on the current time.

So that I can use the function `time()`, I include the file `ctime` at the top of the program.

```
#include <ctime>
```

Then, in `main()`, I seed the random number generator with a number based on the current system time.

```
srand(time(0));  // seed random number generator based on current time
```

In the preceding code, I used the function call `time(0)` as an argument when calling `srand()`. This is perfectly fine because the value returned by `time(0)` can be used by `srand()`. In general, you can use a function call as an argument to another function as long as the first function returns a value that will always be a valid argument for the second function.

In the function call `time(0)`, I pass the function `0`. A call to `time(0)` returns a number based on the current time, which I pass to `srand()`, which seeds the random number generator.

Calculating a Number within a Range

After generating a random number, `randomNumber` holds a value between 0 and 32,767 (based on my implementation of C++). But I need a number between 1 and 6, so next I use the modulus operator to produce a number in that range.

```
int die = (randomNumber % 6) + 1;  // get a number between 1 and 6
```

Any positive number divided by 6 will give a remainder between 0 and 5. In the preceding code, I take this remainder and add 1, giving me the possible range of 1 through 6—exactly what I wanted. You can use this technique to convert a random number to a number within a range you're looking for.

trap

Using the modulus operator to create a number within a range from a random number might not always produce uniform results. Some numbers in the range might be more likely to appear than others. However, this isn't a problem for simple games.

Understanding the Game Loop

The *game loop* is a generalized representation of the flow of events in a game. The core of the events repeats, which is why it's called a loop. Although the implementation might be quite different from game to game, the fundamental structure is the same for almost all games across genres. Whether you're talking about a simple space shooter or a complex role-playing game (RPG), you can usually break the game down into the same repeating components of the game loop. Figure 2.12 provides a visual representation of the game loop.

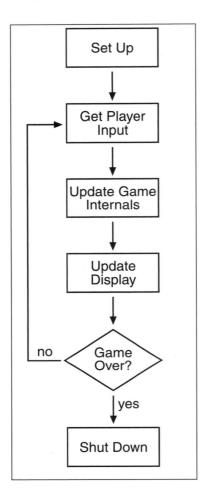

Figure 2.12
The game loop describes a basic flow of events that fits just about any game.

Here's an explanation of the parts of the game loop:

- **Setting up.** This often involves accepting initial settings or loading game assets, such as sound, music, and graphics. The player might also be presented with the game backstory and his objectives.

- **Getting player input.** Whether it comes from the keyboard, mouse, joystick, track-ball, or some other device, input from the player is captured.

- **Updating game internals.** The game logic and rules are applied to the game world, taking into account player input. This might take the shape of a physics system determining the interaction of objects or it might involve calculations of enemy AI, for example.

- **Updating the display.** In the majority of games, this process is the most taxing on the computer hardware because it often involves drawing graphics. However, this process can be as simple as displaying a line of text.

- **Checking whether the game is over.** If the game isn't over (if the player's character is still alive and the player hasn't quit, for example), control branches back to the getting player input stage. If the game is over, control falls through to the shutting down stage.

- **Shutting down.** At this point, the game is over. The player is often given some final information, such as his score. The program frees any resources, if necessary, and exits.

Introducing Guess My Number

The final project for this chapter, Guess My Number, is the classic number-guessing game. For those who missed out on this game in their childhood, it goes like this: The computer chooses a random number between 1 and 100, and the player tries to guess the number in as few attempts as possible. Each time the player enters a guess, the computer tells him whether the guess is too high, too low, or right on the money. Once the player guesses the number, the game is over. Figure 2.13 shows Guess My Number in action. The code for the program is in the Chapter 2 folder on the CD-ROM that came with this book; the file name is guess_my_number.cpp.

Figure 2.13
I guessed the computer's number in just three tries.

Applying the Game Loop

It's possible to examine even this simple game through the construct of the game loop. Figure 2.14 shows how nicely the game loop paradigm fits the flow of the game.

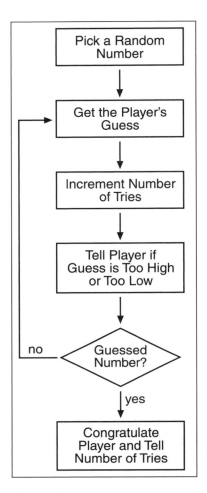

Figure 2.14
The game loop applied to Guess My Number

Setting Up the Game

As always, I start off with some comments and include the necessary files.

```
// Guess My Number
// The classic number guessing game

#include <iostream>
#include <cstdlib>
#include <ctime>

using namespace std;
```

I include `cstdlib` because I plan to generate a random number. I include `ctime` because I want to seed the random number generator with the current time.

Next, I start the `main()` function by picking a random number, setting the number of tries to 0, and establishing a variable for the player's guess.

```
int main()
{
    srand(time(0)); // seed random number generator

    int theNumber = rand() % 100 + 1; // random number between 1 and 100
    int tries = 0, guess;

    cout << "\tWelcome to Guess My Number\n\n";
```

Creating the Guessing Loop

Next, I write the guessing loop.

```
    do
    {
        cout << "Enter a guess: ";
        cin >> guess;
        ++tries;

        if (guess > theNumber)
            cout << "Too high!\n\n";

        if (guess < theNumber)
            cout << "Too low!\n\n";

    } while (guess != theNumber);
```

I get the player's guess, increment the number of tries, and then tell the player if his guess is too high or too low. If the player's guess is correct, the loop ends. Notice that the `if` statements are nested inside the `while` loop.

Wrapping Up the Game

I wrap up the program by congratulating the player and telling him how many tries it took to guess the number.

```
    cout << "\nThat's it! You got it in " << tries << " guesses!\n";

    return 0;
}
```

Summary

In this chapter, you should have learned the following concepts:

- You can use the truth or falsity of an expression to branch to (or skip) sections of code.

- You can represent truth and falsity with their keywords, true and false.

- You can evaluate any value or expression for truth or falsity.

- Any non-zero value can be interpreted as true, while 0 can be interpreted as false.

- The most common way to create an expression to be evaluated as true or false is to compare values with the relational operators.

- The if statement tests an expression and executes a section of code only if the expression is true.

- The else clause in an if statement specifies code that should be executed only if the expression tested in the if statement is false.

- The switch statement tests a value that can be treated as an int and executes a section of code labeled with the corresponding value.

- The default keyword, when used in a switch statement, specifies code to be executed if the value tested in the switch statement matches no listed values.

- The while loop executes a section of code if an expression is true and repeats the code as long as the expression is true.

- A do loop executes a section of code and then repeats the code as long as the expression is true.

- Used in a loop, the break statement immediately ends the loop.

- Used in a loop, the continue statement immediately causes control of the program to branch to the top of the loop.

- The && (AND) operator combines two simpler expressions to create a new expression that is true only if both simpler expressions are true.

- The || (OR) operator combines two simpler expressions to create a new expression that is true if either simpler expression is true.

- The ! (NOT) operator creates a new expression that is the opposite truth value of the original.

- The game loop is a generalized representation of the flow of events in a game, the core of which repeats.

- The file cstdlib contains functions that deal with generating random numbers.

- The function srand(), defined in cstdlib, seeds the random number generator.

- The function rand(), defined in cstdlib, returns a random number.

Questions and Answers

Q: Do you have to use the keywords `true` and `false`?

A: No, but it's a good idea. Before the advent of the keywords `true` and `false`, programmers often used 1 to represent true and 0 to represent false. However, now that `true` and `false` are available, it's best to use them instead of the old-fashioned 1 and 0.

Q: Can you assign a `bool` variable something other than `true` or `false`?

A: Yes. You can assign an expression to a `bool` variable, which will store the truth or falsity of the expression.

Q: Can you use a `switch` statement to test some non-integer value?

A: No. `switch` statements only work with values that can be interpreted as integers (including `char` values).

Q: How can you test a single non-integer value against multiple values if you can't use a `switch` statement?

A: You can use a series of `if` statements.

Q: What's an infinite loop?

A: A loop that will never end, regardless of user input.

Q: Why are infinite loops considered bad?

A: Because a program stuck in an infinite loop will never end on its own. It has to be shut down by the operating system. In the worst case, a user will have to shut his computer off to end a program stuck in an infinite loop.

Q: Won't a compiler catch an infinite loop and flag it as an error?

A: No. An infinite loop is a logical error—the kind of error a programmer must track down.

Q: If infinite loops are a bad thing, then isn't a `while (true)` loop a bad thing?

A: No. When a programmer creates a `while (true)` loop, he should provide a way for the loop to end (usually through a `break` statement).

Q: Why would a programmer create a `while (true)` loop?

A: `while (true)` loops are often used for the main loop of a program, like the game loop.

Q: Why do some people feel that using a `break` statement to exit a loop is poor programming?

A: Because indiscriminate use of `break` statements can make it hard to understand the conditions under which a loop ends. However, sometimes the use of a `while (true)` loop along with a `break` statement can be clearer than creating the same loop in a more traditional way.

Q: What's a pseudorandom number?

A: A random number that's usually generated by a formula. As a result, a series of pseudorandom numbers is not truly random, but good enough for most purposes.

Q: What's seeding a random number generator?

A: It's giving the random number generator a seed, such as an integer, which affects the way the generator produces random numbers. If you don't seed a random number generator, it will produce the same series of numbers each time it's run from the beginning of a program.

Q: Don't you always want to seed the random number generator before using it?

A: Not necessarily. You might want a program to produce the exact same sequence of "random" numbers each time it runs for testing purposes, for example.

Q: How can I generate more truly random numbers?

A: There are third-party libraries that produce better pseudorandom numbers than the ones that typically come with C++ compilers.

Q: Do all games use the game loop?

A: The game loop is just a way of looking at a typical game's flow of events. And just because this paradigm fits a particular game, that doesn't necessarily mean that the game is implemented with a loop around the bulk of its code.

Discussion Questions

1. What kinds of things would be difficult to program without loops?

2. What are the advantages and disadvantages of the switch statement versus a series of if statements?

3. When might you omit a break statement from the end of a case in a switch statement?

4. When should you use a while loop instead of a do loop?

5. Describe your favorite game in terms of the game loop. Is the game loop a good fit?

Exercises

1. Rewrite the Menu Chooser program from this chapter using an enumeration to represent difficulty levels.

2. What's wrong with the following loop?

```
int x = 0;
while (x)
{
    ++x;
    cout << x << endl;
}
```

3. Write a new version of the Guess My Number program in which the player and the computer switch roles. That is, the player picks a number and the computer must guess what it is.

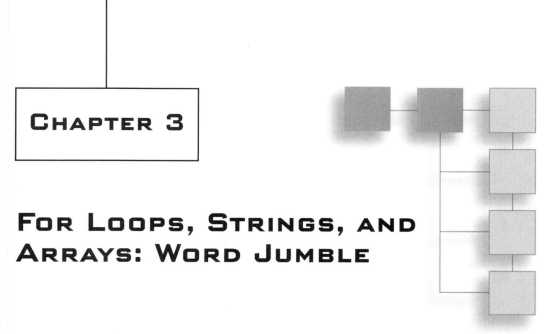

CHAPTER 3

FOR LOOPS, STRINGS, AND ARRAYS: WORD JUMBLE

You've seen how to work with single values, but in this chapter you'll learn how to work with sequences of data. You'll learn more about *strings*—objects for sequences of characters. You'll also see how to work with sequences of any type. And you'll discover a new type of loop that's perfect for use with these sequences. Specifically, you'll learn to:

- Use for loops to iterate over sequences
- Use objects, which combine data and functions
- Use string objects and their member functions to work with sequences of characters
- Use arrays to store, access, and manipulate sequences of any type
- Use multidimensional arrays to better represent certain groups of information

Using for Loops

In Chapter 2, you met two kinds of loops—the while loop and the do loop. Well, it's time to meet another—the for loop. Like the two kinds of loops you know, the for loop lets you repeat a section of code, but for loops are particularly suited for counting and moving through a sequence of things (like the items in an RPG character's inventory).

Here's the generic form of a for loop:

```
for (initialization; test; action)
    statement;
```

initialization is a statement that sets up some initial condition for the loop. (For example, it might set a counter variable to 0.) The expression *test* is tested each time before the loop body executes, just as in a while loop. If *test* is false, the program moves on to the statement after the loop. If *test* is true, the program executes *statement*. Next, *action* is executed (which often involves incrementing a counter variable). The cycle repeats until *test* tests false, at which point the loop ends.

Introducing the Counter Program

The Counter program counts forward, backward, and by fives. It even counts out a grid with rows and columns. It accomplishes all of this through the use of for loops. Figure 3.1 shows the program in action.

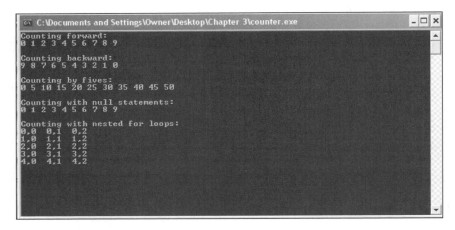

Figure 3.1
for loops do all of the counting, while a pair of nested for loops displays the grid.

The code for the program is in the Chapter 3 folder on the CD-ROM that came with this book; the file name is counter.cpp.

```cpp
// Counter
// Demonstrates for loops

#include <iostream>

using namespace std;

int main()
{
    cout << "Counting forward:\n";
    for (int i = 0; i < 10; ++i)
        cout << i << " ";

    cout << "\n\nCounting backward:\n";
    for (int i = 9; i >= 0; --i)
        cout << i << " ";
```

```
cout << "\n\nCounting by fives:\n";
for (int i = 0; i <= 50; i+=5)
    cout << i << " ";

cout << "\n\nCounting with null statements:\n";
int count = 0;
for ( ; count < 10; )
{
    cout << count << " ";
    ++count;
}

cout << "\n\nCounting with nested for loops:\n";
const int ROWS = 5;
const int COLUMNS = 3;
for (int i = 0; i < ROWS; ++i)
{
    for (int j = 0; j < COLUMNS; ++j)
        cout << i << "," << j << "  ";
    cout << endl;
}

    return 0;
}
```

trap

If you're using an older compiler that doesn't fully implement the current C++ standard, when you try to compile this program, you might get an error that says something like: `error: 'i'  : redefinition; multiple initialization`. Microsoft's old Visual C++ 6.0 is an IDE that will produce this type of error message.

The best solution is to use a modern, compliant compiler. Luckily for you, I've included on this book's CD-ROM a great IDE called Dev-C++ with a modern compiler. I highly recommend that you install and use this IDE when you're working on the programs in this book. After you install Dev-C++, check out Appendix A, "Creating Your First C++ Program," on the book's CD-ROM for a tutorial of how to get your programs running with Dev-C++.

If you must use your old compiler, you should declare any `for` loop counter variables just once for all `for` loops in a scope. I cover the topic of scopes in Chapter 5, "Functions: Mad Lib."

Counting with for Loops

The first `for` loop counts from 0 to 9. The loop begins:

```
for (int i = 0; i < 10; ++i)
```

The initialization statement, `int i = 10`, declares `i` and initializes it to 0. The expression `i < 10` says that the loop will continue as long as `i` is less than 10. Lastly, the action statement,

++i, says i is to be incremented each time the loop body finishes. As a result, the loop *iterates* 10 times—once for each of the values 0 through 9. And during each iteration, the loop body displays the value of i.

The next for loop counts from 9 down to 0. The loop begins:

```
for (int i = 9; i >= 0; --i)
```

Here, i is initialized to 9, and the loop continues as long as i is greater than or equal to 0. Each time the loop body finishes, i is decremented. As a result, the loop displays the values 9 through 0.

The next loop counts from 0 to 50, by fives. The loop begins:

```
for (int i = 0; i <= 50; i += 5)
```

Here, i is initialized to 0, and the loop continues as long as i is less than or equal to 50. But notice the action statement, i += 5. This statement increases i by five each time the loop body finishes. As a result, the loop displays the values 0, 5, 10, 15, and so on. The expression i <= 50 says to execute the loop body as long as i is less than or equal to 50.

You can initialize a counter variable, create a test condition, and update the counter variable with any values you want. However, the most common thing to do is to start the counter at 0 and increment it by 1 after each loop iteration.

Finally, the caveats regarding infinite loops that you learned about while studying while loops apply equally well to for loops. Make sure you create loops that can end; otherwise, you'll have a very unhappy gamer on your hands.

Using Empty Statements in for Loops

You can use empty statements in creating your for loop, as I did in the following loop:

```
for ( ; count < 10; )
```

I used an empty statement for the initialization and action statements. That's fine because I declared and initialized count before the loop and incremented it inside the loop body. This loop displays the same sequence of integers as the very first loop in the program. Although the loop might look odd, it's perfectly legal.

hint

Different game programmers have different traditions. In the last chapter, you saw that you can create a loop that continues until it reaches an exit statement—such as a break—using while (true). Well, some programmers prefer to create these kinds of loops using a for statement that begins for (;;). Because the test expression in this loop is the empty statement, the loop will continue until it encounters some exit statement.

Nesting for Loops

You can nest for loops by putting one inside the other. That's what I did in the following section of code, which counts out the elements of a grid. The outer loop, which begins:

```
for (int i = 0; i < ROWS; ++i)
```

simply executes its loop body ROWS (five) times. But it just so happens that there's another for loop inside this loop, which begins:

```
for (int j = 0; j < COLUMNS; ++j)
```

As a result, the inner loop executes in full for each iteration of the outer loop. In this case, that means the inner loop executes COLUMNS (three) times, for the ROWS (five) times the outer loop iterates, for a total of 15 times. Specifically, here's what happens:

1. The outer for loop declares i and initializes it to 0. Since i is less than ROWS (five), the program enters the outer loop's body.

2. The inner loop declares j and initializes it to 0. Since j is less than COLUMNS (three), the program enters its loop body, sending the values of i and j to cout, which displays 0, 0.

3. The program reaches the end of the body of the inner loop and increments j to 1. Since j is still less than COLUMNS (three), the program executes the inner loop's body again, displaying 0, 1.

4. The program reaches the end of the inner loop's body and increments j to 2. Since j is still less than COLUMNS (three), the program executes the inner loop's body again, displaying 0, 2.

5. The program reaches the end of the inner loop's body and increments j to 3. This time, however, j is not less than COLUMNS (three) and the inner loop ends.

6. The program finishes the first iteration of the outer loop by sending endl to cout, ending the first row.

7. The program reaches the end of the outer loop's body and increments i to 1. Since i is less than ROWS (five), the program enters the outer loop's body again.

8. The program reaches the inner loop, which starts from the beginning once again, by declaring and initializing j to 0. The program goes through the process I described in Steps 2 through 7, displaying the second row of the grid. This process continues until all five rows have been displayed.

Again, the important thing to remember is that the inner loop is executed in full for each iteration of the outer loop.

Understanding Objects

So far you've seen how to store individual pieces of information in variables and how to manipulate those variables using operators and functions. But most of the things you want to represent in games—such as, say alien spacecrafts—are objects. They're encapsulated, cohesive things that combine qualities (such as an energy level) and abilities (for example, firing weapons). Often it makes no sense to talk about the individual qualities and abilities in isolation from each other.

Fortunately, most modern programming languages let you work with software objects (often just called *objects*) that combine data and functions. A data element of an object is called a *data member*, while a function of an object is called a *member function*. As a concrete example, think about that alien spacecraft. An alien spacecraft object might be of a new type called Spacecraft, defined by a game programmer, and might have a data member for its energy level and a member function to fire its weapons. In practice, an object's energy level might be stored in its data member energy as an int, and its ability to fire its weapons might be defined in a member function called fireWeapons().

Every object of the same type has the same basic structure, so each object will have the same set of data members and member functions. However, as an individual, each object will have its own values for its data members. If you had a squadron of five alien spacecrafts, each would have its own energy level. One might have an energy level of 75, while another might have a level of only 10, and so on. Even if two crafts have the same energy level, each would belong to a unique spacecraft. Each craft could also fire its own weapons with a call to its member function, fireWeapons(). Figure 3.2 illustrates the concept of an alien spacecraft.

The cool thing about objects is that you don't need to know the implementation details to use them—just as you don't need to know how to build a car in order to drive one. You only have to know the object's data members and member functions—just as you only need to know where a car's steering wheel, gas pedal, and brake pedal are located.

You can store objects in variables, just like with built-in types. Therefore, you could store an alien spacecraft object in a variable of the Spacecraft type. You can access data members and member functions using the member selection operator (.), by placing the operator after the variable name of the object. So if you want your alien spacecraft, ship, to fire its weapons only if its energy level is greater than 10, you could write the following code.

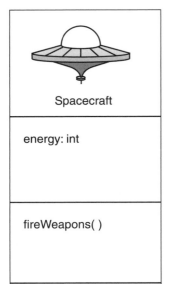

Spacecraft

energy: int

fireWeapons( )

Figure 3.2
This representation of the definition of an alien spacecraft says that each object will have a data member called energy and a member function called fireWeapons().

```
// ship is an object of Spacecraft type
if (ship.energy > 10)
    ship.fireWeapons()
```

`ship.energy` accesses the object's `energy` data member, while `ship.fireWeapons()` calls the object's `fireWeapons()` member function.

Although you can't make your own new types (like for an alien spacecraft) just yet, you can work with previously defined object types. And that's next on the agenda.

Using string Objects

`string` objects, which you met briefly in Chapter 1, are the perfect way to work with sequences of characters, whether you're writing a complete word puzzle game or simply storing a player's name. A `string` is actually an object, and it provides its own set of member functions that allow you to do a range of things with the `string` object—everything from simply getting its length to performing complex character substitutions. In addition, `string` objects are defined so that they work intuitively with a few of the operators you already know.

Introducing the String Tester Program

The String Tester program uses the `string` object equal to `"Game Over!!!"` and tells you its length, the index (position number) of each character, and whether or not certain substrings can be found in it. In addition, the program erases parts of the `string` object. Figure 3.3 shows the results of the program.

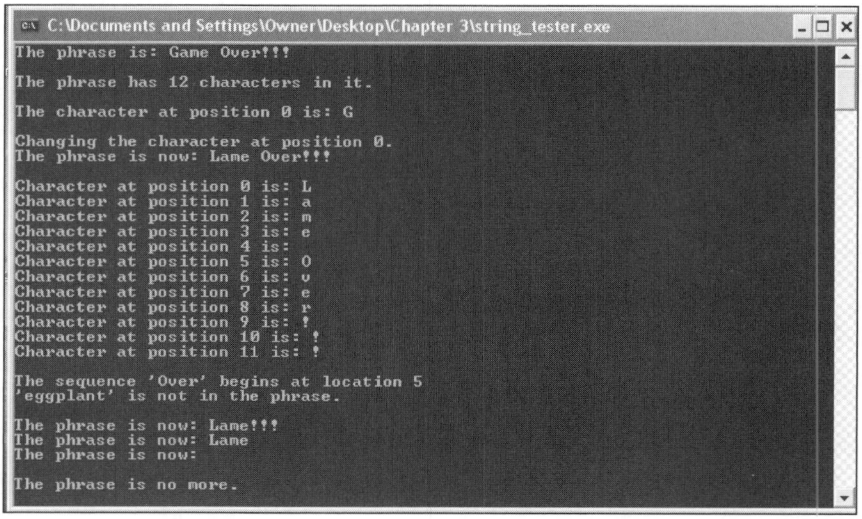

Figure 3.3
`string` objects are combined, changed, and erased through familiar operators and `string` member functions.

The code for the program is in the Chapter 3 folder on the CD-ROM that came with this book; the file name is string_tester.cpp.

```cpp
// String Tester
// Demonstrates string objects

#include <iostream>
#include <string>

using namespace std;

int main()
{
    string word1 = "Game";
    string word2("Over");
    string word3(3, '!');

    string phrase = word1 + " " + word2 + word3;
    cout << "The phrase is: " << phrase << "\n\n";

    cout << "The phrase has " << phrase.size() << " characters in it.\n\n";

    cout << "The character at position 0 is: " << phrase[0] << "\n\n";

    cout << "Changing the character at position 0.\n";
    phrase[0] = 'L';
    cout << "The phrase is now: " << phrase << "\n\n";

    for (int i = 0; i < phrase.size(); ++i)
        cout << "Character at position " << i << " is: " << phrase[i] << endl;

    cout << "\nThe sequence 'Over' begins at location " << phrase.find("Over")
        << endl;

    if (phrase.find("eggplant") == string::npos)
        cout << "'eggplant' is not in the phrase.\n\n";

    phrase.erase(4, 5);
    cout << "The phrase is now: " << phrase << endl;
    phrase.erase(4);
    cout << "The phrase is now: " << phrase << endl;
    phrase.erase();
    cout << "The phrase is now: " << phrase << endl;

    if (phrase.empty())
        cout << "\nThe phrase is no more.\n";

  return 0;
}
```

Creating string Objects

The first thing I do in `main()` is create three strings in three different ways:

```
string word1 = "Game";
string word2("Over");
string word3(3, '!');
```

In the first line of this group, I simply create the `string` object `word1` using the assignment operator, the same way you've seen for other variables. As a result, `word1` is `"Game"`.

Next, I create `word2` by placing the `string` object to which I want the variable set between a pair of parentheses. As a result, `word2` is `"Over"`.

Finally, I create `word3` by supplying between a pair of parentheses a number followed by a single character. This produces a `string` object made up of the provided character, which has a length equal to the number. As a result, `word3` is `"!!!"`.

Concatenating string Objects

Next I create a new `string` object, `phrase`, by concatenating the first three `string` objects.

```
string phrase = word1 + " " + word2 + word3;
```

As a result, `phrase` is `"Game Over!!!"`.

Notice that the + operator, which you've seen work only with numbers, also concatenates `string` objects. That's because the + operator has been overloaded. Now, when you first hear the term *overloaded*, you might think it's a bad thing—the operator is about to blow! But it's a good thing. *Operator overloading* redefines a familiar operator so it works differently when used in a new, previously undefined context. In this case, I use the + operator not to add numbers, but to join `string` objects. I'm able to do this only because the `string` type specifically overloads the + operator and defines it so the operator means `string` object concatenation when used with `string`s.

Using the size() Member Function

Okay, it's time to take a look at a `string` member function. Next, I use the member function `size()`.

```
cout << "The phrase has " << phrase.size() << " characters in it.\n\n";
```

`phrase.size()` calls the member function `size()` of the `string` object `phrase` through the member selection operator . (the dot). The `size()` member function simply returns an unsigned integer value of the size of the `string` object—its number of characters. Because the `string` object is `"Game Over!!!"`, the member function returns 12. (Every character counts, including spaces.) Of course, calling `size()` for another `string` object might return a different result based on the number of characters in the `string` object.

string objects also have a member function `length()`, which, just like `size()`, returns the number of characters in the `string` object.

Indexing a string Object

A `string` object stores a sequence of `char` values. You can access any individual `char` value by providing an index number with the subscripting operator (`[]`). That's what I do next.

```
cout << "The character at position 0 is: " << phrase[0] << "\n\n";
```

The first element in a sequence is at position 0. In the previous statement, `phrase[0]` is the character G. And because counting begins at 0, the last character in the `string` object is `phrase[11]`, even though the `string` object has 12 characters in it.

It's a common mistake to forget that indexing begins at position 0. Remember, a `string` object with n characters in it can be indexed from position 0 to position n–1.

Not only can you access characters in a `string` object with the subscripting operator, but you can also reassign them. That's what I do next.

```
phrase[0] = 'L';
```

I change the first character of `phrase` to the character L, which means `phrase` becomes `"Lame Over!!!"`

C++ compilers do not perform bounds checking when working with `string` objects and the subscripting operator. This means that the compiler doesn't check to see whether you're attempting to access an element that doesn't exist. Accessing an invalid sequence element can lead to disastrous results because it's possible to write over critical data in your computer's memory. By doing this, you can crash your program, so take care when using the subscripting operator.

Iterating through string Objects

Given your new knowledge of `for` loops and `string` objects, it's a snap to iterate through the individual characters of a `string` object. That's what I do next.

```
for (int i = 0; i < phrase.size(); ++i)
    cout << "Character at position " << i << " is: " << phrase[i] << endl;
```

The loop iterates through all of the valid positions of phrase. It starts with 0 and goes through 11. During each iteration, a character of the string object is displayed with phrase[i].

in the real world

Iterating through a sequence is a powerful and often-used technique in games. You might, for example, iterate through hundreds of individual units in a strategy game, updating their status and order. Or you might iterate through the list of vertices of a 3D model to apply some geometric transformation.

Using the find() Member Function

Next I use the member function find() to check whether either of two string literals is contained in phrase. First, I check for the string literal "Over".

```
cout << "\nThe sequence 'Over' begins at location " << phrase.find("Over")
     << endl;
```

The find() member function searches the calling string object for the string supplied as an argument. The member function returns the position number of the first occurrence where the string object for which you are searching begins in the calling string object. This means that phrase.find("Over") returns the position number where the first occurrence of "Over" begins in phrase. Since phrase is "Lame Over!!!", find() returns 5. (Remember, position numbers begin at 0, so 5 means the sixth character.)

But what if the string for which you are searching doesn't exist in the calling string? I tackle that situation next:

```
if (phrase.find("eggplant") == string::npos)
    cout << "'eggplant' is not in the phrase.\n\n";
```

Because "eggplant" does not exist in phrase, find() returns a special constant defined in the file string, which I access with string::npos. As a result, the screen displays the message, 'eggplant' is not in the phrase.

The constant I access through string::npos represents the largest possible size of a string object, so it is greater than any possible valid position number in a string object. Informally, it means "a position number that can't exist." It's the perfect return value to indicate that one string couldn't be found in another.

hint

When using find(), you can supply an optional argument that specifies a character number for the program to start looking for the substring. The following line will start looking for the string literal "eggplant" beginning at position 5 in the string object phrase.

```
location = phrase.find("eggplant", 5);
```

Using the erase() Member Function

The erase() member function removes a specified substring from a string object. One way to call the member function is to specify the beginning position and the length of the substring, as I did in this code:

```
phrase.erase(4, 5);
```

The previous line removes the four-character substring starting at position 5. Because phrase is "Lame Over!!!", the member function removes the substring Over and, as a result, phrase becomes "Lame!!!".

Another way to call erase() is to supply just the beginning position of the substring. This removes all of the characters starting at that position number to the end of the string object. That's what I do next.

```
phrase.erase(4);
```

This line removes all of the characters of the string object starting at position 4. Since phrase is "Lame!!!", the member function removes the substring !!! and, as a result, phrase becomes "Lame".

Yet another way to call erase() is to supply no arguments, as I did in this code:

```
phrase.erase();
```

The previous line erases every character in phrase. As a result, phrase becomes the empty string, which is equal to "".

Using the empty() Member Function

The empty() member function returns a bool value—true if the string object is empty and false otherwise. I use empty() in the following code:

```
if (phrase.empty())
    cout << "\nThe phrase is no more.\n";
```

Because phrase is equal to the empty string, phrase().empty returns true, and the screen displays the message, The phrase is no more.

hint

The string file from the standard library defines many other useful member functions for string objects. These include member functions for appending, copying, inserting, replacing, and swapping string objects. For a full listing of all string member functions, check out Appendix F on the CD-ROM that came with this book, which documents the Standard Template Library. Look for the topic basic_string.

Using Arrays

While `string` objects provide a great way to work with a sequence of characters, arrays provide a way to work with elements of any type. That means you can use an array to store a sequence of integers for, say, a high-score list. But it also means that you can use arrays to store elements of programmer-defined types, such as a sequence of items that an RPG character might carry.

Introducing the Hero's Inventory Program

The Hero's Inventory program maintains the inventory of a hero from a typical RPG. As in most RPGs, the hero is from a small, insignificant village, and his father was killed by an evil warlord. (What's a quest without a dead father?) Now that the hero has come of age, it's time for him to seek his revenge.

In this program, the hero's inventory is represented by an array. The array is a sequence of `string` objects—one for each item in the hero's possession. The hero trades and even finds new items. Figure 3.4 shows the program in action.

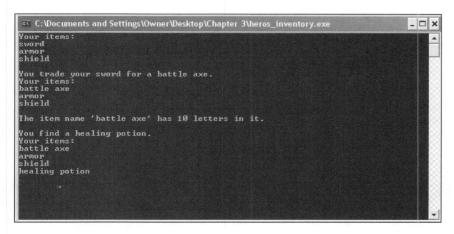

Figure 3.4
The hero's inventory is a sequence of `string` objects stored in an array.

The code for the program is in the Chapter 3 folder on the CD-ROM that came with this book; the file name is heros_inventory.cpp.

```cpp
// Hero's Inventory
// Demonstrates arrays

#include <iostream>
#include <string>

using namespace std;
```

```
int main()
{
    const int MAX_ITEMS = 10;
    string inventory[MAX_ITEMS];

    int numItems = 0;
    inventory[numItems++] = "sword";
    inventory[numItems++] = "armor";
    inventory[numItems++] = "shield";

    cout << "Your items:\n";
    for (int i = 0; i < numItems; ++i)
        cout << inventory[i] << endl;

    cout << "\nYou trade your sword for a battle axe.";
    inventory[0] = "battle axe";
    cout << "\nYour items:\n";
    for (int i = 0; i < numItems; ++i)
        cout << inventory[i] << endl;

    cout << "\nThe item name '" << inventory[0] << "' has ";
    cout << inventory[0].size() << " letters in it.\n";

    cout << "\nYou find a healing potion.";
    if (numItems < MAX_ITEMS)
        inventory[numItems++] = "healing potion";
    else
        cout << "You have too many items and can't carry another.";
    cout << "\nYour items:\n";
    for (int i = 0; i < numItems; ++i)
        cout << inventory[i] << endl;

 return 0;
}
```

Creating Arrays

It's often a good idea to define a constant for the number of elements in an array. That's what I did with MAX_ITEMS, which represents the maximum number of items the hero can carry.

```
const int MAX_ITEMS = 10;
```

You declare an array much the same way you would declare any variable you've seen so far: You provide a type followed by a name. In addition, your compiler must know the size of the array so it can reserve the necessary memory space. You can provide that information following the array name, surrounded by square brackets. Here's how I declare the array for the hero's inventory:

```
string inventory[MAX_ITEMS];
```

The preceding code declares an array `inventory` of `MAX_ITEMS` `string` objects. (Because `MAX_ITEMS` is 10, that means 10 `string` objects.)

trick

You can initialize an array with values when you declare it by providing an *initializer list*—a sequence of elements separated by commas and surrounded by curly braces. Here's an example:

```
string inventory[MAX_ITEMS] = {"sword", "armor", "shield"};
```

The preceding code declares an array of `string` objects, `inventory`, that has a size of `MAX_ITEMS`. The first three elements of the array are initialized to `"sword"`, `"armor"`, and `"shield"`.

If you omit the number of elements when using an initializer list, the array will be created with a size equal to the number of elements in the list. Here's an example:

```
string inventory[] = {"sword", "armor", "shield"};
```

Because there are three elements in the initializer list, the preceding line creates an array, `inventory`, that is three elements in size. Its elements are `"sword"`, `"armor"`, and `"shield"`.

Indexing Arrays

You index arrays much like you index `string` objects. You can access any individual element by providing an index number with the subscripting operator (`[]`).

Next I add three items to the hero's inventory using the subscripting operator.

```
int numItems = 0;
inventory[numItems++] = "sword";
inventory[numItems++] = "armor";
inventory[numItems++] = "shield";
```

I start by defining `numItems` for the number of items the hero is carrying at the moment. Next I assign `"sword"` to position 0 of the array. Because I use the postfix increment operator, `numItems` is incremented after the assignment to the array. The next two lines add `"armor"` and `"shield"` to the array, leaving `numItems` at the correct value of 3 when the code finishes.

Now that the hero is stocked with some items, I display his inventory.

```
cout << "Your items:\n";
for (int i = 0; i < numItems; ++i)
    cout << inventory[i] << endl;
```

This should remind you of string indexing. The code loops through the first three elements of `inventory`, displaying each `string` object in order.

Next the hero trades his sword for a battle axe. I accomplish this through the following line:

```
inventory[0] = "battle axe";
```

The previous code reassigns the element at position 0 in inventory the string object "battle axe". Now the first three elements of inventory are "battle axe", "armor", and "shield".

trap

Array indexing begins at 0, just as you saw with string objects. This means that the following code defines a five-element array.

```
int highScores[5];
```

Valid position numbers are 0 through 4, inclusive. There is no element highScores[5]! An attempt to access highScores[5] could lead to disastrous results, including a program crash.

Accessing Member Functions of an Array Element

You can access the member functions of an array element by writing the array element, followed by the member selection operator, followed by the member function name. This sounds a bit complicated, but it's not. Here's an example:

```
cout << inventory[0].size() << " letters in it.\n";
```

The code inventory[0].size() means the program should call the size() member function of the element inventory[0]. In this case, because inventory[0] is "battle axe", the call returns 10, the number of characters in the string object.

Being Aware of Array Bounds

As you learned, you have to be careful when you index an array. Because an array has a fixed size, you can create an integer constant to store the size of an array. Again, that's just what I did in the beginning of the program.

```
const int MAX_ITEMS = 10;
```

In the following lines, I use MAX_ITEMS to protect myself before adding another item to the hero's inventory.

```
if (numItems < MAX_ITEMS)
    inventory[numItems++] = "healing potion";
else
    cout << "You have too many items and can't carry another.";
```

In the preceding code, I first checked to see whether numItems is less than MAX_ITEMS. If it is, then I can safely use numItems as an index and assign a new string object to the array. In this case numItems is 3, so I assign the string "healing potion" to array position 3. If this hadn't been the case, then I would have displayed the message, You have too many items and can't carry another.

So what happens if you do attempt to access an array element outside the bounds of the array? It depends, because you'd be accessing some unknown part of the computer's memory. At worst, if you attempt to assign some value to an element outside the bounds of an array you could cause your program to do unpredictable things, and it might even crash.

Testing to make sure that an index number is a valid array position before using it is called *bounds checking*. It's critical for you to perform bounds checking when there's a chance that an index you want to use might not be valid.

Understanding C-Style Strings

Before string objects came along, C++ programmers represented strings with arrays of characters terminated by a null character. These arrays of characters are now called *C-style strings* because the practice began in C programs. You can declare and initialize a C-style string like you would any other array.

```
char phrase[] = "Game Over!!!";
```

C-style strings terminate with a character called the *null character* to signify their end. You can write the null character as '\0'. I didn't need to use the null character in the previous code because it is stored at the end of the string for me. So technically, phrase has 13 elements. (However, functions that work with C-style strings will say that phrase has a length of 12, which makes sense and is in line with how string objects work.)

As with any other type of array, you can specify the array size when you define it. So another way to declare and initialize a C-style string is

```
char phrase[81] = "Game Over!!!";
```

The previous code creates a C-style string that can hold 80 printable characters (plus its terminating null character).

C-style strings don't have member functions. But the cstring file, which is part of the standard library, contains a variety of functions for working with C-style strings.

A nice thing about string objects is that they're designed to work seamlessly with C-style strings. For example, all of the following are completely valid uses of C-style strings with string objects:

```
string word1 = "Game";
char word2[] = " Over";

string phrase = word1 + word2;

if (word1 != word2)
    cout << "word1 and word2 are not equal.\n";

if (phrase.find(word2) != string::npos)
    cout << "word2 is contained in phrase.\n";
```

You can concatenate `string` objects and C-style strings, but the result is always a `string` object (so the code `char phrase2[] = word1 + word2;` would produce an error). You can compare `string` objects and C-style strings using the relational operators. And you can even use C-style strings as arguments in `string` object member functions.

C-style strings have the same shortcomings as arrays. One of the biggest is that their lengths are fixed. So the moral is: Use `string` objects whenever possible, but be prepared to work with C-style strings if necessary.

Using Multidimensional Arrays

As you've seen, sequences are great for games. You can use them in the form of a string to store a player's name, or you can use them in the form of any array to store a list of items in an RPG. But sometimes part of a game cries out for more than a linear list of things. Sometimes part of a game literally requires more dimension. For example, while you could represent a chessboard with a 64-element array, it really is much more intuitive to work with it as a two-dimensional entity of 8×8 elements. Fortunately, you can create an array of two or three (or even more dimensions) to best fit your game's needs.

Introducing the Tic-Tac-Toe Board Program

The Tic-Tac-Toe Board program displays a tic-tac-toe board. The program displays the board and declares X the winner. Although the program could have been written using a one-dimensional array, it uses a two-dimensional array to represent the board. Figure 3.5 illustrates the program.

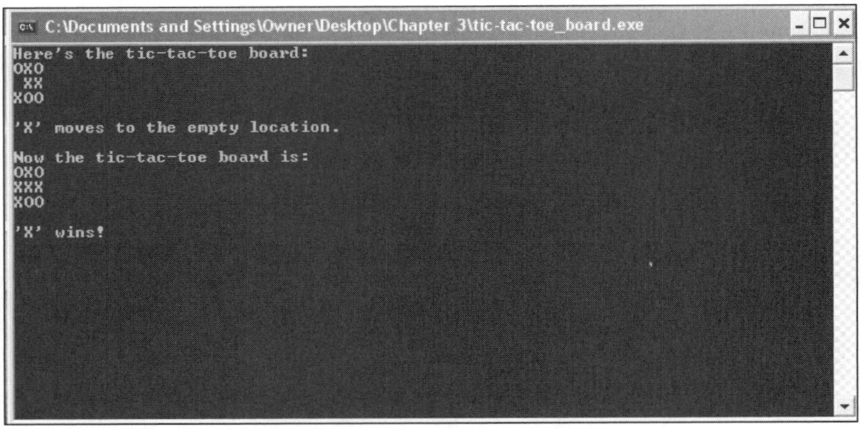

```
C:\Documents and Settings\Owner\Desktop\Chapter 3\tic-tac-toe_board.exe
Here's the tic-tac-toe board:
OXO
 XX
XOO

'X' moves to the empty location.

Now the tic-tac-toe board is:
OXO
XXX
XOO

'X' wins!
```

Figure 3.5
The tic-tac-toe board is represented by a two-dimensional array.

The code for the program is in the Chapter 3 folder on the CD-ROM that came with this book; the file name is tic-tac-toe_board.cpp.

```cpp
// Tic-Tac-Toe Board
// Demonstrates multidimensional arrays

#include <iostream>

using namespace std;

int main()
{
    const int ROWS = 3;
    const int COLUMNS = 3;
    char board[ROWS][COLUMNS] = { {'O', 'X', 'O'},
                                  {' ', 'X', 'X'},
                                  {'X', 'O', 'O'} };

    cout << "Here's the tic-tac-toe board:\n";
    for (int i = 0; i < ROWS; ++i)
    {
        for (int j = 0; j < COLUMNS; ++j)
            cout << board[i][j];
        cout << endl;
    }

    cout << "\n'X' moves to the empty location.\n\n";
    board[1][0] = 'X';

    cout << "Now the tic-tac-toe board is:\n";
    for (int i = 0; i < ROWS; ++i)
    {
        for (int j = 0; j < COLUMNS; ++j)
            cout << board[i][j];
        cout << endl;
    }

    cout << "\n'X' wins!";

    return 0;
}
```

Creating Multidimensional Arrays

One of the first things I do in the program is declare and initialize an array for the tic-tac-toe board.

```cpp
char board[ROWS][COLUMNS] = { {'O', 'X', 'O'},
                              {' ', 'X', 'X'},
                              {'X', 'O', 'O'} };
```

The preceding code declares a 3×3 (since ROWS and COLUMNS are both three) two-dimensional character array. It also initializes all of the elements.

hint

It's possible to simply declare a multidimensional array without initializing it. Here's an example:

```
char chessBoard[8][8];
```

The preceding code declares an 8×8, two-dimensional character array, chessBoard. By the way, multidimensional arrays aren't required to have the same size for each dimension. The following is a perfectly valid declaration for a game map represented by individual characters:

```
char map[12][20];
```

Indexing Multidimensional Arrays

The next thing I do in the program is display the tic-tac-toe board. But before I get into the details of that, I want to explain how to index an individual array element. You index an individual element of a multidimensional array by supplying a value for each dimension of the array. That's what I do to place an X in the array where a space was.

```
board[1][0] = 'X';
```

The previous code assigns the character to the element at board[1][0] (which was ' '). Then I display the tic-tac-toe board after the move the same way I displayed it before the move.

```
for (int i = 0; i < ROWS; ++i)
{
    for (int j = 0; j < COLUMNS; ++j)
        cout << board[i][j];
    cout << endl;
}
```

By using a pair of nested for loops, I move through the two-dimensional array and display the character elements as I go, forming a tic-tac-toe board.

Introducing Word Jumble

Word Jumble is a puzzle game in which the computer creates a version of a word where the letters are in random order. The player has to guess the word to win the game. If the player is stuck, he or she can ask for a hint. Figure 3.6 shows the game.

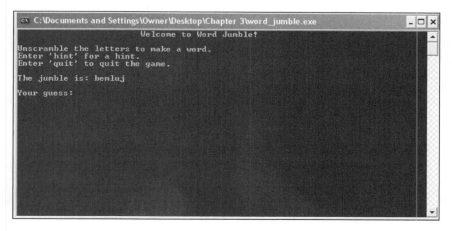

Figure 3.6
Hmm…the word looks "jumbled."

in the real world

Even though puzzle games don't usually break into the top-ten list of games, major companies still publish them year after year. Why? For one simple reason: They're profitable. Puzzle games, while not usually blockbusters, can still sell well. There are many gamers out there (casual and hardcore) who are drawn to the Zen of a well-designed puzzle game. And puzzle games cost much less to produce than the high-profile games that require large production teams and years of development time.

Setting Up the Program

As usual, I start with some comments and include the files I need.

```cpp
// Word Jumble
// The classic word jumble game where the player can ask for a hint

#include <iostream>
#include <string>
#include <cstdlib>
#include <ctime>

using namespace std;
```

Picking a Word to Jumble

My next task is to pick a word to jumble—the word the player will try to guess. First, I create a list of words and hints.

```
int main()
{
    enum fields {WORD, HINT, NUM_FIELDS};
    const int NUM_WORDS = 5;
    const string WORDS[NUM_WORDS][NUM_FIELDS] =
    {
        {"wall", "Do you feel you're banging your head against something?"},
        {"glasses", "These might help you see the answer."},
        {"labored", "Going slowly, is it?"},
        {"persistent", "Keep at it."},
        {"jumble", "It's what the game is all about."}
    };
```

I declare and initialize a two-dimensional array with words and corresponding hints. The enumeration defines enumerators for accessing the array. For example, WORDS[x][WORD] is always a string object that is one of the words, while WORDS[x][HINT] is the corresponding hint.

trick

You can list a final enumerator in an enumeration as a convenient way to store the number of elements. Here's an example:

```
enum difficulty {EASY, MEDIUM, HARD, NUM_DIFF_LEVELS};
cout << "There are " << NUM_DIFF_LEVELS << " difficulty levels."
```

In the previous code, NUM_DIFF_LEVELS is 3, the exact number of difficulty levels in the enumeration. As a result, the second line of code displays the message, There are 3 difficulty levels.

Next, I pick a random word from my choices.

```
srand(time(0));
int choice = (rand() % NUM_WORDS);
string theWord = WORDS[choice][WORD];   // word to guess
string theHint = WORDS[choice][HINT];   // hint for word
```

I generate a random index based on the number of words in the array. Then I assign both the random word at that index and its corresponding hint to the variables theWord and theHint.

Jumbling the Word

Now that I have the word for the player to guess, I need to create a jumbled version of it.

```
string jumble = theWord;   // jumbled version of word
int length = jumble.size();
for (int i = 0; i < length; ++i)
{
    int index1 = (rand() % length);
    int index2 = (rand() % length);
```

```
            char temp = jumble[index1];
            jumble[index1] = jumble[index2];
            jumble[index2] = temp;
    }
```

In the preceding code, I created a copy of the word jumble to...well, jumble. I generated two random positions in the string object and swapped the characters at those positions. I did this a number of times equal to the length of the word.

Welcoming the Player

Now it's time to welcome the player, which is what I do next.

```
    cout << "\t\t\tWelcome to Word Jumble!\n\n";
    cout << "Unscramble the letters to make a word.\n";
    cout << "Enter 'hint' for a hint.\n";
    cout << "Enter 'quit' to quit the game.\n\n";
    cout << "The jumble is: " << jumble;

    string guess;
    cout << "\n\nYour guess: ";
    cin >> guess;
```

I gave the player instructions on how to play, including how to quit and how to ask for a hint.

hint

As enthralling as you think your game is, you should always provide a way for the player to exit it.

Entering the Game Loop

Next, I enter the game loop.

```
    while ((guess != theWord) && (guess != "quit"))
    {
        if (guess == "hint")
            cout << theHint;
        else
            cout << "Sorry, that's not it.";

        cout <<"\n\nYour guess: ";
        cin >> guess;
    }
```

The loop continues to ask the player for a guess until the player either guesses the word or asks to quit.

Saying Goodbye

When the loop ends, the player has either won or quit, so it's time to say goodbye.

```
if (guess == theWord)
    cout << "\nThat's it! You guessed it!\n";

cout << "\nThanks for playing.\n";

return 0;
}
```

If the player has guessed the word, I congratulate him. Finally, I thank the player for playing.

Summary

In this chapter, you should have learned the following concepts:

- The for loop lets you repeat a section of code. In a for loop, you can provide an initialization statement, an expression to test, and an action to take after each loop iteration.

- for loops are often used for counting or looping through a sequence.

- Objects are encapsulated, cohesive entities that combine data (called *data members*) and functions (called *member functions*).

- string objects (often just called *strings*) are defined in the file string, which is part of the standard library. string objects allow you to store a sequence of characters and also have member functions.

- string objects are defined so that they work intuitively with familiar operators, such as the concatenation operator and the relational operators.

- All string objects have member functions, including those for determining a string object's length, determining whether or not a string object is empty, finding substrings, and removing substrings.

- Arrays provide a way to store and access sequences of any type.

- A limitation of arrays is that they have fixed lengths.

- You can access individual elements of string objects and arrays through the subscripting operator.

- Bounds checking is not enforced when attempts are made to access individual elements of string objects or arrays. Therefore, bounds checking is up to the programmer.

- C-style strings are character arrays terminated with the null character. They are the standard way to represent strings in the C language. And even though C-style strings are perfectly legal in C++, string objects are the preferred way to work with sequences of characters.
- Multidimensional arrays allow for access to array elements using multiple subscripts. For example, a chessboard can be represented as a two-dimensional array, 8×8 elements.

Questions and Answers

Q: Which is better, a while loop or a for loop?

A: Neither is inherently better than the other. Use the loop that best fits your needs.

Q: When might it be better to use a for loop than a while loop?

A: You can create a while loop to do the job of any for loop; however, there are some cases that cry out for a for loop. Those include counting and iterating through a sequence.

Q: Can I use break and continue statements with for loops?

A: Sure. And they behave just like they do in while loops: break ends the loop and continue jumps control back to the top of the loop.

Q: Why do programmers tend to use variable names such as i, j, and k as counters in for loops?

A: Believe it or not, programmers use i, j, and k mainly out of tradition. The practice started in early versions of the FORTRAN language, in which integer variables had to start with certain letters, including i, j, and k.

Q: I don't have to include a file to use int or char types, so why do I have to include the string file to use strings?

A: int and char are built-in types. They're always accessible in any C++ program. The string type, on the other hand, is not a built-in type. It's defined as part of the standard library in the file string.

Q: How did C-style strings get their name?

A: In the C programming language, programmers represent strings with arrays of characters terminated by a null character. This practice carried over to C++. After the new string type was introduced in C++, programmers needed a way to differentiate between the two. Therefore, the old method was dubbed C-style strings.

Q: Why should I use string objects instead of C-style strings?

A: string objects have advantages over C-style strings. The most obvious is that they are dynamically sizeable. You don't have to specify a length limit when you create one.

Q: Should I ever use C-style strings?

A: You should opt for `string` objects whenever possible. If you're working on an existing project that uses C-style strings, then you might have to work with C-style strings.

Q: What is operator overloading?

A: It's a process that allows you to define the use of familiar operators in different contexts with different but predictable results. For example, the + operator that is used to add numbers is overloaded by the `string` type to join strings.

Q: Can't operator overloading be confusing?

A: It's true that by overloading an operator you give it another meaning. But the new meaning applies only in a specific new context. For example, it's clear in the expression 4 + 6 that the + operator adds numbers, while in the expression `myString1 + myString2`, the + operator joins strings.

Q: Can I use the += operator to concatenate strings?

A: Yes, the += operator is overloaded so it works with strings.

Q: To get the number of characters in a `string` object, should I use the `length()` member function or the `size()` member function?

A: Both `length()` and `size()` return the same value, so you can use either.

Q: What's a predicate function?

A: A function that returns either `true` or `false`. The `string` object member function `empty()` is an example of a predicate function.

Q: What happens if I try to assign a value to an element beyond the bounds of an array?

A: C++ will allow you to make the assignment. However, the results are unpredictable and might cause your program to crash. That's because you're altering some unknown part of your computer's memory.

Q: Why should I use multidimensional arrays?

A: To make working with a group of elements more intuitive. For example, you could represent a chessboard with a one-dimensional array, as in `chessBoard[64]`, or you could represent it with a more intuitive, two-dimensional array, as in `chessBoard[8][8]`.

Discussion Questions

1. What are some of the things from your favorite game that you could represent as objects? What might their data members and member functions be?

2. What are the advantages of using an array over using a group of individual variables?

3. What are some limitations imposed by a fixed array size?

4. What are the advantages and disadvantages of operator overloading?

5. What kinds of games could you create using string objects, arrays, and for loops as your main tools?

Exercises

1. Improve the Word Jumble game by adding a scoring system. Make the point value for a word based on its length. Deduct points if the player asks for a hint.

2. What's wrong with the following code?

```
for (int i = 0; i <= phrase.size(); ++i)
    cout << "Character at position " << i << " is: " << phrase[i] << endl;
```

3. What's wrong with the following code?

```
const int ROWS = 2;
const int COLUMNS = 3;
char board[COLUMNS][ROWS] = { {'O', 'X', 'O'},
                             {' ', 'X', 'X'} };
```

CHAPTER 4

THE STANDARD TEMPLATE
LIBRARY: HANGMAN

So far you've seen how to work with sequences of values using arrays. But there are more sophisticated ways to work with collections of values. In fact, working with collections is so common that part of standard C++ is dedicated to doing just that. In this chapter, you'll get an introduction to this important library. Specifically, you'll learn to:

- Use vectors to work with sequences of values
- Use `vector` member functions to manipulate sequence elements
- Use iterators to move through sequences
- Use library algorithms to work with groups of elements
- Plan your programs with pseudocode

Introducing the Standard Template Library

Good game programmers are lazy. It's not that they don't want to work; it's just that they don't want to redo work that's already been done—especially if it has been done well. The STL (*Standard Template Library*) represents a powerful collection of programming work that's been done well. It provides a group of containers, algorithms, and iterators, among other things.

So what's a container and how can it help you write games? Well, containers let you store and access collections of values of the same type. Yes, arrays let you do the same thing, but the STL containers offer more flexibility and power than a simple but trusty array. The STL defines a variety of container types; each works in a different way to meet different needs.

The algorithms defined in the STL work with its containers. The *algorithms* are common functions that game programmers find themselves repeatedly applying to groups of values. They include algorithms for sorting, searching, copying, merging, inserting, and removing container elements. The cool thing is that the same algorithm can work its magic on many different container types.

Iterators are objects that identify elements in containers and can be manipulated to move among elements. They're great for, well, iterating through containers. In addition, iterators are required by the STL algorithms.

All of this makes a lot more sense when you see an actual implementation of one of the container types, so that's up next.

Using Vectors

The vector class defines one kind of container provided by the STL. It meets the general description of a *dynamic array*—an array that can grow and shrink in size as needed. In addition, vector defines member functions to manipulate vector elements. This means that the vector has all of the functionality of the array plus more.

Introducing the Hero's Inventory 2.0 Program

From the user's point of view, the Hero's Inventory 2.0 program is similar to its predecessor, the Hero's Inventory program from Chapter 3. The new version stores and works with a collection of string objects that represent a hero's inventory. However, from the programmer's perspective the program is quite different. That's because the new program uses a vector instead of an array to represent the inventory. Figure 4.1 shows the results of the program.

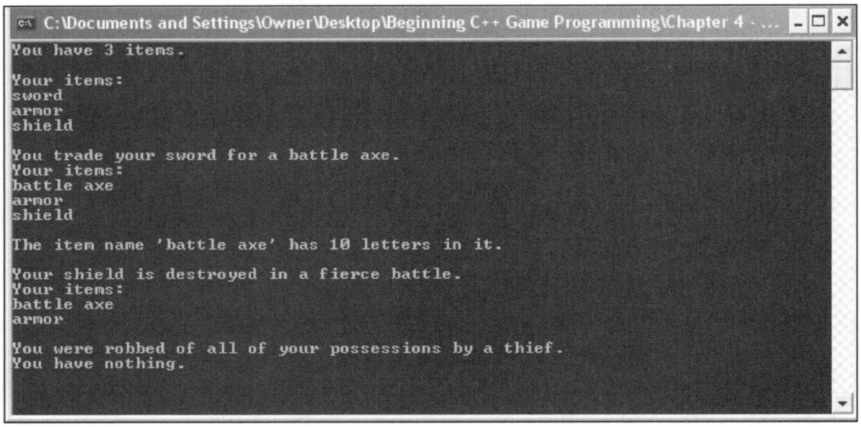

Figure 4.1
This time the hero's inventory is represented by a vector.

The code for the program is in the Chapter 4 folder on the CD-ROM that came with this book; the file name is heros_inventory2.cpp.

```cpp
// Hero's Inventory 2.0
// Demonstrates vectors

#include <iostream>
#include <string>
#include <vector>

using namespace std;

int main()
{
    vector<string> inventory;
    inventory.push_back("sword");
    inventory.push_back("armor");
    inventory.push_back("shield");

    cout << "You have " << inventory.size() << " items.\n";

    cout << "\nYour items:\n";
    for (int i = 0; i < inventory.size(); ++i)
        cout << inventory[i] << endl;

    cout << "\nYou trade your sword for a battle axe.";
    inventory[0] = "battle axe";
    cout << "\nYour items:\n";
    for (int i = 0; i < inventory.size(); ++i)
        cout << inventory[i] << endl;

    cout << "\nThe item name '" << inventory[0] << "' has ";
    cout << inventory[0].size() << " letters in it.\n";

    cout << "\nYour shield is destroyed in a fierce battle.";
    inventory.pop_back();
    cout << "\nYour items:\n";
    for (int i = 0; i < inventory.size(); ++i)
        cout << inventory[i] << endl;

    cout << "\nYou were robbed of all of your possessions by a thief.";
    inventory.clear();
    if (inventory.empty())
        cout << "\nYou have nothing.\n";
    else
        cout << "\nYou have at least one item.\n";

 return 0;
}
```

Preparing to Use Vectors

Before I can declare a vector, I have to include the file that contains its definition.

```
#include <vector>
```

All STL components live in the `std` namespace, so by using the following code (as I typically do) I can refer to `vector` without having to precede it with `std::`.

```
using namespace std;
```

Declaring a Vector

Okay, the first thing I do in `main()` is declare a new vector.

```
vector<string> inventory;
```

The preceding line declared an empty vector named `inventory`, which can contain `string` object elements. Declaring an empty vector is fine because it grows in size when you add new elements.

To declare a vector of your own, write `vector` followed by the type of objects you want to use with the vector (surrounded by the ⟨ and ⟩ symbols), followed by the vector name.

hint

There are additional ways to declare a vector. You can declare one with a starting size by specifying a number in parentheses after the vector name.

```
vector<string> inventory(10);
```

The preceding code declared a vector to hold `string` object elements with a starting size of 10. You can also initialize all of a vector's elements to the same value when you declare it. You simply supply the number of elements followed by the starting value, as in:

```
vector<string> inventory(10, "nothing");
```

The preceding code declared a vector with a size of 10 and initialized all 10 elements to "nothing". Finally, you can declare a vector and initialize it with the contents of another vector.

```
vector<string> inventory(myStuff);
```

The preceding code created a new vector with the same contents as the vector myStuff.

Using the push_back() Member Function

Next I give the hero the same three starting items as in the previous version of the program.

```
inventory.push_back("sword");
inventory.push_back("armor");
inventory.push_back("shield");
```

The push_back() member function adds a new element to the end of a vector. In the preceding lines I added "sword", "armor", and "shield" to inventory. As a result, inventory[0] is equal to "sword", inventory[1] is equal to "armor", and inventory[2] is equal to "shield".

Using the size() Member Function

Next I display the number of items the hero has in his possession.

```
cout << "You have " << inventory.size() << " items.\n";
```

I get the size of inventory by calling the size() member function with inventory.size(). The size() member function simply returns the size of a vector. In this case, it returns 3.

Indexing Vectors

Next I display all of the hero's items.

```
cout << "\nYour items:\n";
for (int i = 0; i < inventory.size(); ++i)
    cout << inventory[i] << endl;
```

Just as with arrays, you can index vectors by using the subscripting operator. In fact, the preceding code is nearly identical to the same section of code from the original Hero's Inventory program. The only difference is that I used inventory.size() to specify when the loop should end.

Next I replace the hero's first item.

```
inventory[0] = "battle axe";
```

Again, just as with arrays, I use the subscripting operator to assign a new value to an existing element position.

trap

Although vectors are dynamic, you can't increase a vector's size by applying the subscripting operator. For example, the following highly dangerous code snippet does not increase the size of the vector `inventory`:

```
vector<string> inventory; //creating an empty vector
inventory[0] = "sword";   //may cause your program to crash!
```

Just as with arrays, you can attempt to access a nonexistent element position—but with potentially disastrous results. The preceding code changed some unknown section of your computer's memory and could cause your program to crash. To add a new element at the end of a vector, use the `push_back()` member function.

Calling Member Functions of an Element

Next I show the number of letters in the name of the first item in the hero's inventory.

```
cout << inventory[0].size() << " letters in it.\n";
```

Just as with arrays, you can access the member functions of a vector element by writing the element, followed by the member selection operator, followed by the member function name. Because `inventory[0]` is equal to `"battle axe"`, `inventory[0].size()` returns 10.

Using the pop_back() Member Function

I remove the hero's shield using

```
inventory.pop_back();
```

The `pop_back()` member function removes the last element of a vector and reduces the vector size by one. In this case, `inventory.pop_back()` removes `"shield"` from `inventory` because that was the last element in the vector. Also, the size of `inventory` is reduced from 3 to 2.

Using the clear() Member Function

Next I simulate the act of a thief robbing the hero of all of his items.

```
inventory.clear();
```

The `clear()` member function removes all of the items of a vector and sets its size to 0. After the previous line of code executes, `inventory` is an empty vector.

Using the empty() Member Function

Finally, I check to see whether the hero has any items in his inventory.

```
if (inventory.empty())
    cout << "\nYou have nothing.\n";
else
    cout << "\nYou have at least one item.\n";
```

The vector member function empty() works just like the string member function empty(). It returns true if the vector is empty; otherwise, it returns false. Because inventory is empty in this case, the program displays the message, You have nothing.

Using Iterators

Iterators are the key to using containers to their fullest potential. With iterators you can, well, iterate through a sequence container. In addition, important parts of the STL require iterators. Many container member functions and STL algorithms take iterators as arguments. So if you want to reap the benefits of these member functions and algorithms, you've got to use iterators.

Introducing the Hero's Inventory 3.0 Program

The Hero's Inventory 3.0 program acts like its two predecessors, at least at the start. The program shows off a list of items, replaces the first item, and displays the number of letters in the name of an item. But then the program does something new: It inserts an item at the beginning of the group, and then it removes an item from the middle of the group. The program accomplishes all of this by working with iterators. Figure 4.2 shows the program in action.

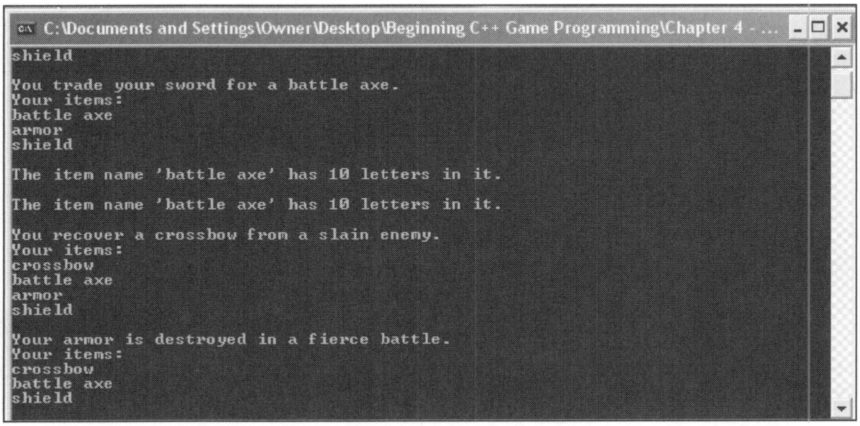

Figure 4.2
The program performs a few vector manipulations that you can accomplish only with iterators.

The code for the program is in the Chapter 4 folder on the CD-ROM that came with this book; the file name is heros_inventory3.cpp.

```cpp
// Hero's Inventory 3.0
// Demonstrates iterators

#include <iostream>
#include <string>
#include <vector>

using namespace std;

int main()
{
    vector<string> inventory;
    inventory.push_back("sword");
    inventory.push_back("armor");
    inventory.push_back("shield");

    vector<string>::iterator myIterator;
    vector<string>::const_iterator iter;

    cout << "Your items:\n";
    for (iter = inventory.begin(); iter != inventory.end(); ++iter)
        cout << *iter << endl;

    cout << "\nYou trade your sword for a battle axe.";
    myIterator = inventory.begin();
    *myIterator = "battle axe";
    cout << "\nYour items:\n";
    for (iter = inventory.begin(); iter != inventory.end(); ++iter)
        cout << *iter << endl;

    cout << "\nThe item name '" << *myIterator << "' has ";
    cout << (*myIterator).size() << " letters in it.\n";

    cout << "\nThe item name '" << *myIterator << "' has ";
    cout << myIterator->size() << " letters in it.\n";

    cout << "\nYou recover a crossbow from a slain enemy.";
    inventory.insert(inventory.begin(), "crossbow");
    cout << "\nYour items:\n";
    for (iter = inventory.begin(); iter != inventory.end(); ++iter)
        cout << *iter << endl;

    cout << "\nYour armor is destroyed in a fierce battle.";
    inventory.erase((inventory.begin() + 2));
    cout << "\nYour items:\n";
    for (iter = inventory.begin(); iter != inventory.end(); ++iter)
        cout << *iter << endl;
```

```
  return 0;
}
```

Declaring Iterators

After I declare a vector for the hero's inventory and add the same three string objects from the previous incarnations of the program, I declare an iterator.

```
vector<string>::iterator myIterator;
```

The preceding line declared an iterator named myIterator for a vector that contains string objects. To declare an iterator of you own, follow the same pattern. Write the container type, followed by the type of objects the container will hold (surrounded by the < and > symbols), followed by the scope resolution operator (the :: symbol), followed by iterator, followed by a name for your new iterator.

So what are iterators? *Iterators* are values that identify a particular element in a container. Given an iterator, you can access the value of the element. Given the right kind of iterator, you can change the value. Iterators can also move among elements via familiar arithmetic operators.

A way to think about iterators is to imagine them as Post-it notes that you can stick on a specific element in a container. An iterator is not one of the elements, but a way to refer to one. Specifically, I can use myIterator to refer to a particular element of the vector inventory. That is, I can stick the myIterator Post-it note on a specific element in inventory. Once I've done that, I can access the element or even change it through the iterator.

Next, I declare another iterator.

```
vector<string>::const_iterator iter;
```

The preceding line of code created a constant iterator named iter for a vector that contains string objects. A *constant iterator* is just like a regular iterator except that you can't use it to change the element to which it refers; the element must remain constant. You can think of a constant iterator as providing read-only access. However, the iterator itself can change. This means you can move iter all around the vector inventory as you see fit. You can't, however, change the value of any of the elements through iter. With a constant iterator the Post-it can change, but the thing it's stuck to can't.

Why would you want to use a constant iterator if it's a limited version of a regular iterator? First, it makes your intentions clearer. When you use a constant iterator, it's clear that you won't be changing any element to which it refers. Second, it's safer. You can use a constant iterator to avoid accidentally changing a container element. (If you attempt to change an element through a constant iterator, you'll generate a compile error.)

trap

Using push_back() might invalidate all iterators referencing the vector.

Is all of this iterator talk a little too abstract for you? Are you tired of analogies about Post-it notes? Fear not—next, I put an actual iterator to work.

Looping through a Vector

Next I loop through the contents of the vector and display the hero's inventory.

```
cout << "Your items:\n";
for (iter = inventory.begin(); iter != inventory.end(); ++iter)
    cout << *iter << endl;
```

In the preceding code, I used a for loop to move from the first to the last element of inventory. At this general level, this is exactly how I looped through the contents of the vector in Hero's Inventory 2.0. But instead of using an integer and the subscripting operator to access each element, I used an iterator. Basically, I moved the Post-it note through the entire sequence of elements and displayed the value of each element to which the note is stuck. There are a lot of new ideas in this little loop, so I'll tackle them one at a time.

Calling the begin() vector Member Function

In the initialization statement of the loop, I assign the return value of inventory.begin() to iter. The begin() member function returns an iterator that refers to a container's first element. So in this case, the statement assigns an iterator that refers to the first element of inventory (the string object equal to "sword") to iter. Figure 4.3 shows an abstract view of the iterator returned by a call to inventory.begin(). (Note that the figure is abstract because the vector inventory doesn't contain the string literals "sword", "armor", and "shield"; it contains string objects.)

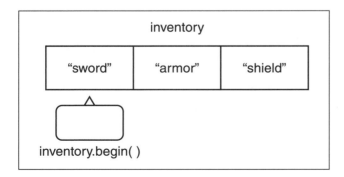

Figure 4.3
A call to inventory.begin() returns an iterator that refers to the first element in the vector.

Calling the end() vector Member Function

In the test statement of the loop, I test the return value of `inventory.end()` against `iter` to make sure the two are not equal. The `end()` member function returns an iterator one past the last element in a container. This means the loop will continue until `iter` has moved through all of the elements in `inventory`. Figure 4.4 shows an abstract view of the iterator returned by a call to this member function. (Note that the figure is abstract because the vector `inventory` doesn't contain the string literals `"sword"`, `"armor"`, and `"shield"`; it contains `string` objects.)

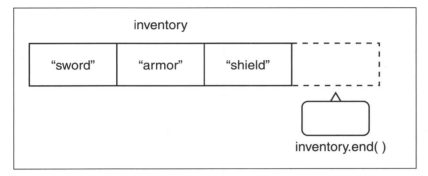

Figure 4.4
A call to `inventory.end()` returns an iterator one past the last element of the vector.

trap

The `end()` `vector` member function returns an iterator that's one *past* the last element in the vector—not the last element. Therefore, you can't get a value from the iterator returned by `end()`. This might seem counterintuitive, but it works well for loops that move through a container.

Altering an Iterator

The action statement in the loop, `++iter`, increments `iter`, which moves it to the next element in the vector. Depending upon the iterator, you can perform other mathematical operations on iterators to move them around a container. Most often, though, you'll find that you simply want to increment an iterator.

Dereferencing an Iterator

In the loop body, I send `*iter` to `cout`. By placing the dereference operator (*) in front of `iter`, I display the value of the element to which the iterator refers (not the iterator itself). By placing the dereference operator in front of an iterator, you're saying, "Treat this as the thing that the iterator references, not as the iterator itself."

Changing the Value of a Vector Element

Next I change the first element in the vector from the `string` object equal to `"sword"` to the `string` object equal to `"battle axe"`. First I set `myIterator` to reference the first element of `inventory`.

```
myIterator = inventory.begin();
```

Then I change the value of the first element.

```
*myIterator = "battle axe";
```

Remember, by dereferencing `myIterator` with `*`, the preceding assignment statement says, "Assign `"battle axe"` to the element that `myIterator` references." It does not change `myIterator`. After the assignment statement, `myIterator` still refers to the first element in the vector.

Just to prove that the assignment worked, I then display all of the elements in `inventory`.

Accessing Member Functions of a Vector Element

Next I display the number of characters in the name of the first item in the hero's inventory.

```
cout << "\nThe item name '" << *myIterator << "' has ";
cout << (*myIterator).size() << " letters in it.\n";
```

The code `(*myIterator).size()` says, "Take the result of dereferencing `myIterator` and call that object's `size()` member function." Because `myIterator` refers to the `string` object equal to `"battle axe"`, the code returns 10.

hint

Whenever you dereference an iterator to access a data member or member function, surround the dereferenced iterator with a pair of parentheses. This ensures that the dot operator will be applied to the object the iterator references.

The code `(*myIterator).size()` is not the prettiest, so C++ offers an alternative, more intuitive way to express the same thing, which I demonstrate in the next two lines of the program.

```
cout << "\nThe item name '" << *myIterator << "' has ";
cout << myIterator->size() << " letters in it.\n";
```

The preceding code does exactly the same thing as the first pair of lines I presented in this section; it displays the number of characters in `"battle axe"`. However, notice that I substitute `myIterator->size()` for `(*myIterator).size()`. You can see that the first version (with the `->` symbol) is more readable. The two pieces of code mean exactly the same thing to the computer, but the second is easier for humans to use. In general, you can use the `->` operator to access the member functions or data members of an object that an iterator references.

Using the insert() vector Member Function

Next I add a new item to the hero's inventory. This time, though, I don't add the item to the end of the sequence; instead, I insert it at the beginning.

```
inventory.insert(inventory.begin(), "crossbow");
```

One form of the `insert()` member function inserts a new element into a vector just before the element referred to by a given iterator. You supply two arguments to this version of `insert()`—the first is an iterator, and the second is the element to be inserted. In this case, I inserted `"crossbow"` into `inventory` just before the first element. As a result, all of the other elements will move down by one. This version of the `insert()` member function returns an iterator that references the newly inserted element. In this case, I don't assign the returned iterator to a variable.

Next I show the contents of the vector to prove the insertion worked.

Using the erase() vector Member Function

Next I remove an item from the hero's inventory. However, this time I don't remove the item at the end of the sequence; instead, I remove one from the middle.

```
inventory.erase((inventory.begin() + 2));
```

One form of the `erase()` member function removes an element from a vector. You supply one argument to this version of `erase()`—the iterator that references the element you want to remove. In this case, I passed `(inventory.begin() + 2)`, which is equal to the iterator that references the third element in `inventory`. This removes the `string` object equal to `"armor"`.

As a result, all of the following elements will move up by one. This version of the `erase()` member function returns an iterator that references the element after the element that was removed. In this case, I don't assign the returned iterator to a variable.

trap

Calling the `erase()` member function on a vector invalidates all of the iterators that reference elements after the removal point because all of the elements after the removal point are shifted up by one.

Next I show the contents of the vector to prove the removal worked.

Using Algorithms

The STL defines a group of algorithms that allow you to manipulate elements in containers through iterators. Algorithms exist for common tasks such as searching, sorting, and copying container elements. These algorithms are your built-in arsenal of flexible and efficient weapons. By using them, you can leave the mundane task of manipulating container elements in common ways to the STL so you can concentrate on writing your game. The powerful thing about these algorithms is that they are generic—the same algorithm can work with elements of different container types.

Introducing the High Scores Program

The High Scores program creates a vector of high scores. It uses STL algorithms to randomize and then sort the scores. Then the program creates another vector of scores and merges the two—again with an algorithm. Figure 4.5 illustrates the program.

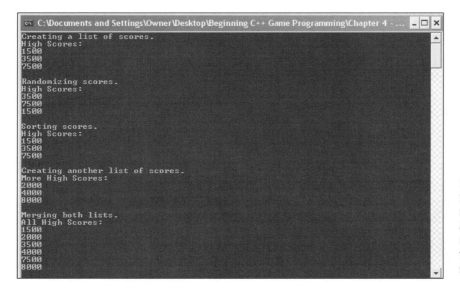

Figure 4.5
STL algorithms randomize, sort, and merge elements of vectors of high scores.

The code for the program is in the Chapter 4 folder on the CD-ROM that came with this book; the file name is high_scores.cpp.

```cpp
// High Scores
// Demonstrates algorithms

#include <iostream>
#include <vector>
#include <algorithm>
#include <ctime>
#include <cstdlib>

using namespace std;

int main()
{
    vector<int>::const_iterator iter;

    cout << "Creating a list of scores.";
    vector<int> scores;
    scores.push_back(1500);
    scores.push_back(3500);
    scores.push_back(7500);

    cout << "\nHigh Scores:\n";
    for (iter = scores.begin(); iter != scores.end(); ++iter)
        cout << *iter << endl;

    cout << "\nRandomizing scores.";
    srand(time(0));
    random_shuffle(scores.begin(), scores.end());
    cout << "\nHigh Scores:\n";
    for (iter = scores.begin(); iter != scores.end(); ++iter)
        cout << *iter << endl;

    cout << "\nSorting scores.";
    sort(scores.begin(), scores.end());
    cout << "\nHigh Scores:\n";
    for (iter = scores.begin(); iter != scores.end(); ++iter)
        cout << *iter << endl;

    cout << "\nCreating another list of scores." ;
    vector<int> moreScores;
    moreScores.push_back(2000);
    moreScores.push_back(4000);
    moreScores.push_back(8000);

    cout << "\nMore High Scores:\n";
    for (iter = moreScores.begin(); iter != moreScores.end(); ++iter)
        cout << *iter << endl;
```

```
cout << "\nMerging both lists.";
vector<int> allScores(6);  //need container big enough to hold results
merge(scores.begin(), scores.end(),
      moreScores.begin(), moreScores.end(),
      allScores.begin());

cout << "\nAll High Scores:\n";
for (iter = allScores.begin(); iter != allScores.end(); ++iter)
    cout << *iter << endl;

return 0;
}
```

Preparing to Use Algorithms

So that I can use the STL algorithms, I include the file with their definitions.

```
#include <algorithm>
```

As you know, all STL components live in the std namespace. By using the following code (as I typically do), I can refer to algorithms without having to precede them with std::.

```
using namespace std;
```

Using the random_shuffle() Algorithm

After I display the contents of the vector scores, which contains three high scores in ascending order, I prepare to randomize the scores using the random_shuffle() STL algorithm. Just as when I generate a single random number, I seed the random number generator before I call random_shuffle(), so the order of the scores might be different each time I run the program.

```
srand(time(0));
```

Then I reorder the scores in a random way.

```
random_shuffle(scores.begin(), scores.end());
```

The random_shuffle() algorithm randomizes the elements of a sequence. You must supply as iterators the starting and ending points of the sequence to shuffle. In this case, I passed the iterators returned by scores.begin() and scores.end(). These two iterators indicate that I want to shuffle all of the elements in scores. As a result, scores contains the same scores, but in some random order.

Finally, I display the scores to prove the randomization worked.

trick

Although you might not want to randomize a list of high scores, random_shuffle() is a valuable algorithm for games. You can use it for everything from shuffling a deck of cards to mixing up the order of the enemies a player will encounter in a game level.

Using the sort() Algorithm

Next I sort the scores.

```
sort(scores.begin(), scores.end());
```

The sort() algorithm sorts the elements of a sequence in ascending order. You must supply as iterators the starting and ending points of the sequence to sort. In this particular case, I passed the iterators returned by scores.begin() and scores.end(). These two iterators indicate that I want to sort all of the elements in scores. As a result, scores contains all of the scores in ascending order.

Next I display the scores to prove the sorting worked.

Using the merge() Algorithm

Next I prepare to use the merge() algorithm to combine two vectors that contain high scores. First, I create a new vector named moreScores, which contains three additional scores. Then I create an empty vector with a size of 6 named allScores to hold the results of the merge. Finally, I merge the vectors scores and moreScores and place the resulting sequence in allScores.

```
merge(scores.begin(), scores.end(),
      moreScores.begin(), moreScores.end(),
      allScores.begin());
```

The merge() algorithm combines two sorted sequences into another sorted sequence. An iterator to the resulting sequence is returned. The algorithm requires the beginning and ending points of the two sequences to be merged and the beginning point of the resulting sequence. The resulting container must be large enough to accommodate the merged sequence.

In this case, I passed the iterators returned by scores.begin() and scores.end(), followed by moreScores.begin() and moreScores.end(), to indicate that I want to merge the entire sequence of elements in scores with the entire sequence of elements in moreScores. I passed allScores.begin() to indicate that I want the results put in allScores, starting at the beginning position of the vector.

trap

The container you specify to hold the results of merge() must be large enough to accommodate all of the elements in the newly merged sequence. merge() does not increase the size of the container.

trick

A very cool property of STL algorithms is that they can work with containers defined outside of the STL. These containers only have to meet certain requirements. For example, even though `string` objects are not part of the STL, you can use appropriate STL algorithms on them. The following code snippet demonstrates this:

```
string word = "High Scores";
random_shuffle(word.begin(), word.end());
```

The preceding code randomly shuffles the characters in `word`. As you can see, `string` objects have both `begin()` and `end()` member functions, which return iterators to the first character and one past the last character, respectively. That's part of the reason why STL algorithms work with `string`s—because they're designed to.

Understanding Vector Performance

Like all STL containers, vectors provide game programmers with sophisticated ways to work with information, but this level of sophistication can come at a performance cost. And if there's one thing game programmers obsess about, it's performance. But fear not, vectors and other STL containers are incredibly efficient. In fact, they've already been used in published PC and console games. However, these containers have their strengths and weaknesses; a game programmer needs to understand the performance characteristics of the various container types so that he can choose the right one for the job.

Examining Vector Growth

Although vectors grow dynamically as needed, every vector has a specific size. When a new element added to a vector pushes the vector beyond its current size, the computer reallocates memory and might even copy all of the vector elements to this newly seized chunk of memory real estate. This can cause a performance hit.

The most important thing to keep in mind about program performance is whether or not you need to care. For example, vector memory reallocation might not occur at a performance-critical part of your program. In that case, you can safely ignore the cost of reallocation. Also, with small vectors, the reallocation cost might be insignificant, so again you can safely ignore it. However, if you need greater control over when these memory reallocations occur, you have it.

Using the capacity() Member Function

The `capacity()` vector member function returns the capacity of a vector—in other words, the number of elements that a vector can hold before a program must reallocate more memory for it. A vector's capacity is not the same thing as its size (the number of elements a vector currently holds). Here's a code snippet to help drive this point home:

```
cout << "Creating a 10 element vector to hold scores.\n";
vector<int> scores(10, 0);  //initialize all 10 elements to 0
cout << "Vector size is :" << scores.size() << endl;
cout << "Vector capacity is:" << scores.capacity() << endl;

cout << "Adding a score.\n";
scores.push_back(0);  //memory is reallocated to accommodate growth
cout << "Vector size is :" << scores.size() << endl;
cout << "Vector capacity is:" << scores.capacity() << endl;
```

Right after I declare and initialize the vector, this code reports that its size and capacity are both 10. However, after an element is added, the code reports that the vector's size is 11 while its capacity is 20. That's because the capacity of a vector doubles every time a program reallocates additional memory for it. In this case, when a new score was added, memory was reallocated and the capacity of the vector doubled from 10 to 20.

Using the reserve() Member Function

The reserve() member function increases the capacity of a vector to the number supplied as an argument. Using reserve() gives you control over when a reallocation of additional memory occurs. Here's an example:

```
cout << "Creating a list of scores.\n";
vector<int> scores(10, 0);  //initialize all 10 elements to 0
cout << "Vector size is :" << scores.size() << endl;
cout << "Vector capacity is:" << scores.capacity() << endl;

cout << "Reserving more memory.\n";
scores.reserve(20);  //reserve memory for 10 additional elements
cout << "Vector size is :" << scores.size() << endl;
cout << "Vector capacity is:" << scores.capacity() << endl;
```

Right after I declare and initialize the vector, this code reports that its size and capacity are both 10. However, after I reserve memory for 10 additional elements, the code reports that the vector's size is still 10 while its capacity is 20.

By using reserve() to keep a vector's capacity large enough for your purposes, you can delay memory reallocation to a time of your choosing.

hint

As a beginning game programmer, it's good to be aware of how vector memory allocation works; however, don't obsess over it. The first game programs you'll write probably won't benefit from a more manual process of vector memory allocation.

Examining Element Insertion and Deletion

Adding or removing an element from the end of a vector using the `push_back()` or `pop_back()` member function is extremely efficient. However, adding or removing an element at any other point in a vector (for example, using `insert()` or `erase()`) can require more work because you might have to move multiple elements to accommodate the insertion or deletion. With small vectors the overhead is usually insignificant, but with larger vectors (with, say, thousands of elements), inserting or erasing elements from the middle of a vector can cause a performance hit.

Fortunately, the STL offers another sequence container type, `list`, which allows for efficient insertion and deletion regardless of the sequence size. The important thing to remember is that one container type isn't the solution for every problem. Although `vector` is versatile and perhaps the most popular STL container type, there are times when another container type might make more sense.

trap

Just because you want to insert or delete elements from the middle of a sequence, that doesn't mean you should abandon the vector. It might still be a good choice for your game program. It really depends on how you use the sequence. If your sequence is small or there are only a few insertion and deletions, then a vector might still be your best bet.

Examining Other STL Containers

The STL defines a variety of container types that fall into two basic categories—sequential and associative. With a *sequential container*, you can retrieve values in sequence, while an *associative container* lets you retrieve values based on keys. `vector` is an example of a sequential container.

How might you use these different container types? Consider an online, turned-based strategy game. You could use a sequential container to store a group of players that you want to cycle through in, well, sequence. On the other hand, you could use an associative container to retrieve player information in a random-access fashion by looking up a unique identifier, such as a player's IP address.

Finally, the STL defines container adaptors that adapt one of the sequence containers. *Container adaptors* represent standard computer science data structures. Although they are not official containers, they look and feel just like them. Table 4.1 lists the container types offered by the STL.

Table 4.1 STL Containers

Container	Type	Description
deque	Sequential	Double-ended queue
list	Sequential	Linear list
map	Associative	Collection of key/value pairs in which each key is associated with exactly one value
multimap	Associative	Collection of key/value pairs in which each key may be associated with more than one value
multiset	Associative	Collection in which each element is not necessarily unique
priority_queue	Adaptor	Priority queue
queue	Adaptor	Queue
set	Associative	Collection in which each element is unique
stack	Adaptor	Stack
vector	Sequential	Dynamic array

Planning Your Programs

So far all the programs you've seen have been pretty simple. The idea of formally planning any of them on paper probably seems like overkill. It's not—planning your programs (even the small ones) will almost always result in time (and frustration) saved.

Programming is a lot like construction. Imagine a contractor building a house for you without a blueprint. Yikes! You might end up with a house that has 12 bathrooms, no windows, and a front door on the second floor. Plus, it probably would cost you 10 times the estimated price. Programming is the same way. Without a plan, you'll likely struggle through the process and waste time. You might even end up with a program that doesn't quite work.

Using Pseudocode

Many programmers sketch out their programs using *pseudocode*—a language that falls somewhere between English and a formal programming language. Anyone who understands English should be able to follow pseudocode. Here's an example: Suppose I want to make a million dollars. A worthy goal, but what do I do to achieve it? I need a plan. So I come up with one and put it in pseudocode.

```
If you can think of a new and useful product
    Then that's your product
Otherwise
    Repackage an existing product as your product
Make an infomercial about your product
Show the infomercial on TV
Charge $100 per unit of your product
Sell 10,000 units of your product
```

Even though anyone, even a non-programmer, can understand my plan, my pseudocode feels vaguely like a program. The first four lines resemble an `if` statement with an `else` clause, and that's intentional. When you write your plan, you should try to incorporate the feel of the code that you're representing with pseudocode.

Using Stepwise Refinement

Your programming plan might not be finished after only one draft. Often pseudocode needs multiple passes before it can be implemented in programming code. *Stepwise refinement* is one process used to rewrite pseudocode to make it ready for implementation. Stepwise refinement is pretty simple. Basically, it means, "Make it more detailed." By taking each step described in pseudocode and breaking it down into a series of simpler steps, the plan becomes closer to programming code. Using stepwise refinement, you keep breaking down each step until you feel the entire plan could be fairly easily translated into a program. As an example, take a step from my master plan to make a million dollars.

```
Create an infomercial about your product
```

This might seem like too vague of a task. How do you create an infomercial? Using stepwise refinement, you can break down the single step into several others. So it becomes

```
Write a script for an infomercial about your product
Rent a TV studio for a day
Hire a production crew
Hire an enthusiastic audience
Film the infomercial
```

If you feel these five steps are clear and achievable, then that part of the pseudocode has been thoroughly refined. If you're still unclear about a step, refine it some more. Continue with this process and you will have a complete plan—and a million dollars.

Introducing Hangman

In the Hangman program, the computer picks a secret word and the player tries to guess it one letter at a time. The player is allowed eight incorrect guesses. If he or she fails to guess the word in time, the player is hanged and the game is over. Figure 4.6 shows the game.

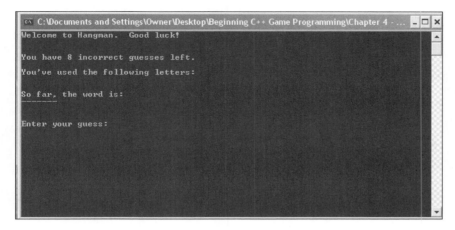

Figure 4.6
The Hangman game in action

Planning the Game

Before I write a single line in C++, I plan the game program using pseudocode.

```
Create a group of words
Pick a random word from the group as the secret word
While player hasn't made too many incorrect guesses and hasn't guessed
the secret word
        Tell player how many incorrect guesses he or she has left
        Show player the letters he or she has guessed
        Show player how much of the secret word he or she has guessed
        Get player's next guess
        While player has entered a letter that he or she has already guessed
                Get player's guess
        Add the new guess to the group of used letters
        If the guess is in the secret word
                Tell the player the guess is correct
                Update the word guessed so far with the new letter
        Otherwise
                Tell the player the guess is incorrect
                Increment the number of incorrect guesses the player has made
If the player has made too many incorrect guesses
        Tell the player that he or she has been hanged
Otherwise
        Congratulate the player on guessing the secret word
```

Although the pseudocode doesn't account for every line of C++ I'll write, I think it does a good job describing what I need to do. Then I begin writing the program.

Setting Up the Program

As usual, I start with some comments and include the files I need.

```
// Hangman
// The classic game of hangman

#include <iostream>
#include <string>
#include <vector>
#include <algorithm>
#include <ctime>
#include <cctype>

using namespace std;
```

Notice that I include a new file—cctype. It's part of the standard library and it includes functions for converting characters to uppercase, which I use so I can compare apples to apples (uppercase to uppercase) when I compare individual characters.

Initializing Variables and Constants

Next I start the main() function and initialize variables and constants for the game.

```
int main()
{
    //setup
    const int MAX_WRONG = 8;   //maximum number of incorrect guesses allowed

    vector<string> words;  //collection of possible words to guess
    words.push_back("GUESS");
    words.push_back("HANGMAN");
    words.push_back("DIFFICULT");

    srand(time(0));
    random_shuffle(words.begin(), words.end());
    const string THE_WORD = words[0];          //word to guess
    int wrong = 0;                             //number of incorrect guesses
    string soFar(THE_WORD.size(), '-');        //word guessed so far
    string used = "";                          //letters already guessed

    cout << "Welcome to Hangman. Good luck!\n";
```

MAX_WRONG is the maximum number of incorrect guesses the player can make. words is a vector of possible words to guess. I randomize words using the random_shuffle() algorithm, and then I assign the first word in the vector to THE_WORD, which is the secret word the player must guess. wrong is the number of incorrect guesses the player has made. soFar is the word guessed so far by the player. soFar starts out as a series of dashes—one for each letter in the secret word. When the player guesses a letter that's in the secret word, I replace the dash at the corresponding position with the letter.

Entering the Main Loop

Next I enter the main loop, which continues until the player has made too many incorrect guesses or has guessed the word.

```
//main loop
while ((wrong < MAX_WRONG) && (soFar != THE_WORD))
{
    cout << "\n\nYou have " << (MAX_WRONG - wrong) << " incorrect guesses left.\n";
    cout << "\nYou've used the following letters:\n" << used << endl;
    cout << "\nSo far, the word is:\n" << soFar << endl;
```

Getting the Player's Guess

Next I get the player's guess.

```
char guess;
cout << "\n\nEnter your guess: ";
cin >> guess;
guess = toupper(guess); //make uppercase since secret word in uppercase
while (used.find(guess) != string::npos)
{
    cout << "\nYou've already guessed " << guess << endl;
    cout << "Enter your guess: ";
    cin >> guess;
    guess = toupper(guess);
}

used += guess;

if (THE_WORD.find(guess) != string::npos)
{
    cout << "That's right! " << guess << " is in the word.\n";

    //update soFar to include newly guessed letter
    for (int i = 0; i < THE_WORD.length(); ++i)
        if (THE_WORD[i] == guess)
            soFar[i] = guess;
}
else
{
    cout << "Sorry, " << guess << " isn't in the word.\n";
    ++wrong;
}
}
```

I convert the guess to uppercase using the function uppercase(), which is defined in the file cctype. I do this so I can compare uppercase letters to uppercase letters when I'm checking a guess against the letters of the secret word.

If the player guesses a letter that he or she has already guessed, I make the player guess again. If the player guesses a letter correctly, I update the word guessed so far. Otherwise, I tell the player the guess is not in the secret word and I increase the number of incorrect guesses the player has made.

Ending the Game

At this point, the player has guessed the word or has made one too many incorrect guesses. Either way, the game is over.

```
//shut down
if (wrong == MAX_WRONG)
    cout << "\nYou've been hanged!";
else
    cout << "\nYou guessed it!";

cout << "\nThe word was " << THE_WORD << endl;

return 0;
}
```

I congratulate the player or break the bad news that he or she has been hanged. Then I reveal the secret word.

Summary

In this chapter, you should have learned the following concepts:

- The Standard Template Library (STL) is a powerful collection of programming code that provides containers, algorithms, and iterators.
- Containers are objects that let you store and access collections of values of the same type.
- Algorithms defined in the STL can be used with its containers and provide common functions for working with groups of objects.
- Iterators are objects that identify elements in containers and can be manipulated to move among elements.
- Iterators are the key to using containers to their fullest. Many of the container member functions require iterators, and the STL algorithms require them, too.
- To get the value referenced by an iterator, you must dereference the iterator using the dereference operator (*).
- A vector is one kind of sequential container provided by the STL. It acts like a dynamic array.

- It's very efficient to iterate through a vector. It's also very efficient to insert or remove an element from the end of a vector.

- It can be inefficient to insert or delete elements from the middle of a vector, especially if the vector is large.

- Pseudocode, which falls somewhere between English and a programming language, is used to plan programs.

- Stepwise refinement is a process used to rewrite pseudocode to make it ready for implementation.

Questions and Answers

Q: Why is the STL important?

A: Because it saves game programmers time and effort. The STL provides commonly used container types and algorithms.

Q: Is the STL fast?

A: Definitely. The STL has been honed by hundreds of programmers to eke out as much performance as possible on each supported platform.

Q: When should I use a vector instead of an array?

A: Almost always. Vectors are efficient and flexible. They do require a little more memory than arrays, but this tradeoff is almost always worth the benefits.

Q: Is a vector as fast as an array?

A: Accessing a vector element can be just as fast as accessing an array element. Also, iterating though a vector can be just as fast as iterating through an array.

Q: If I can use the subscripting operator with vectors, why would I ever need iterators?

A: There are several reasons. First, many of the vector member functions require iterators. (insert() and erase() are two examples.) Second, STL algorithms require iterators. And third, you can't use the subscripting operator with most of the STL containers, so you're going to have to learn to use iterators sooner or later.

Q: Which is the best way to access elements of a vector—through iterators or through the subscripting operator?

A: It depends. If you need random-element access, then the subscripting operator is a natural fit. If you need to use STL algorithms, then you must use iterators.

Q: What about iterating through the elements of a vector? Should I use the subscripting operator or an iterator?

A: You can use either method. However, an advantage of using an iterator is that it gives you the flexibility to substitute a different STL container in place of a vector (such as a list) without much code changing.

Q: Why does the STL define more than one sequential container type?

A: Different sequential container types have different performance properties. They're like tools in a toolbox; each tool is best suited for a different job.

Q: What are container adaptors?

A: Container adaptors are based on one of the STL sequence containers; they represent standard computer data structures. Although they are not official containers, they look and feel just like them.

Q: What's a stack?

A: A data structure in which elements are removed in the reverse order from how they were added. This means that the last element added is the first one removed. This is just like a real-life stack, from which you remove the last item you placed on the top of the stack.

Q: What's a queue?

A: A data structure in which elements are removed in the same order in which they were added. This is just like a real-life queue, such as a line of people in which the first person in line gets served first.

Q: What's a double-ended queue?

A: A queue in which elements can be added or removed from either end.

Q: What's a priority queue?

A: A data structure that supports finding and removing the element with the highest priority.

Q: When would I use pseudocode?

A: Any time you want to plan a program or section of code.

Q: When would I use stepwise refinement?

A: When you want to get even more detailed with your pseudocode.

Discussion Questions

1. Why should a game programmer use the STL?

2. What are the advantages of a vector over an array?

3. What types of game objects might you store with a vector?

4. How do performance characteristics of a container type affect the decision to use it?

5. Why is program planning important?

Exercises

1. Write a program using vectors and iterators that allows a user to maintain a list of his or her favorite games. The program should allow the user to list all game titles, add a game title, and remove a game title.

2. Assuming that `scores` is a vector that holds elements of type `int`, what's wrong with the following code snippet (meant to increment each element)?

    ```
    vector<int>::iterator iter;
    //increment each score
    for (iter = scores.begin(); iter != scores.end(); ++iter)
        iter++;
    ```

3. Write pseudocode for the Word Jumble game from Chapter 3.

CHAPTER 5

FUNCTIONS: MAD LIB

E very program you've seen so far has consisted of one function—main(). However, once your programs reach a certain size or level of complexity, it becomes hard to work with them like this. Fortunately, there are ways to break up big programs into smaller, bite-sized chunks of code. In this chapter, you'll learn about one way—creating new functions. Specifically, you'll learn to:

- Write new functions
- Accept values into your new functions through parameters
- Return information from your new functions through return values
- Work with global variables and constants
- Overload functions
- Inline functions

Creating Functions

C++ lets you write programs with multiple functions. Your new functions work just like the ones that are part of the standard language—they go off and perform a task and then return control to your program. A big advantage of writing new functions is it allows you to break up your code into manageable pieces. Just like the functions you've already learned about from the standard library, your new functions should do one job well.

Introducing the Instructions Program

The results of the Instructions program are pretty basic—a few lines of text that are the beginning of some game instructions. From the looks of the output, Instructions seems like a program you could have written way back in Chapter 1. But this program has a fresh element working behind the scenes—a new function. Take a look at Figure 5.1 to see the modest results of the code.

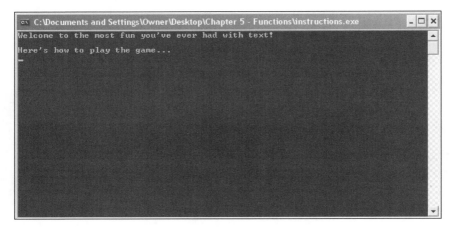

Figure 5.1
The instructions are displayed by a function.

The code for the program is in the Chapter 5 folder on the CD-ROM that came with this book; the file name is instructions.cpp.

```cpp
// Instructions
// Demonstrates writing new functions

#include <iostream>

using namespace std;

// function prototype (declaration)
void instructions();

int main()
{
    instructions();
    return 0;
}

// function definition
void instructions()
{
    cout << "Welcome to the most fun you've ever had with text!\n\n";
    cout << "Here's how to play the game...\n";
}
```

Declaring Functions

Before you can call a function you've written, you have to declare it. One way to declare a function is to write a *function prototype*—code that describes the function. You write a prototype by listing the return value of the function (or void if the function returns no value), followed by the name of the function, followed by a list of parameters between a set of parentheses. *Parameters* receive the values sent as arguments in a function call.

Just before the main() function, I write a function prototype.

```
void instructions();
```

In the preceding code, I declared a function named instructions that doesn't return a value. (You can tell this because I used void as the return type.) The function also takes no values so it has no parameters. (You can tell this because there's nothing between the parentheses.)

Prototypes are not the only way to declare a function. Another way to accomplish the same thing is to let the function definition act as its own declaration. To do that, you simply have to put your function definition before the call to the function.

hint

Although you don't have to use prototypes, they offer a lot of benefits—not the least of which is making your code clearer.

Defining Functions

Defining functions means writing all the code that makes the function tick. You define a function by listing the return value of the function (or void if the function returns no value), followed by the name of the function, followed by a list of parameters between a set of parentheses—just like a function prototype (except you don't end the line with a semicolon). This is called the *function header*. Then you create a block with curly braces that contains the instructions to be executed when the function is executed. This is called the *function body*.

At the end of the Instructions program, I define my simple instructions() function, which displays some game instructions. Because the function doesn't return any value, I don't need to use a return statement like I do in main(). I simply end the function definition with a closing curly brace.

```
void instructions()
{
    cout << "Welcome to the most fun you've ever had with text!\n\n";
    cout << "Here's how to play the game...\n";
}
```

trap

A function definition must match its prototype in return type and function name; otherwise, you'll generate a compile error.

Calling Functions

You call your own functions the same way you call any other function—by writing the function's name followed by a pair of parentheses that encloses a valid list of arguments. In main(), I call my newly minted function simply with:

```
instructions();
```

This line invokes instructions(). Whenever you call a function, control of the program jumps to that function. In this case, it means control jumps to instructions() and the program executes the function's code, which displays the game instructions. When a function finishes, control returns to the calling code. In this case, it means control returns to main(). The next statement in main() (return 0;) is executed and the program ends.

Understanding Abstraction

By writing and calling functions, you practice what's known as *abstraction*. Abstraction lets you think about the big picture without worrying about the details. In this program, I can simply use the function instructions() without worrying about the details of displaying the text. All I have to do is call the function with one line of code, and it gets the job done.

You might be surprised where you find abstraction, but people use it all the time. For example, consider two employees at a fast-food restaurant. If one tells the other that he just filled a Number 3 and "sized it," the other employee knows that the first employee took a customer's order, went to the heat lamps, grabbed a burger, went over to the deep fryer, filled their biggest cardboard container with french fries, went to the soda fountain, grabbed their biggest cup, filled it with soda, gave it all to the customer, took the customer's money, and gave the customer change. Not only would this level of detail make for a boring conversation, but it's unnecessary. Both employees understand what it means to fill a Number 3 and "size it." They don't have to concern themselves with all the details because they're using abstraction.

Using Parameters and Return Values

As you've seen with standard library functions, you can provide a function with values and get a value back. For example, with the toupper() function, you provide a character, and the function returns the uppercase version of it. Your own functions can also receive values and return a value. This allows your functions to communicate with the rest of your program.

Introducing the Yes or No Program

The Yes or No program asks the user typical questions a gamer might have to answer. First, the program asks the user to indicate yes or no. Then the program gets more specific and asks whether the user wants to save his game. Again, the results of the program are not remarkable; it's their implementation that's interesting. Each question is posed by a different function that communicates with main(). Figure 5.2 shows a sample run of the program.

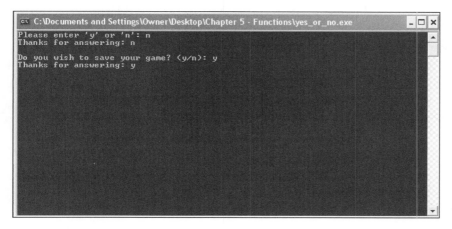

Figure 5.2
Each question is asked by a separate function, and information is passed between these functions and main().

The code for the program is in the Chapter 5 folder on the CD-ROM that came with this book; the file name is yes_or_no.cpp.

```cpp
// Yes or No
// Demonstrates return values and parameters

#include <iostream>
#include <string>

using namespace std;

char askYesNo1();
char askYesNo2(string question);

int main()
{
    char answer1 = askYesNo1();
    cout << "Thanks for answering: " << answer1 << "\n\n";

    char answer2 = askYesNo2("Do you wish to save your game?");
    cout << "Thanks for answering: " << answer2 << "\n";
```

```
    return 0;
}

char askYesNo1()
{
    char response1;
    do
    {
        cout << "Please enter 'y' or 'n': ";
        cin >> response1;
    } while (response1 != 'y' && response1 != 'n');

    return response1;
}

char askYesNo2(string question)
{
    char response2;
    do
    {
        cout << question << " (y/n): ";
        cin >> response2;
    } while (response2 != 'y' && response2 != 'n');

    return response2;
}
```

Returning a Value

You can return a value from a function to send information back to the calling code. To return a value, you need to specify a return type and then return a value of that type from the function.

Specifying a Return Type

The first function I declare, `askYesNo1()`, returns a `char` value. You can tell this from the function prototype before `main()`.

```
char askYesNo1();
```

You can also see this from the function definition after `main()`.

```
char askYesNo1()
```

Using the return Statement

`askYesNo1()` asks the user to enter y or n and keeps asking until he does. Once the user enters a valid character, the function wraps up with the following line, which returns the value of `response1`.

```
return response1;
```

Notice that `response1` is a `char` value. It has to be because that's what I promised to return in both the function prototype and function definition.

A function ends whenever it hits a `return` statement. It's perfectly acceptable for a function to have more than one `return`. This just means that the function has several points at which it can end.

trick

You don't have to return a value with a `return` statement. You can use `return` by itself in a function that returns no value (one that indicates `void` as its return type) to end the function.

Using a Returned Value

In `main()`, I call the function with the following line, which assigns the return value of the function to `answer1`.

```
char answer1 = askYesNo1();
```

This means that `answer1` is assigned either `'y'` or `'n'`—whichever character the user entered when prompted by `askYesNo1()`.

Next in `main()`, I display the value of `answer1` for all to see.

Accepting Values into Parameters

You can send a function values that it accepts into its parameters. This is the most common way to get information into a function.

Specifying Parameters

The second function I declare, `askYesNo2()`, accepts a value into a parameter. Specifically, it accepts a value of type `string`. You can tell this from the function prototype before `main()`.

```
char askYesNo2(string question);
```

hint

You don't have to use parameter names in a prototype; all you have to include are the parameter types. For example, the following is a perfectly valid prototype that declares `askYesNo2()`, a function with one `string` parameter that returns a `char`.

```
char askYesNo2(string);
```

Even though you don't have to use parameter names in prototypes, it's a good idea to do so. It makes your code clearer, and it's worth the minor effort.

From the header of askYesNo2(), you can see that the function accepts a string object as a parameter and names that parameter question.

```
char askYesNo2(string question)
```

Unlike prototypes, you must specify parameter names in a function definition. You use a parameter name inside a function to access the parameter value.

trap

The parameter types specified in a function prototype must match the parameter types listed in the function definition. If they don't, you'll generate a nasty compile error.

Passing Values to Parameters

The askYesNo2() function is an improvement over askYesNo1(). The new function allows you to ask your own personalized question by passing a string prompt to the function. In main(), I call askYesNo2() with:

```
char answer2 = askYesNo2("Do you wish to save your game?");
```

This statement calls askYesNo2() and passes the string literal argument "Do you wish to save your game?" to the function.

Using Parameter Values

askYesNo2() accepts "Do you wish to save your game?" into its parameter question, which acts like any other variable in the function. In fact, I display question with:

```
cout << question << " (y/n): ";
```

hint

Actually, there's a little more going on behind the scenes here. When the string literal "Do you wish to save your game?" is passed to question, a string object equal to the string literal is created and the string object gets assigned to question.

Just like askYesNo1(), askYesNo2() continues to prompt the user until he enters y or n. Then the function returns that value and ends.

Back in main(), the returned char value is assigned to answer2, which I then display.

Understanding Encapsulation

You might not see the need for return values when you are using your own functions. Why not just use the variables response1 and resopnse2 back in the main()? Because you can't; response1 and resopnse2 don't exist outside of the functions in which they were defined. In fact, no variable you create in a function, including its parameters, can be directly accessed outside its function. This is a good thing, and it is called *encapsulation*. Encapsulation helps keep independent code truly separate by hiding or encapsulating the details. That's why you use parameters and return values—to communicate only the information that needs to be exchanged. Plus, you don't have to keep track of variables you create within a function in the rest of your program. As your programs get large, this is a great benefit.

Encapsulation might sound a lot like abstraction. That's because they're closely related. Encapsulation is a principal of abstraction. Abstraction saves you from worrying about the details, while encapsulation hides the details from you. As an example, consider a television remote control with volume up and down buttons. When you use a TV remote to change the volume, you're employing abstraction because you don't need to know what happens inside the TV for it to work. Now suppose the TV remote has 10 volume levels. You can get to them all through the remote, but you can't directly access them. That is, you can't get a specific volume number directly. You can only press the up volume and down volume buttons to eventually get to the level you want. The actual volume number is encapsulated and not directly available to you.

Understanding Software Reuse

You can reuse functions in other programs. For example, since asking the user a yes or no question is such a common thing to do in a game, you could create an askYesNo() function and use it in all of your future game programs. So writing good functions not only saves you time and energy in your current game project, but it can save you effort in future ones, too.

in the real world

It's always a waste of time to reinvent the wheel, so *software reuse*—employing existing software and other elements in new projects—is a technique that game companies take to heart. The benefits of software reuse include

- **Increased company productivity.** By reusing code and other elements that already exist, such as a graphics engine, game companies can get their projects done with less effort.
- **Improved software quality.** If a game company already has a tested piece of code, such as a networking module, then the company can reuse the code with the knowledge that it's bug-free.
- **Improved software performance.** Once a game company has a high-performance piece of code, using it again not only saves the company the trouble of reinventing the wheel, it saves them from reinventing a less efficient one.

You can reuse code you've written by copying from one program and pasting it into another, but there is a better way. You can divide up a big game project into multiple files. You'll learn about this technique in Chapter 10, "Inheritance and Polymorphism: Blackjack."

Working with Scopes

A variable's *scope* determines where the variable can be seen in your program. Scopes allow you to limit the accessibility of variables and are the key to encapsulation, helping keep separate parts of your program, such as functions, apart from each other.

Introducing the Scoping Program

The Scoping program demonstrates scopes. The program creates three variables with the same name in three separate scopes. It displays the values of these variables, and you can see that even though they all have the same name, the variables are completely separate entities. Figure 5.3 shows the results of the program.

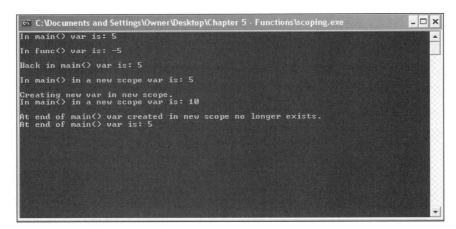

Figure 5.3
Even though they have the same name, all three variables have a unique existence in their own scopes.

The code for the program is in the Chapter 5 folder on the CD-ROM that came with this book; the file name is scoping.cpp.

```
// Scoping
// Demonstrates scopes

#include <iostream>
```

```
using namespace std;

void func();

int main()
{
    int var = 5;  // local variable in main()
    cout << "In main() var is: " << var << "\n\n";

    func();

    cout << "Back in main() var is: " << var << "\n\n";

    {
        cout << "In main() in a new scope var is: " << var << "\n\n";

        cout << "Creating new var in new scope.\n";
        int var = 10;  // variable in new scope, hides other variable named var
        cout << "In main() in a new scope var is: " << var << "\n\n";
    }

    cout << "At end of main() var created in new scope no longer exists.\n";
    cout << "At end of main() var is: " << var << "\n";

    return 0;
}

void func()
{
    int var = -5;  // local variable in func()
    cout << "In func() var is: " << var << "\n\n";
}
```

Working with Separate Scopes

Every time you use curly braces to create a block, you create a scope. Functions are one example of this. Variables declared in a scope aren't visible outside of that scope. This means that variables declared in a function aren't visible outside of that function.

Variables declared inside a function are considered *local variables*—they're local to the function. This is what makes functions encapsulated.

You've seen many local variables in action already. I define yet another local variable in main() with:

```
int var = 5;  // local variable in main()
```

This line declares and initializes a local variable named var. I send the variable to cout in the next line of code.

```
cout << "In main() var is: " << var << "\n\n";
```

This works just as you'd expect—5 is displayed.

Next I call func(). Once I enter the function, I'm in a separate scope outside of the scope defined by main(). As a result, I can't access the variable var that I defined in main(). This means that when I next define a variable named var in func() with the following line, this new variable is completely separate from the variable named var in main().

```
int var = -5;   // local variable in func()
```

The two have no effect on each other, and that's the beauty of scopes. When you write a function, you don't have to worry if another function uses the same variable names.

Then, when I display the value of var in func() with the following line, the computer displays -5.

```
cout << "In func() var is: " << var << "\n\n";
```

That's because, as far as the computer can see in this scope, there's only one variable named var—the local variable I declared in this function.

Once a scope ends, all of the variables declared in that scope cease to exist. They're said to go *out of scope*. So next, when func() ends, its scope ends. This means all of the variables declared in func() are destroyed. As a result, the var I declared in func() with a value of -5 is destroyed.

After func() ends, control returns to main() and picks up right where it left off. Next the following line is executed, which sends var to cout.

```
cout << "Back in main() var is: " << var << "\n\n";
```

The value of the var local to main() (5) is displayed again.

You might be wondering what happened to the var I created in main() while I was in func(). Well, the variable wasn't destroyed because main() hadn't yet ended. (Program control simply took a small detour to func().) When a program momentarily exits one function to enter another, the computer saves its place in the first function, keeping safe the values of all of its local variables, which are reinstated when control returns to the first function.

hint

Parameters act just like local variables in functions.

Working with Nested Scopes

You can create a nested scope with a pair of curly braces in an existing scope. That's what I do next in main(), with:

```
{
    cout << "In main() in a new scope var is: " << var << "\n\n";

    cout << "Creating new var in new scope.\n";
    int var = 10;  // variable in new scope, hides other variable named var
    cout << "In main() in a new scope var is: " << var << "\n\n";
}
```

This new scope is a nested scope in main(). The first thing I do in this nested scope is display var. If a variable hasn't been declared in a scope, the computer looks up the levels of nested scopes one at a time to find the variable you requested. In this case, because var hasn't been declared in this nested scope, the computer looks one level up to the scope that defines main() and finds var. As a result, the program displays that variable's value—5.

However, the next thing I do in this nested scope is declare a new variable named var and initialize it to 10. Now when I send var to cout, 10 is displayed. This time the computer doesn't have to look up any levels of nested scopes to find var; there's a var local to this scope. And don't worry, the var I first declared in main() still exists; it's simply hidden in this nested scope by the new var.

trap

Although you can declare variables with the same name in a series of nested scopes, it's not a good idea because it can lead to confusion.

Next, when the nested scope ends, the var that was equal to 10 goes out of scope and ceases to exist. However, the first var I created is still around, so when I display var for the last time in main() with the following line, the program displays 5.

```
cout << "At end of main() var is: " << var << "\n";
```

hint

When you define variables inside for loops, while loops, if statements, and switch statements, these variables don't exist outside their structures. They act like variables declared in a nested scope. For example, in the following code, the variable i doesn't exist outside the loop.

```
for(int i = 0; i < 10; ++i)
    cout << i;
// i doesn't exist outside the loop
```

But beware—some older compilers, such as Microsoft Visual C++ 6.0, don't properly implement this functionality of standard C++.

I recommend that you use an IDE with a modern compiler, such as Dev-C++, which is on the CD-ROM that came with this book. After you install Dev-C++, check out Appendix A, "Creating Your First C++ Program," on the book's CD-ROM for a tutorial of how to get your programs running with Dev-C++.

Using Global Variables

Through the magic of encapsulation, the functions you've seen are all totally sealed off and independent from each other. The only way to get information into them is through their parameters, and the only way to get information out of them is from their return values. Well, that's not completely true. There is another way to share information among parts of your program—through *global variables* (variables that are accessible from any part of your program).

Introducing the Global Reach Program

The Global Reach program demonstrates global variables. The program shows how you can access a global variable from anywhere in your program. It also shows how you can hide a global variable in a scope. Finally, it shows that you can change a global variable from anywhere in your program. Figure 5.4 shows the results of the program.

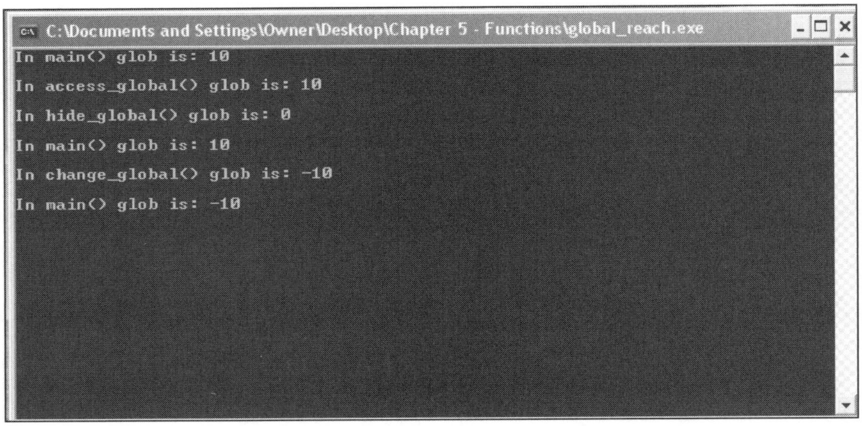

Figure 5.4
You can access and change global variables from anywhere in a program—but they can also be hidden in a scope as well.

The code for the program is in the Chapter 5 folder on the CD-ROM that came with this book; the file name is global_reach.cpp.

```
// Global Reach
// Demonstrates global variables

#include <iostream>

using namespace std;

int glob = 10;   // global variable
```

```
void access_global();
void hide_global();
void change_global();

int main()
{
    cout << "In main() glob is: " << glob << "\n\n";
    access_global();

    hide_global();
    cout << "In main() glob is: " << glob << "\n\n";

    change_global();
    cout << "In main() glob is: " << glob << "\n\n";

    return 0;
}

void access_global()
{
    cout << "In access_global() glob is: " << glob << "\n\n";
}

void hide_global()
{
    int glob = 0;  // hide global variable glob
    cout << "In hide_global() glob is: " << glob << "\n\n";
}

void change_global()
{
    glob = -10;  // change global variable glob
    cout << "In change_global() glob is: " << glob << "\n\n";
}
```

Declaring Global Variables

You declare global variables outside of any function in your program file. That's what I do in the following line, which creates a global variable named glob initialized to 10.

```
int glob = 10;  // global variable
```

Accessing Global Variables

You can access a global variable from anywhere in your program. To prove it, I display glob in main() with:

```
cout << "In main() glob is: " << glob << "\n\n";
```

The program displays 10 because as a global variable, `glob` is available to any part of the program. To show this again, I next call `access_global()`, and the computer executes the following code in that function.

```
cout << "In access_global() glob is: " << glob << "\n\n";
```

Again, 10 is displayed. That makes sense because I'm displaying the exact same variable in each function.

Hiding Global Variables

You can hide a global variable like any other variable in a scope; you simply declare a new variable with the same name. That's exactly what I do next, when I call `hide_global()`. The key line in that function doesn't change the global variable `glob`; instead, it creates a new variable named `glob`, local to `hide_global()`, that hides the global variable.

```
int glob = 0;   // hide global variable glob
```

As a result, when I send `glob` to `cout` next in `hide_global()` with the following line, 0 is displayed.

```
cout << "In hide_global() glob is: " << glob << "\n\n";
```

The global variable `glob` remains hidden in the scope of `hide_global()` until the function ends.

To prove that the global variable was only hidden and not changed, next I display `glob` back in `main()` with:

```
cout << "In main() glob is: " << glob << "\n\n";
```

Once again, 10 is displayed.

trap

Although you can declare variables in a function with the same name as a global variable, it's not a good idea because it can lead to confusion.

Altering Global Variables

Just as you can access a global variable from anywhere in your program, you can alter one from anywhere in your program, too. That's what I do next, when I call the `change_global()` function. The key line of the function assigns –10 to the global variable `glob`.

```
glob = -10;   // change global variable glob
```

To show that it worked, I display the variable in `change_global()` with:

```
cout << "In change_global() glob is: " << glob << "\n\n";
```

Then, back in `main()`, I send `glob` to `cout` with:

```
cout << "In main() glob is: " << glob << "\n\n";
```

Because the global variable `glob` was changed, –10 is displayed.

Minimizing the Use of Global Variables

Just because you can doesn't mean you should. This is a good programming motto. Sometimes things are technically possible, but not a good idea. Using global variables is an example of this. In general, global variables make programs confusing because it can be difficult to keep track of their changing values. You should limit your use of global variables as much as possible.

Using Global Constants

Unlike global variables, which can make your programs confusing, *global constants*—constants that can be accessed from anywhere in your program—can help make programs clearer. You declare a global constant much like you declare a global variable—by declaring it outside of any function. And because you're declaring a constant, you need to use the `const` keyword. For example, the following line defines a global constant (assuming the declaration is outside of any function) named `MAX_ENEMIES` with a value of 10 that can be accessed anywhere in the program.

```
const int MAX_ENEMIES = 10;
```

trap

Just like with global variables, you can hide a global constant by declaring a local constant with the same name. However, you should avoid this because it can lead to confusion.

How exactly can global constants make game programming code clearer? Well, suppose you're writing an action game in which you want to limit the total number of enemies that can blast the poor player at once. Instead of using a numeric literal everywhere, such as 10, you could define a global constant `MAX_ENEMIES` that's equal to 10. Then whenever you see that global constant name, you know exactly what it stands for.

One caveat: You should only use global constants if you need a constant value in more than one part of your program. If you only need a constant value in a specific scope (such as in a single function), use a local constant instead.

Using Default Arguments

When you write a function in which a parameter almost always gets passed the same value, you can save the caller the effort of constantly specifying this value by using a *default argument*—a value assigned to a parameter if none is specified. Here's a concrete example. Suppose you have a function that sets the graphics display. One of your parameters might be `bool fullScreen`, which tells the function whether to display the game in full screen or windowed mode. Now, if you think the function will often be called with `true` for `fullScreen`, you could give that parameter a default argument of `true`, saving the caller the effort of passing `true` to `fullScreen` whenever the caller invokes this display-setting function.

Introducing the Give Me a Number Program

The Give Me a Number program asks the user for two different numbers in two different ranges. The same function is called each time the user is prompted for a number. However, each call to this function uses a different number of arguments because this function has a default argument for the lower limit. This means the caller can omit an argument for the lower limit, and the function will use a default value automatically. Figure 5.5 shows the results of the program.

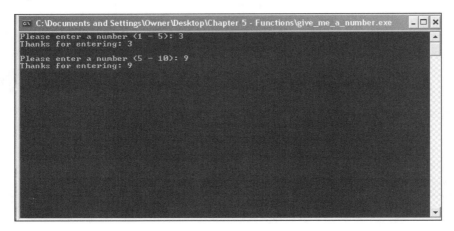

Figure 5.5
A default argument is used for the lower limit the first time the user is prompted for a number.

The code for the program is in the Chapter 5 folder on the CD-ROM that came with this book; the file name is give_me_a_number.cpp.

```cpp
// Give Me a Number
// Demonstrates default function arguments

#include <iostream>
#include <string>

using namespace std;
```

```
int askNumber(int high, int low = 1);

int main()
{
    int number = askNumber(5);
    cout << "Thanks for entering: " << number << "\n\n";

    number = askNumber(10, 5);
    cout << "Thanks for entering: " << number << "\n\n";

    return 0;
}

int askNumber(int high, int low)
{
    int num;
    do
    {
        cout << "Please enter a number" << " (" << low << " - " << high
            << "): ";
        cin >> num;
    } while (num > high || num < low);

    return num;
}
```

Specifying Default Arguments

The function askNumber() has two parameters—high and low. You can tell this from the function prototype.

```
int askNumber(int high, int low = 1);
```

Notice that the second parameter, low, looks like it's assigned a value. In a way, it is. The 1 is a default argument meaning that if a value isn't passed to low when the function is called, low is assigned 1. You specify default arguments by using = followed by a value after a parameter name.

trap

Once you specify a default argument in a list of parameters, you must specify default arguments for all remaining parameters. So the following prototype is valid:

```
void setDisplay(int height, int width, int depth = 32, bool fullScreen = true);
```

while this one is illegal:

```
void setDisplay(int width, int height, int depth = 32, bool fullScreen);
```

By the way, you don't repeat the default argument in the function definition, as you can see in the function definition of `askNumber()`.

```
int askNumber(int high, int low)
```

Assigning Default Arguments to Parameters

The `askNumber()` function asks the user for a number between an upper and a lower limit. The function keeps asking until the user enters a number within the range, and then it returns the number. I first call the function in `main()` with:

```
int number = askNumber(5);
```

As a result of this code, the parameter `high` in `askNumber()` is assigned 5. Because I don't provide any value for the second parameter, `low`, it gets assigned the default value of 1. This means the function prompts the user for a number between 1 and 5.

---

trap

> When you are calling a function with default arguments, once you omit an argument, you must omit arguments for all remaining parameters. For example, given the prototype `void setDisplay(int height, int width, int depth = 32, bool fullScreen = true);` a valid call to the function would be
>
> `setDisplay(800, 600);`
>
> while an illegal call would be
>
> `setDisplay(800, 600, false);`

Once the user enters a valid number, `askNumber()` returns that value and ends. Back in `main()`, the value is assigned to `number` and displayed.

Overriding Default Arguments

Next I call `askNumber()` again with:

```
number = askNumber(10, 5);
```

This time I pass a value for `low`—5. This is perfectly fine; you can pass an argument for any parameter with a default argument, and the value you pass will override the default. In this case, it means that `low` is assigned 5.

As a result, the user is prompted for a number between 5 and 10. Once the user enters a valid number, `askNumber()` returns that value and ends. Back in `main()`, the value is assigned to `number` and displayed.

Overloading Functions

You've seen how you must specify a parameter list and a single return type for each function you write. But what if you want a function that's more versatile—one that can accept different sets of arguments? For example, suppose you want to write a function that performs a 3D transformation on a set of vertices that are represented as floats, but you want the function to work with ints as well. Instead of writing two separate functions with two different names, you could use function overloading so that a single function could handle the different parameter lists. This way, you could call one function and pass vertices as either floats or ints.

Introducing the Triple Program

The Triple program triples the values 5 and gamer. The program triples these values using a single function that's been overloaded to work with an argument of two different types: int and string. Figure 5.6 shows a sample run of the program.

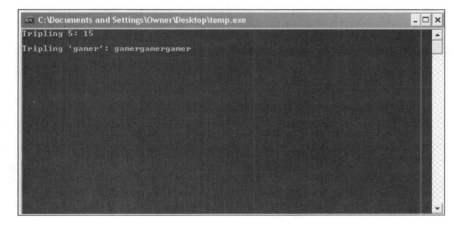

Figure 5.6
Function overloading allows you to triple the values of two different types using the same function name.

The code for the program is in the Chapter 5 folder on the CD-ROM that came with this book; the file name is triple.cpp.

```
// Triple
// Demonstrates function overloading

#include <iostream>
#include <string>

using namespace std;
```

```
int triple(int number);
string triple(string text);

int main()
{
    cout << "Tripling 5: " << triple(5) << "\n\n";
    cout << "Tripling 'gamer': " << triple("gamer");

    return 0;
}

int triple(int number)
{
    return (number * 3);
}

string triple(string text)
{
    return (text + text + text);
}
```

Creating Overloaded Functions

To create an overloaded function, you simply need to write multiple function definitions with the same name and different parameter lists. In the Triple program, I write two definitions for the function triple(), each of which specifies a different type as its single argument. Here are the function prototypes:

```
int triple(int number);
string triple(string text);
```

The first takes an int argument and returns an int. The second takes a string object and returns a string object.

In each function definition, you can see that I return triple the value sent. In the first function, I return the int sent, tripled. In the second function, I return the string sent, repeated three times.

trap

To implement function overloading, you need to write multiple definitions for the same function with different parameter lists. Notice that I didn't mention anything about return types. That's because if you write two function definitions in which only the return type is different, you'll generate a compile error. For example, you cannot have both of the following prototypes in a program:

```
int Bonus(int);

float Bonus(int);
```

Calling Overloaded Functions

You can call an overloaded function the same way you call any other function, by using its name with a set of valid arguments. But with overloaded functions, the compiler (based on the argument values) determines which definition to invoke. For example, when I call `triple()` with the following line and use an `int` as the argument, the compiler knows to invoke the definition that takes an `int`. As a result, the function returns the `int` 15.

```
cout << "Tripling 5: " << triple(5) << "\n\n";
```

I call `triple()` again with:

```
cout << "Tripling 'gamer': " << triple("gamer");
```

Because I use a string literal as the argument, the compiler knows to invoke the definition of the function that takes a `string` object. As a result, the function returns the `string` object equal to `gamergamergamer`.

Inlining Functions

There's a small performance cost associated with calling a function. Normally this isn't a big deal because the cost is pretty small. However, for tiny functions (such as one or two lines), it's sometimes possible to speed up program performance by inlining them. By *inlining* a function, you ask the compiler to make a copy of the function everywhere it's called. As a result, program control doesn't have to jump to a different location each time the function is called.

Introducing the Taking Damage Program

The Taking Damage program simulates what happens to a character's health as the character takes radiation damage. The character loses half of his health each round. Fortunately, the program runs only three rounds, so we're spared the sad end of the character. The program inlines the tiny function that calculates the character's new health. Figure 5.7 shows the program results.

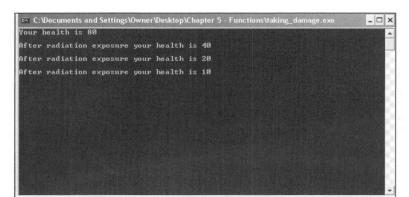

Figure 5.7
The character approaches his demise quite efficiently as his health decreases through an inlined function.

The code for the program is in the Chapter 5 folder on the CD-ROM that came with this book; the file name is taking_damage.cpp.

```
// Taking Damage
// Demonstrates function inlining

#include <iostream>

int radiation(int health);

using namespace std;

int main()
{
    int health = 80;
    cout << "Your health is " << health << "\n\n";

    health = radiation(health);
    cout << "After radiation exposure your health is " << health << "\n\n";

    health = radiation(health);
    cout << "After radiation exposure your health is " << health << "\n\n";

    health = radiation(health);
    cout << "After radiation exposure your health is " << health << "\n\n";

    return 0;
}

inline int radiation(int health)
{
    return (health / 2);
}
```

Specifying Functions for Inlining

To mark a function for inlining, simply put `inline` before the function defintion. That's what I do when I define the following function:

```
inline int radiation(int health)
```

Note that you don't use `inline` in the function declaration.

```
int radiation(int health);
```

By flagging the function with `inline`, you ask the compiler to copy the function directly into the calling code. This saves the overhead of making the function call. That is, program control doesn't have to jump to another part of your code. For small functions, this can result in a performance boost.

However, inlining is not a silver bullet for performance. In fact, indiscriminate inlining can lead to worse performance because inlining a function creates extra copies of it, which can dramatically increase memory consumption.

hint

When you inline a function, you really make a request to the compiler, which has the ultimate decision on whether or not to inline the function. If your compiler thinks that inlining won't boost performance, it won't inline the function.

Calling Inlined Functions

Calling an inlined function is no different than calling a non-inlined function, as you see with my first call to `radiation()`.

```
health = radiation(health);
```

This line of code assigns `health` one half of its original value.

Assuming that the compiler grants my request for inlining, this code doesn't result in a function call. Instead, the compiler places the code to halve `health` right at this place in the program. In fact, the compiler does this for all three calls to the function.

in the real world

Although obsessing about performance is a game programmer's favorite hobby, there's a danger in focusing too much on speed. In fact, the approach many developers take is to first get their game programs working well before they tweak for small performance gains. At that point, programmers will *profile* their code by running a utility (a profiler) that analyzes where the game program spends its time. If a programmer sees bottlenecks, he or she might consider hand optimizations such as function inlining.

Introducing the Mad Lib Game

The Mad Lib game asks for the user's help in creating a story. The user supplies the name of a person, a plural noun, a number, and a verb. The program takes all of this information and uses it to create a personalized story. Figure 5.8 shows a sample run of the program.

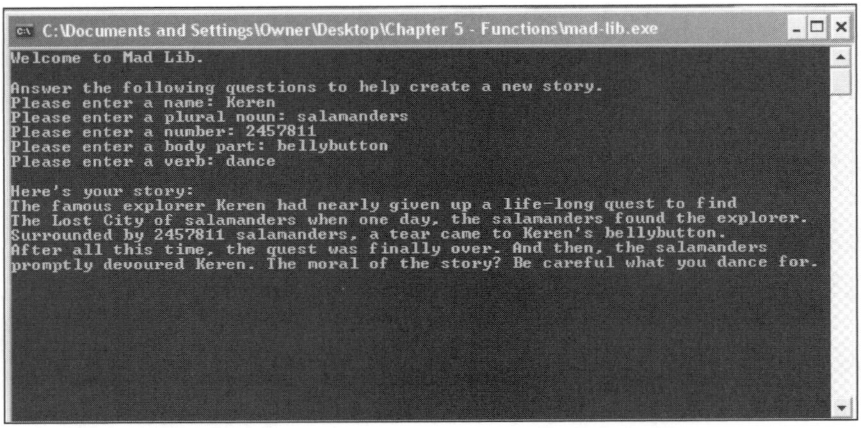

Figure 5.8
After the user provides all of the necessary information, the program displays the
literary masterpiece.

The code for the program is in the Chapter 5 folder on the CD-ROM that came with this
book; the file name is mad_lib.cpp.

Setting Up the Program

As usual, I start the program with some comments and include the necessary files.

```
// Mad-Lib
// Creates a story based on user input

#include <iostream>
#include <string>

using namespace std;

string askText(string prompt);
int askNumber(string prompt);
void tellStory(string name, string noun, int number, string bodyPart,
               string verb);
```

You can tell from my function prototypes that I have three functions in addition to
main()—askText(), askNumber(), and tellStory().

The main() Function

The main() function calls all of the other functions. It calls the function askText() to get a
name, plural noun, body part, and verb from the user. It calls askNumber() to get a number
from the user. It calls tellStory() with all of the user-supplied information to generate and
display the story.

```
int main()
{
    cout << "Welcome to Mad Lib.\n\n";
    cout << "Answer the following questions to help create a new story.\n";

    string name = askText("Please enter a name: ");
    string noun = askText("Please enter a plural noun: ");
    int number = askNumber("Please enter a number: ");
    string bodyPart = askText("Please enter a body part: ");
    string verb = askText("Please enter a verb: ");

    tellStory(name, noun, number, bodyPart, verb);

    return 0;
}
```

The askText() Function

The askText() function gets a string from the user. The function is versatile and takes a parameter of type string, which it uses to prompt the user. Because of this, I'm able to call this single function to ask the user for a variety of different pieces of information, including a name, plural noun, body part, and verb.

```
string askText(string prompt)
{
    string text;
    cout << prompt;
    cin >> text;
    return text;
}
```

trap

Remember that this simple use of cin only works with strings that have no whitespace in them (such as tabs or spaces). So when a user is prompted for a body part, he can enter bellybutton, but medulla oblongata will cause a problem for the program.

There are ways to compensate for this, but that really requires a discussion of something called *streams*, which is beyond the scope of this book. So use cin in this way, but just be aware of its limitations.

The askNumber() Function

The askNumber() function gets a number from the user. Although I only call it once in the program, it's versatile because it takes a parameter of type string that it uses to prompt the user.

```
int askNumber(string prompt)
{
    int num;
    cout << prompt;
    cin >> num;
    return num;
}
```

The tellStory() Function

The tellStory() function takes all of the information entered by the user and uses it to display a personalized story.

```
void tellStory(string name, string noun, int number, string bodyPart,
               string verb)
{
    cout << "\nHere's your story:\n";
    cout << "The famous explorer ";
    cout << name;
    cout << " had nearly given up a life-long quest to find\n";
    cout << "The Lost City of ";
    cout << noun;
    cout << " when one day, the ";
    cout << noun;
    cout << " found the explorer.\n";
    cout << "Surrounded by ";
    cout << number;
    cout << " " << noun;
    cout << ", a tear came to ";
    cout << name << "'s ";
    cout << bodyPart << ".\n";
    cout << "After all this time, the quest was finally over. ";
    cout << "And then, the ";
    cout << noun << "\n";
    cout << "promptly devoured ";
    cout << name << ". ";
    cout << "The moral of the story? Be careful what you ";
    cout << verb;
    cout << " for.";
}
```

Summary

In this chapter, you should have learned the following concepts:

- Functions allow you to break up your programs into manageable chunks.
- One way to declare a function is to write a function prototype—code that lists the return value, name, and parameter types of a function.

- Defining a function means writing all the code that makes the function tick.
- You can use the `return` statement to return a value from a function. You can also use `return` to end a function that has `void` as its return type.
- A variable's scope determines where the variable can be seen in your program.
- Global variables are accessible from any part of your program. In general, you should try to limit your use of global variables.
- Global constants are accessible from any part of your program. Using global constants can make your program code clearer.
- Default arguments are assigned to a parameter if no value for the parameter is specified in the function call.
- Function overloading is the process of creating multiple definitions for the same function, each of which has a different set of parameters.
- Function inlining is the process of asking the compiler to inline a function—meaning that the compiler should make a copy of the function everywhere in the code where the function is called. Inlining very small functions can sometimes yield a performance boost.

Questions and Answers

Q: Why should I write functions?

A: Functions allow you to break up your programs into logical pieces. These pieces result in smaller, more manageable chunks of code, which are easier to work with than a single monolithic program.

Q: What's encapsulation?

A: At its core, encapsulation is about keeping things separate. Function encapsulation provides that variables declared in a function are not accessible outside the function, for example.

Q: What's the difference between an argument and a parameter?

A: An argument is what you use in a function call to pass a value to a function. A parameter is what you use in a function definition to accept values passed to a function.

Q: Can I have more than one `return` statement in a function?

A: Sure. In fact, you might want multiple `return` statements to specify different end points of a function.

Q: What's a local variable?

A: A variable that's defined in a scope. All variables defined in a function are local variables; they're local to that function.

Q: What does it mean to hide a variable?

A: A variable is hidden when you declare it inside a new scope with the same name as a variable in an outer scope. As a result, you can't get to the variable in the outer scope by using its variable name in the inner scope.

Q: When does a variable go out of scope?

A: A variable goes out of scope when the scope in which it was created ends.

Q: What does it mean when a variable goes out of scope?

A: It means the variable ceases to exist.

Q: What's a nested scope?

A: A scope created within an existing scope.

Q: Must an argument have the same name as the parameter to which it's passed?

A: No. You're free to use different names. It's only the value that's passed from a function call to a function.

Q: Can I write one function that calls another?

A: Of course. In fact, whenever you write a function that you call from main(), you're doing just that. In addition, you can write a function (other than main()) that calls another function.

Q: What is code profiling?

A: It's the process of recording how much CPU time various parts of a program use.

Q: Why profile code?

A: To determine any bottlenecks in a program. Sometimes it makes sense to revisit these sections of code in an attempt to optimize them.

Q: When do programmers profile code?

A: Usually toward the end of the programming of a game project.

Q: What's premature optimization?

A: An attempt to optimize code too early in the development process. Code optimization usually makes sense near the end of programming a game project.

Discussion Questions

1. How does function encapsulation help you write better programs?
2. How can global variables make code confusing?
3. How can global constants make code clearer?
4. What are the pros and cons of optimizing code?
5. How can software reuse benefit the game industry?

Exercises

1. What's wrong with the following prototype?

   ```
   int askNumber(int low = 1, int high);
   ```

2. Rewrite the Hangman game from Chapter 4 using functions. Include a function to get the player's guess and another function to determine whether the player's guess is in the secret word.

3. Using default arguments, write a function that asks the user for a number and returns that number. The function should accept a string prompt from the calling code. If the caller doesn't supply a string for the prompt, the function should use a generic prompt. Next, using function overloading, write a function that achieves the same results.

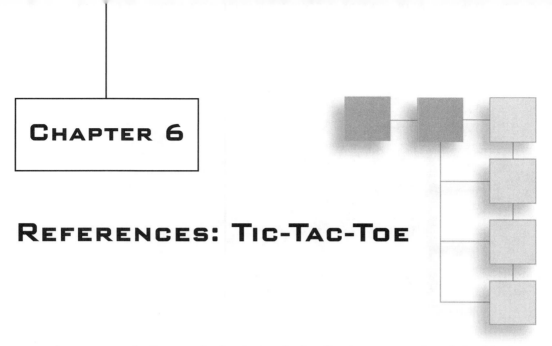

CHAPTER 6

REFERENCES: TIC-TAC-TOE

The concept of references is simple, but its implications are profound. In this chapter, you'll learn about references and how they can help you write more efficient game code. Specifically, you'll learn to:

- Create references
- Access and change referenced values
- Pass references to functions to alter argument values or for efficiency
- Return references from a function for efficiency or to alter values

Using References

A *reference* provides another name for a variable. Whatever you do to a reference is done to the variable to which it refers. You can think of a reference as a nickname for a variable—another name that the variable goes by. In the first program in this chapter, I'll show you how to create references. Then, in the next few programs, I'll show you why you'd want to use references and how they can improve your game programs.

Introducing the Referencing Program

The Referencing program demonstrates references. The program declares and initializes a variable to hold a score and then creates a reference that refers to the variable. The program displays the score using the variable and the reference to show that they access the same single value. Next, the program shows that this single value can be altered through either the variable or the reference. Figure 6.1 illustrates the program.

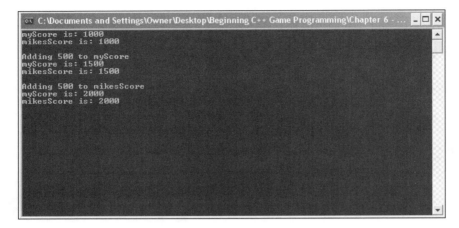

Figure 6.1
The variable myScore and the reference mikesScore are both names for the
single score value.

The code for the program is in the Chapter 6 folder on the CD-ROM that came with this
book; the file name is referencing.cpp.

```cpp
// Referencing
// Demonstrates using references

#include <iostream>

using namespace std;

int main()
{
    int myScore = 1000;
    int& mikesScore = myScore;   //create a reference

    cout << "myScore is: " << myScore << "\n";
    cout << "mikesScore is: " << mikesScore << "\n\n";

    cout << "Adding 500 to myScore\n";
    myScore += 500;
    cout << "myScore is: " << myScore << "\n";
    cout << "mikesScore is: " << mikesScore << "\n\n";

    cout << "Adding 500 to mikesScore\n";
    mikesScore += 500;
    cout << "myScore is: " << myScore << "\n";
    cout << "mikesScore is: " << mikesScore << "\n\n";

    return 0;
}
```

Creating References

The first thing I do in `main()` is create a variable to hold my score.

```
int myScore = 1000;
```

Then I create a reference that refers to `myScore`.

```
int& mikesScore = myScore;  //create a reference
```

The preceding line declares and initializes `mikesScore`, a reference that refers to `myScore`. `mikesScore` is an alias for `myScore`. `mikesScore` does not hold its own `int` value; it's simply another way to get at the `int` value that `myScore` holds.

To declare and initialize a reference, start with the type of value to which the reference will refer, followed by the reference operator (`&`), followed by the reference name, followed by =, followed by the variable to which the reference will refer.

trick

Sometimes programmers prefix a reference name with the letter "r" to remind them that they're working with a reference. A programmer might include the following lines:

```
int playerScore = 1000;
int& rScore = playerScore;
```

One way to understand references is to think of them as nicknames. For example, suppose you've got a friend named Eugene, and he (understandably) asks to be called by a nickname—Gibby (not much of an improvement, but it's what Eugene wants). So when you're at a party with your friend, you can call him over using either Eugene or Gibby. Your friend is only one person, but you can call him using either his name or a nickname. This is the same as how a variable and a reference to that variable work. You can get to a single value stored in a variable by using its variable name or the name of a reference to that variable. Finally, whatever you do, try not to name your variables `Eugene`—for their sakes.

trap

Because a reference must always refer to another value, you must initialize the reference when you declare it. If you don't, you'll get a compile error. The following line is quite illegal:

```
int& mikesScore;  //don't try this at home!
```

Accessing Referenced Values

Next I send both `myScore` and `mikesScore` to `cout`.

```
cout << "myScore is: " << myScore << "\n";
cout << "mikesScore is: " << mikesScore << "\n\n";
```

Both lines of code display 1000 because they each access the same single chunk of memory that stores the number 1000. Remember, there is only one value, and it is stored in the variable myScore. mikesScore simply provides another way to get to that value.

Altering Referenced Values

Next I increase the value of myScore by 500.

```
myScore += 500;
```

When I send myScore to cout, 1500 is displayed, just as you'd expect. When I send mikesScore to cout, 1500 is also displayed. Again, that's because mikesScore is just another name for the variable myScore. In essence, I'm sending the same variable to cout both times.

Next I increase mikesScore by 500.

```
mikesScore += 500;
```

Because mikesScore is just another name for myScore, the preceding line of code increases the value of myScore by 500. So when I next send myScore to cout, 2000 is displayed. When I send mikesScore to cout, 2000 is displayed again.

trap

A reference always refers to the variable with which it was initialized. You can't reassign a reference to refer to another variable so, for example, the results of the following code might not be obvious.

```
int myScore = 1000;
int& mikesScore = myScore;
int larrysScore = 2500;
mikesScore = larrysScore;   //may not do what you think!
```

The line mikesScore = larrysScore; does not reassign the reference mikesScore so it refers to larrysScore because a reference can't be reassigned. However, because mikesScore is just another name for myScore, the code mikesScore = larrysScore; is equivalent to myScore = larrysScore;, which assigns 2500 to myScore. And after all is said and done, myScore becomes 2500 and mikesScore still refers to myScore.

Passing References to Alter Arguments

Now that you've seen how references work, you might be wondering why you'd ever use them. Well, references come in quite handy when you are passing variables to functions because when you pass a variable to a function, the function gets a copy of the variable. This means that the original variable you passed (called the *argument variable*) can't be changed. Sometimes this might be exactly what you want because it keeps the argument variable safe and unalterable. But other times you might want to change an argument variable from inside the function to which it was passed. You can accomplish this by using references.

Introducing the Swap Program

The Swap program defines two variables—one that holds my pitifully low score and another that holds your impressively high score. After displaying the scores, the program calls a function meant to swap the scores. But because only copies of the score values are sent to the function, the argument variables that hold the scores are unchanged. Next, the program calls another swap function. This time, through the use of references, the argument variables' values are successfully exchanged—giving me the great big score and leaving you with the small one. Figure 6.2 shows the program in action.

Figure 6.2
Passing references allows goodSwap() to alter the argument variables.

The code for the program is in the Chapter 6 folder on the CD-ROM that came with this book; the file name is referencing.cpp.

```
// Swap
// Demonstrates passing references to alter argument variables

#include <iostream>

using namespace std;

void badSwap(int x, int y);
void goodSwap(int& x, int& y);
```

```
int main()
{
    int myScore = 150;
    int yourScore = 1000;
    cout << "Original values\n";
    cout << "myScore: " << myScore << "\n";
    cout << "yourScore: " << yourScore << "\n\n";

    cout << "Calling badSwap()\n";
    badSwap(myScore, yourScore);
    cout << "myScore: " << myScore << "\n";
    cout << "yourScore: " << yourScore << "\n\n";

    cout << "Calling goodSwap()\n";
    goodSwap(myScore, yourScore);
    cout << "myScore: " << myScore << "\n";
    cout << "yourScore: " << yourScore << "\n";

    return 0;
}

void badSwap(int x, int y)
{
    int temp = x;
    x = y;
    y = temp;
}

void goodSwap(int& x, int& y)
{
    int temp = x;
    x = y;
    y = temp;
}
```

Passing by Value

After declaring and initializing myScore and yourScore, I send them to cout. As you'd expect, 150 and 1000 are displayed. Next I call badSwap().

When you specify a parameter the way you've seen so far (as an ordinary variable, not as a reference), you're indicating that the argument for that parameter will be *passed by value*, meaning that the parameter will get a *copy* of the argument variable and not access to the argument variable itself. By looking at the function header of badSwap(), you can tell that a call to the function passes both arguments by value.

```
void badSwap(int x, int y)
```

This means that when I call badSwap() with the following line, copies of myScore and yourScore are sent to the parameters, x and y.

```
badSwap(myScore, yourScore);
```

Specifically, x is assigned 150 and y is assigned 1000. As a result, nothing I do with x and y in the function badSwap() will have any effect on myScore and yourScore.

When the guts of badSwap() execute, x and y do exchange values—x becomes 1000 and y becomes 150. However, when the function ends, both x and y go out of scope and cease to exist. Control then returns to main(), where myScore and yourScore haven't changed. Then, when I send myScore and yourScore to cout, 150 and 1000 are displayed again. Sadly, I still have the small score and you still have the large one.

Passing by Reference

It's possible to give a function access to an argument variable by passing a parameter a reference to the argument variable. As a result, anything done to the parameter will be done to the argument variable. To *pass by reference*, you must first declare the parameter as a reference.

You can tell that a call to goodSwap() passes both arguments by reference by looking at the function header.

```
void goodSwap(int& x, int& y)
```

This means that when I call goodSwap() with the following line, the parameter x will refer to myScore and the parameter y will refer to yourScore.

```
goodSwap(myScore, yourScore);
```

This means that x is just another name for myScore and y is just another name for yourScore. When goodSwap() executes and x and y exchange values, what really happens is that myScore and yourScore exchange values.

After the function ends, control returns to main(), where I send myScore and yourScore to cout. This time 1000 and 150 are displayed. The variables have exchanged values. I've taken the large score and left you with the small one. Success at last!

Passing References for Efficiency

Passing a variable by value creates some overhead because you must copy the variable before you assign it to a parameter. When we're talking about variables of simple, built-in types, such as an int or a float, the overhead is negligible. But a large object, such as one that represents an entire 3D world, could be expensive to copy. Passing by reference, on the other hand, is efficient because you don't make a copy of an argument variable. Instead, you simply provide access to the existing object through a reference.

Introducing the Inventory Displayer Program

The Inventory Displayer program creates a vector of strings that represents a hero's inventory. The program then calls a function that displays the inventory. The program passes the displayer function the vector of items as a reference, so it's an efficient call; the vector isn't copied. However, there's a new wrinkle. The program passes the vector as a special kind of reference that prohibits the displayer function from changing the vector. Figure 6.3 shows you the program.

Figure 6.3
The vector `inventory` is passed in a safe and efficient way to the function that displays the hero's items.

The code for the program is in the Chapter 6 folder on the CD-ROM that came with this book; the file name is inventory_displayer.cpp.

```cpp
// Inventory Displayer
// Demonstrates constant references

#include <iostream>
#include <string>
#include <vector>

using namespace std;

//parameter vec is a constant reference to a vector of strings
void display(const vector<string>& vec);

int main()
{
    vector<string> inventory;
    inventory.push_back("sword");
```

```
    inventory.push_back("armor");
    inventory.push_back("shield");

    display(inventory);

    return 0;
}

//parameter vec is a constant reference to a vector of strings
void display(const vector<string>& vec)
{
    cout << "Your items:\n";
    for (vector<string>::const_iterator iter = vec.begin();
        iter != vec.end(); ++iter)
        cout << *iter << endl;
}
```

Understanding the Pitfalls of Reference Passing

One way to efficiently give a function access to a large object is to pass it by reference. However, this introduces a potential problem. As you saw in the Swap program, it opens up an argument variable to being changed. But what if you don't want to change the argument variable? Is there a way to take advantage of the efficiency of passing by reference while protecting an argument variable's integrity? Yes, there is. The answer is to pass a constant reference.

hint

In general, you should avoid changing an argument variable. Try to write functions that send back new information to the calling code through a return value.

Declaring Parameters as Constant References

The function display() shows the contents of the hero's inventory. In the function's header I specify one parameter—a constant reference to a vector of string objects named vec.

```
void display(const vector<string>& vec)
```

A *constant reference* is a restricted reference. It acts like any other reference, except you can't use it to change the value to which it refers. To create a constant reference, simply put the keyword const before the type in the reference declaration.

What does this all mean for the function display()? Because the parameter vec is a constant reference, it means display() can't change vec. In turn, this means that inventory is safe; it can't be changed by display(). In general, you can efficiently pass an argument to a function as a constant reference so it's accessible, but not changeable. It's like providing the function read-only access to the argument. Although constant references are very useful for specifying function parameters, you can use them anywhere in your program.

hint

A constant reference comes in handy in another way. If you need to assign a constant value to a reference, you have to assign it to a constant reference. (A non-constant reference won't do.)

Passing a Constant Reference

Back in `main()`, I create `inventory` and then call `display()` with the following line, which passes the vector as a constant reference.

```
display(inventory);
```

This results in an efficient and safe function call. It's efficient because only a reference is passed; the vector is not copied. It's safe because the reference to the vector is a constant reference; `inventory` can't be changed by `display()`.

trap

You can't modify a parameter marked as a constant reference. If you try, you'll generate a compile error.

Next, `display()` lists the elements in the vector using a constant reference to `inventory`. Then control returns to `main()` and the program ends.

Deciding How to Pass Arguments

At this point you've seen three different ways to pass arguments—by value, as a reference, and as a constant reference. So how do you decide which method to use? Here are some guidelines:

- **By value.** Pass by value when an argument variable is one of the fundamental built-in types, such as `bool`, `int`, or `float`. Objects of these types are so small that passing by reference doesn't result in any gain in efficiency. You should also pass by value when you want the computer to make a copy of a variable. You might want to use a copy if you plan to alter a parameter in a function, but you don't want the actual argument variable to be affected.

- **As a constant reference.** Pass a constant reference when you want to efficiently pass a value that you don't need to change.

- **As a reference.** Pass a reference only when you want to alter the value of the argument variable. However, you should try to avoid changing argument variables whenever possible.

Returning References

Just like when you pass a value, when you return a value from a function, you're really returning a copy of the value. Again, for values of the basic built-in types, this isn't a big deal. However, it can be an expensive operation if you're returning a large object. Returning a reference is an efficient alternative.

Introducing the Inventory Referencer Program

The Inventory Referencer program demonstrates returning references. The program displays the elements of a vector that holds a hero's inventory by using returned references. Then the program changes one of the items through a returned reference. Figure 6.4 shows the results of the program.

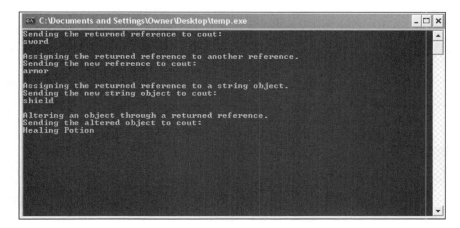

Figure 6.4
The items in the hero's inventory are displayed and changed by using returned references.

The code for the program is in the Chapter 6 folder on the CD-ROM that came with this book; the file name is inventory_referencer.cpp.

```cpp
// Inventory Referencer
// Demonstrates returning a reference

#include <iostream>
#include <string>
#include <vector>

using namespace std;

//returns a reference to a string
string& refToElement(vector<string>& vec, int i);
```

```
int main()
{
    vector<string> inventory;
    inventory.push_back("sword");
    inventory.push_back("armor");
    inventory.push_back("shield");

    //displays string that the returned reference refers to
    cout << "Sending the returned reference to cout:\n";
    cout << refToElement(inventory, 0) << "\n\n";

    //assigns one reference to another -- inexpensive assignment
    cout << "Assigning the returned reference to another reference.\n";
    string& rStr = refToElement(inventory, 1);
    cout << "Sending the new reference to cout:\n";
    cout << rStr << "\n\n";

    //copies a string object -- expensive assignment
    cout << "Assigning the returned reference to a string object.\n";
    string str = refToElement(inventory, 2);
    cout << "Sending the new string object to cout:\n";
    cout << str << "\n\n";

    //altering the string object through a returned reference
    cout << "Altering an object through a returned reference.\n";
    rStr = "Healing Potion";
    cout << "Sending the altered object to cout:\n";
    cout << inventory[1] << endl;

    return 0;
}

//returns a reference to a string
string& refToElement(vector<string>& vec, int i)
{
    return vec[i];
}
```

Returning a Reference

Before you can return a reference from a function, you must specify that you're returning one. That's what I do in the `refToElement()` function header.

```
string& refToElement(vector<string>& vec, int i)
```

By using the reference operator in `string&` when I specify the return type, I'm saying that the function will return a reference to a `string` object (not a `string` object itself). You can use the reference operator like I did to specify that a function returns a reference to an object of a particular type. Simply put the reference operator after the type name.

The body of the function refToElement() contains only one statement, which returns a reference to the element at position i in the vector.

```
return vec[i];
```

Notice that there's nothing in the return statement to indicate that the function returns a reference. The function header and prototype determine whether a function returns an object or a reference to an object.

trap

Although returning a reference can be an efficient way to send information back to a calling function, you have to be careful not to return a reference to an out-of-scope object—an object that ceases to exist. For example, the following function returns a reference to a string object that no longer exists after the function ends—and that's illegal.

```
string& badReference()
{
    string local = "This string will cease to exist once the function ends.";
    return local;
}
```

One way to avoid this problem is to never return a reference to a local variable.

Displaying the Value of a Returned Reference

After creating inventory, a vector of items, I display the first item through a returned reference.

```
cout << refToElement(inventory, 0) << "\n\n";
```

The preceding code calls refToElement(), which returns a reference to the element at position 0 of inventory and then sends that reference to cout. As a result, sword is displayed.

Assigning a Returned Reference to a Reference

Next I assign a returned reference to another reference with the following line, which takes a reference to the element in position 1 of inventory and assigns it to rStr.

```
string& rStr = refToElement(inventory, 1);
```

This is an efficient assignment because assigning a reference to a reference does not involve the copying of an object. Then I send rStr to cout, and armor is displayed.

Assigning a Returned Reference to a Variable

Next I assign a returned reference to a variable.

```
string str = refToElement(inventory, 2);
```

The preceding code doesn't assign a reference to str. It can't, because str is a string object. Instead, the code copies the element to which the returned reference refers (the element in position 2 of inventory) and assigns that new copy of the string object to str. Because this kind of assignment involves copying an object, it's more expensive than assigning one reference to another. Sometimes the cost of copying an object this way is perfectly acceptable, but you should be aware of the extra overhead associated with this kind of assignment and avoid it when necessary.

Next I send the new string object, str, to cout, and shield is displayed.

Altering an Object through a Returned Reference

You can also alter the object to which a returned reference refers. This means you can change the hero's inventory through rStr, as in the following line of code.

```
rStr = "Healing Potion";
```

Because rStr refers to the element in position 1 of inventory, this code changes inventory[1] so it's equal to "Healing Potion". To prove it, I display the element using the following line, which does indeed show Healing Potion.

```
cout << inventory[1] << endl;
```

If I want to protect inventory so a reference returned by refToElement() can't be used to change the vector, I should specify the return type of the function as a constant reference.

Introducing the Tic-Tac-Toe Game

In this chapter project, you'll learn how to create a computer opponent using a dash of AI (*Artificial Intelligence*). In the game, the player and computer square off in a high-stakes, man-versus-machine showdown of Tic-Tac-Toe. The computer plays a formidable (although not perfect) game and comes with enough attitude to make any match fun. Figure 6.5 shows the start of a match.

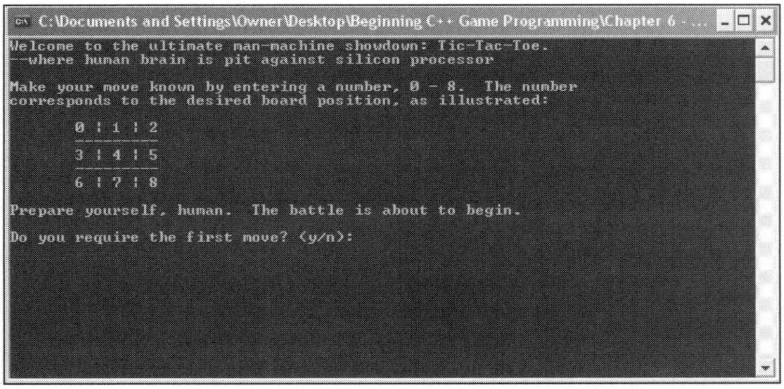

Figure 6.5
The computer is full of... confidence.

Planning the Game

This game is your most ambitious project yet. You certainly have all the skills you need to create it, but I'm going to go through a longer planning section to help you get the big picture and understand how to create a larger program. Remember, the most important part of programming is planning to program. Without a roadmap, you'll never get to where you want to go (or it'll take you a lot longer as you travel the scenic route).

in the real world

Game designers work countless hours on concept papers, design documents, and prototypes before programmers write any game code. Once the design work is done, the programmers start their work—more planning. It's only after programmers write their own technical designs that they then begin coding in earnest. The moral of this story? Plan. It's easier to scrap a blueprint than a 50-story building.

Writing the Pseudocode

It's back to your favorite language that's not really a language—pseudocode. Because I'll be using functions for most of the tasks in the program, I can afford to think about the code at a pretty abstract level. Each line of pseudocode should feel like one function call. Later, all I'll have to do is write the functions that the plan implies. Here's the pseudocode:

```
Create an empty Tic-Tac-Toe board
Display the game instructions
Determine who goes first
Display the board
While nobody's won and it's not a tie
    If it's the human's turn
        Get the human's move
        Update the board with the human's move
    Otherwise
        Calculate the computer's move
        Update the board with the computer's move
    Display the board
    Switch turns
Congratulate the winner or declare a tie
```

Representing the Data

All right, I've got a good plan, but it is pretty abstract and talks about throwing around different elements that aren't really defined in my mind yet. I see the idea of making a move as placing a piece on a game board. But how exactly am I going to represent the game board? Or a piece? Or a move?

Since I'm going to display the game board on the screen, why not just represent a piece as a single character—an X or an O? An empty piece could just be a space. Therefore, the board itself could be a vector of chars. There are nine squares on a Tic-Tac-Toe board, so the vector should have nine elements. Each square on the board will correspond to an element in the vector. Figure 6.6 illustrates what I mean.

0	1	2
3	4	5
6	7	8

Figure 6.6
Each square number corresponds to a position in the vector that represents the board.

Each square or position on the board is represented by a number, 0–8. That means the vector will have nine elements, giving it position numbers 0–8. Because each move indicates a square where a piece should be placed, a move is also just a number, 0–8. That means a move could be represented as an int.

The side the player and computer play could also be represented by a char—either an 'X' or an 'O', just like a game piece. A variable to represent the side of the current turn would also be a char, either an 'X' or an 'O'.

Creating a List of Functions

The pseudocode inspires the different functions I'll need. I created a list of them, thinking about what each will do, what parameters they'll have, and what values they'll return. Table 6.1 shows the results of my efforts.

Table 6.1 Tic-Tac-Toe Functions

Function	Description
void instructions()	Displays the game instructions.
char askYesNo(string *question*)	Asks a yes or no question. Receives a question. Returns either a 'y' or an 'n'.
int askNumber(string *question*, int *high*, int *low* = 0)	Asks for a number within a range. Receives a question, a low number, and a high number. Returns a number in the range from *low* to *high*.
char humanPiece()	Determines the human's piece. Returns either an 'X' or an 'O'.

Table 6.1 Tic-Tac-Toe Functions (continued)

Function	Description
`char opponent(char `*`piece`*`)`	Calculates the opposing piece given a piece. Receives either an `'X'` or an `'O'`. Returns either an `'X'` or an `'O'`.
`void displayBoard(const vector<char>& `*`board`*`)`	Displays the board on the screen. Receives a board.
`char winner(const vector<char>& `*`board`*`)`	Determines the game winner. Receives a board. Returns an `'X'`, `'O'`, `'T'` (to indicate a tie), or `'N'` (to indicate that no one has won yet).
`bool isLegal(const vector<char>& `*`board`*`, int `*`move`*`)`	Determines whether a move is legal. Receives a board and a move. Returns either `true` or `false`.
`int humanMove(const vector<char>& `*`board`*`, char `*`human`*`)`	Gets the human's move. Receives a board and the human's piece. Returns the human's move.
`int computerMove(vector<char> `*`board`*`, char `*`computer`*`)`	Calculates the computer's move. Receives a board and the computer's piece. Returns the computer's move.
`void announceWinner(char `*`winner`*`, char `*`computer`*`, char `*`human`*`)`	Congratulates the winner or declares a tie. Receives the winning side, the computer's piece, and the human's piece.

Setting Up the Program

The code for the program is in the Chapter 6 folder on the CD-ROM that came with this book; the file name is tic-tac-toe.cpp. I'll go over the code here, section by section.

The first thing I do in the program is include the files I need, define some global constants, and write my function prototypes.

```
// Tic-Tac-Toe
// Plays the game of tic-tac-toe against a human opponent

#include <iostream>
#include <string>
#include <vector>
#include <algorithm>

using namespace std;

// global constants
const char X = 'X';
const char O = 'O';
const char EMPTY = ' ';
const char TIE = 'T';
const char NO_ONE = 'N';
```

```
// function prototypes
void instructions();
char askYesNo(string question);
int askNumber(string question, int high, int low = 0);
char humanPiece();
char opponent(char piece);
void displayBoard(const vector<char>& board);
char winner(const vector<char>& board);
bool isLegal(const vector<char>& board, int move);
int humanMove(const vector<char>& board, char human);
int computerMove(vector<char> board, char computer);
void announceWinner(char winner, char computer, char human);
```

In the global constants section, X is shorthand for the char 'X', one of the two pieces in the game. O represents the char 'O', the other piece in the game. EMPTY, also a char, represents an empty square on the board. It's a space because when it's displayed, it will look like an empty square. TIE is a char that represents a tie game. And NO_ONE is a char used to represent neither side of the game, which I use to indicate that no one has won yet.

The main() Function

As you can see, the main() function is almost exactly the pseudocode I created earlier.

```
// main function
int main()
{
    int move;
    const int NUM_SQUARES = 9;
    vector<char> board(NUM_SQUARES, EMPTY);

    instructions();
    char human = humanPiece();
    char computer = opponent(human);
    char turn = X;
    displayBoard(board);

    while (winner(board) == NO_ONE)
    {
        if (turn == human)
        {
            move = humanMove(board, human);
            board[move] = human;
        }
        else
        {
            move = computerMove(board, computer);
            board[move] = computer;
        }
        displayBoard(board);
```

```
        turn = opponent(turn);
    }

    announceWinner(winner(board), computer, human);

    return 0;
}
```

The instructions() Function

This function displays the game instructions and gives the computer opponent a little attitude.

```
void instructions()
{
    cout << "Welcome to the ultimate man-machine showdown: Tic-Tac-Toe.\n";
    cout << "--where human brain is pit against silicon processor\n\n";

    cout << "Make your move known by entering a number, 0 - 8. The number\n";
    cout << "corresponds to the desired board position, as illustrated:\n\n";

    cout << "        0 | 1 | 2\n";
    cout << "        ------\n";
    cout << "        3 | 4 | 5\n";
    cout << "        ------\n";
    cout << "        6 | 7 | 8\n\n";

    cout << "Prepare yourself, human. The battle is about to begin.\n\n";
}
```

The askYesNo() Function

This function asks a yes or no question. It keeps asking the question until the player enters either a y or an n. It receives a question and returns either a 'y' or an 'n'.

```
char askYesNo(string question)
{
    char response;
    do
    {
        cout << question << " (y/n): ";
        cin >> response;
    } while (response != 'y' && response != 'n');

    return response;
}
```

The askNumber() Function

This function asks for a number within a range and keeps asking until the player enters a valid number. It receives a question, a high number, and a low number. It returns a number within the range specified.

```
int askNumber(string question, int high, int low)
{
    int number;
    do
    {
        cout << question << " (" << low << " - " << high << "): ";
        cin >> number;
    } while (number > high || number < low);

    return number;
}
```

If you take a look at this function's prototype, you can see that the low number has a default value of 0. I take advantage of this fact when I call the function later in the program.

The humanPiece() Function

This function asks the player if he wants to go first, and returns the human's piece based on that choice. As the great tradition of Tic-Tac-Toe dictates, the X goes first.

```
char humanPiece()
{
    char go_first = askYesNo("Do you require the first move?");
    if (go_first == 'y')
    {
        cout << "\nThen take the first move. You will need it.\n";
        return X;
    }
    else
    {
        cout << "\nYour bravery will be your undoing... I will go first.\n";
        return O;
    }
}
```

The opponent() Function

This function gets a piece (either an 'X' or an 'O') and returns the opponent's piece (either an 'X' or an 'O').

```
char opponent(char piece)
{
```

```
    if (piece == X)
        return 0;
    else
        return X;
}
```

The displayBoard() Function

This function displays the board passed to it. Because each element in the board is either a space, an 'X', or an '0', the function can display each one. I use a few other characters on my keyboard to draw a decent-looking Tic-Tac-Toe board.

```
void displayBoard(const vector<char>& board)
{
    cout << "\n\t" << board[0] << " | " << board[1] << " | " << board[2];
    cout << "\n\t" << "-----";
    cout << "\n\t" << board[3] << " | " << board[4] << " | " << board[5];
    cout << "\n\t" << "-----";
    cout << "\n\t" << board[6] << " | " << board[7] << " | " << board[8];
    cout << "\n\n";
}
```

Notice that the vector that represents the board is passed through a constant reference. This means that the vector is passed efficiently; it is not copied. It also means that the vector is safeguarded against any changes. Since I plan to simply display the board and not change it in this function, this is perfect.

The winner() Function

This function receives a board and returns the winner. There are four possible values for a winner. The function will return either X or 0 if one of the players has won. If every square is filled and no one has won, it returns TIE. Finally, if no one has won and there is at least one empty square, the function returns NO_ONE.

```
char winner(const vector<char>& board)
{
    // all possible winning rows
    const int WINNING_ROWS[8][3] = { {0, 1, 2},
                                     {3, 4, 5},
                                     {6, 7, 8},
                                     {0, 3, 6},
                                     {1, 4, 7},
                                     {2, 5, 8},
                                     {0, 4, 8},
                                     {2, 4, 6} };
```

The first thing to notice is that the vector that represents the board is passed through a constant reference. This means that the vector is passed efficiently; it is not copied. It also means that the vector is safeguarded against any change.

In this initial section of the function, I define a constant, two-dimensional array of ints called WINNING_ROWS, which represents all eight ways to get three in a row and win the game. Each winning row is represented by a group of three numbers—three board positions that form a winning row. For example, the group {0, 1, 2} represents the top row—board positions 0, 1, and 2. The next group, {3, 4, 5}, represents the middle row—board positions 3, 4, and 5. And so on....

Next I check to see whether either player has won.

```
const int TOTAL_ROWS = 8;

// if any winning row has three values that are the same (and not EMPTY),
// then we have a winner
for(int row = 0; row < TOTAL_ROWS; ++row)
{
    if ( (board[WINNING_ROWS[row][0]] != EMPTY) &&
         (board[WINNING_ROWS[row][0]] == board[WINNING_ROWS[row][1]]) &&
         (board[WINNING_ROWS[row][1]] == board[WINNING_ROWS[row][2]]) )
    {
        return board[WINNING_ROWS[row][0]];
    }
}
```

I loop through each possible way a player can win to see whether either player has three in a row. The if statement checks to see whether the three squares in question all contain the same value and are not EMPTY. If so, it means that the row has either three Xs or Os in it, and one side has won. The function then returns the piece in the first position of this winning row.

If neither player has won, I check for a tie game.

```
// since nobody has won, check for a tie (no empty squares left)
if (count(board.begin(), board.end(), EMPTY) == 0)
    return TIE;
```

If there are no empty squares on the board, then the game is a tie. I use the STL count() algorithm, which counts the number of times a given value appears in a group of container elements, to count the number of EMPTY elements in board. If the number is equal to 0, the function returns TIE.

Finally, if neither player has won and the game isn't a tie, then there is no winner yet. Thus, the function returns NO_ONE.

```
// since nobody has won and it isn't a tie, the game ain't over
return NO_ONE;
}
```

The isLegal() Function

This function receives a board and a move. It returns `true` if the move is a legal one on the board or `false` if the move is not legal. A legal move is represented by the number of an empty square.

```
inline bool isLegal(int move, const vector<char>& board)
{
    return (board[move] == EMPTY);
}
```

Again, notice that the vector that represents the board is passed through a constant reference. This means that the vector is passed efficiently; it is not copied. It also means that the vector is safeguarded against any change.

You can see that I inlined `isLegal()`. Modern compilers are quite good at optimizing on their own; however, since this function is just one line, it's a good candidate for inlining.

The humanMove() Function

This next function receives a board and the human's piece. It returns the square number for where the player wants to move. The function asks the player for the square number to which he wants to move until the response is a legal move. Then the function returns the move.

```
int humanMove(const vector<char>& board, char human)
{
    int move = askNumber("Where will you move?", (board.size() - 1));
    while (!isLegal(move, board))
    {
        cout << "\nThat square is already occupied, foolish human.\n";
        move = askNumber("Where will you move?", (board.size() - 1));
    }
    cout << "Fine...\n";
    return move;
}
```

Again, notice that the vector that represents the board is passed through a constant reference. This means that the vector is passed efficiently; it is not copied. It also means that the vector is safeguarded against any change.

The computerMove() Function

This function receives the board and the computer's piece. It returns the computer's move. The first thing to notice is that I do not pass the board by reference.

```
int computerMove(vector<char> board, char computer)
```

Instead, I choose to pass by value, even though it's not as efficient as passing by reference. I pass by value because I need to work with and modify a copy of the board as I place pieces in empty squares to determine the best computer move. By working with a copy, I keep the original vector that represents the board safe.

Now on to the guts of the function. Okay, how do I program a bit of AI so the computer puts up a decent fight? Well, I came up with a basic three-step strategy for choosing a move.

1. If the computer can win on this move, make that move.

2. If the human can win on his next move, block it.

3. Otherwise, take the best remaining open square. The best square is the center. The next best squares are the corners, and then the rest of the squares.

The next section of the function implements Step 1.

```
{
    cout << "I shall take square number ";

    // if computer can win on next move, make that move
    for(int move = 0; move < board.size(); ++move)
    {
        if (isLegal(move, board))
        {
            board[move] = computer;
            if (winner(board) == computer)
            {
                cout << move << endl;
                return move;
            }
            // done checking this move, undo it
            board[move] = EMPTY;
        }
    }
}
```

I loop through all of the possible moves, 0–8. For each move, I test to see whether the move is legal. If it is, I put the computer's piece in that square and check to see whether this move gives the computer a win. If it does, it means that the computer can win by moving to that square, so I return the move. If the move doesn't produce a win for the computer, I undo the move and try the next move.

If I get to this next section of the function, it means the computer can't win on its next move. So I go to Step 2 of my AI strategy and check to see whether the player can win on his next move.

```
    // if human can win on next move, block that move
    char human = opponent(computer);
```

```
for(int move = 0; move < board.size(); ++move)
{
    if (isLegal(move, board))
    {
        board[move] = human;
        if (winner(board) == human)
        {
            cout << move << endl;
            return move;
        }
        // done checking this move, undo it
        board[move] = EMPTY;
    }
}
```

I loop through all of the possible moves, 0–8. For each move, I test to see whether the move is legal. If it is, I put the human's piece in that square and check to see whether the move gives the human a win. If it does, I return that move for the computer to block. If not, I undo the move and try the next move.

If I get to the next point in the function, it means that neither side can win on its next move. So, implementing Step 3, I look through the list of best moves in order of desirability and take the first legal one.

```
// the best moves to make, in order
const int BEST_MOVES[] = {4, 0, 2, 6, 8, 1, 3, 5, 7};
// since no one can win on next move, pick best open square
for(int i = 0; i < board.size(); ++i)
{
    int move = BEST_MOVES[i];
    if (isLegal(move, board))
    {
        cout << move << endl;
        return move;
    }
}
}
```

in the real world

The Tic-Tac-Toe game considers only the next possible move. Programs that play serious games of strategy, such as chess, look far deeper into the consequences of individual moves and consider many levels of moves and countermoves. In fact, good computer chess programs can consider literally millions of board positions before making a move.

The announceWinner() Function

This function receives the winner of the game, the computer's piece, and the human's piece. The function announces the winner or declares a tie.

```
void announceWinner(char winner, char computer, char human)
{
    if (winner == computer)
    {
        cout << winner << "'s won!\n";
        cout << "As I predicted, human, I am triumphant once more -- proof\n";
        cout << "that computers are superior to humans in all regards.\n";
    }

    else if (winner == human)
    {
        cout << winner << "'s won!\n";
        cout << "No, no! It cannot be! Somehow you tricked me, human.\n";
        cout << "But never again! I, the computer, so swear it!\n";
    }

    else
    {
        cout << "It's a tie.\n";
        cout << "You were most lucky, human, and somehow managed to tie me.\n";
        cout << "Celebrate... for this is the best you will ever achieve.\n";
    }
}
```

Summary

In this chapter, you should have learned the following concepts:

- A reference is an alias; it's another name for a variable.

- You create a reference using &—the referencing operator.

- A reference must be initialized when it's defined.

- A reference can't be changed to refer to a different variable.

- Whatever you do to a reference is done to the variable to which the reference refers.

- When you assign a reference to a variable, you create a new copy of the referenced value.

- When you pass a variable to a function by value, you pass a copy of the variable to the function.

- When you pass a variable to a function by reference, you pass access to the variable.

- Passing by reference can be more efficient than passing by value, especially when you are passing large objects.

- Passing a reference provides direct access to the argument variable passed to a function. As a result, the function can make changes to the argument variable.

- A constant reference can't be used to change the value to which it refers. You declare a constant reference by using the keyword `const`.

- You can't assign a constant reference or a constant value to a non-constant reference.

- Passing a constant reference to a function protects the argument variable from being changed by that function.

- Changing the value of an argument variable passed to a function can lead to confusion, so game programmers consider passing a constant reference before passing a non-constant reference.

- Returning a reference can be more efficient than returning a copy of a value, especially when you are returning large objects.

- You can return a constant reference to an object so the object can't be changed through the returned reference.

- A basic technique of game AI is to have the computer consider all of its legal moves and all of its opponent's legal replies before deciding which move to take next.

Questions and Answers

Q: Different programmers put the reference operator (`&`) in different places when declaring a reference. Where should I put it?

A: Three basic styles exist with regard to using the referencing operator. Some programmers opt for `int& ref = var;`, while others opt for `int & ref = var;`. Still others opt for `int &ref = var;`. The computer is fine with all three. There are cases to be made for each style; however, the most important thing is to be consistent.

Q: Why can't I initialize a non-constant reference with a constant value?

A: Because a non-constant reference allows you to change the value to which it refers.

Q: If I initialize a constant reference with a non-constant variable, can I change the value of the variable?

A: Not through the constant reference because when you declare a constant reference, you're saying that the reference can't be used to change the value to which it refers (even if that value can be changed by other means).

Q: How does passing a constant reference save overhead?

A: When you pass a large object to a function by value, your program makes a copy of the object. This can be an expensive operation depending on the size of the object. Passing a reference is like passing only access to the large object; it is an inexpensive operation.

Q: Can I make a reference to a reference?

A: Not exactly. You can assign one reference to another reference, but the new reference will simply refer to the value to which the original reference refers.

Q: What happens if I declare a reference without initializing it?

A: Your compiler should complain because it's illegal.

Q: Why should I avoid changing the value of a variable that I pass through a reference?

A: Because it could lead to confusion. It's impossible to tell from only a function call whether a variable is being passed to change its value.

Q: Does that mean I should always pass a constant reference?

A: No. You can pass a non-constant reference to a function, but to most game programmers, this signals that you intend to change the argument variable's value.

Q: If I don't change the argument variables passed to functions, how should I get new information back to the calling code?

A: Use return values.

Q: Can I pass a literal through a non-constant reference?

A: No. If you try to pass a literal as a non-constant reference, you'll generate a compile error.

Q: Is it impossible to pass a literal to a parameter that accepts a reference?

A: No, you can pass a literal as a constant reference.

Q: What happens when I return an object from a function?

A: Normally, your program creates a copy of the object and returns that. This can be an expensive operation, depending on the size of the object.

Q: Why return a reference?

A: It can be more efficient because returning a reference doesn't involve copying an object.

Q: How can I lose the efficiency of returning a reference?

A: By assigning the returned reference to a variable. When you assign a reference to a variable, the computer must make a copy of the object to which the reference refers.

Q: What's wrong with returning a reference to a local variable?

A: The local variable doesn't exist once the function ends, which means that you're returning a reference to a non-existent object, which is illegal.

Discussion Questions

1. What are the advantages and disadvantages of passing an argument by value?

2. What are the advantages and disadvantages of passing a reference?

3. What are the advantages and disadvantages of passing a constant reference?

4. What are the advantages and disadvantages of returning a reference?

5. Should game AI cheat in order to create a more worthy opponent?

Exercises

1. Improve the Mad Lib game from Chapter 5 by using references to make the program more efficient.

2. What's wrong with the following program?

```
int main()
{
    int score;
    score = 1000;
    float& rScore = score;
    return 0;
}
```

3. What's wrong with the following function?

```
int& plusThree(int number)
{
    int threeMore = number + 3;
    return threeMore;
}
```

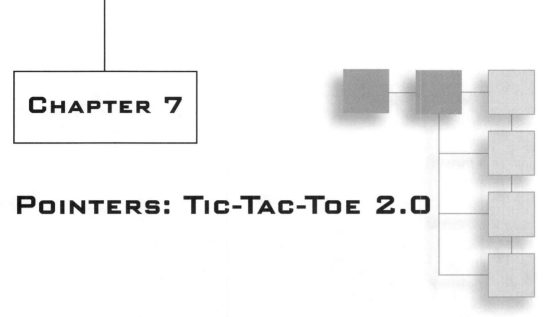

CHAPTER 7

POINTERS: TIC-TAC-TOE 2.0

P ointers are a powerful part of C++. In some ways, they behave like iterators from the STL. Often you can use them in place of references. But pointers offer functionality that no other part of the language can. In this chapter, you'll learn the basic mechanics of pointers and get an idea of what they're good for. Specifically, you'll learn to:

- Declare and initialize pointers
- Dereference pointers
- Use constants and pointers
- Pass and return pointers
- Work with pointers and arrays

Understanding Pointer Basics

Pointers have a reputation for being difficult to understand. In reality, the essence of pointers is quite simple—a *pointer* is a variable that can contain a memory address. Pointers give you the ability to work directly and efficiently with computer memory. Like iterators from the STL, they're often used to access the contents of other variables. But before you can put pointers to good use in your game programs, you have to understand the basics of how they work.

hint

Computer memory is a lot like a neighborhood, but instead of houses in which people store their stuff, you have memory locations where you can store data. Just like a neighborhood where houses sit side by side, labeled with addresses, chunks of computer memory sit side by side, labeled with addresses. In a neighborhood, you can use a slip of paper with a street address on it to get to a particular house (and to the stuff stored inside it). In a computer, you can use a pointer with a memory address in it to get to a particular memory location (and to the stuff stored inside it).

Introducing the Pointing Program

The Pointing program demonstrates the mechanics of pointers. The program creates a variable for a score and then creates a pointer to store the address of that variable. The program shows that you can change the value of a variable directly, and the pointer will reflect the change. It also shows that you can change the value of a variable through a pointer. It then demonstrates that you can change a pointer to point to another variable entirely. Finally, the program shows that pointers can work just as easily with objects. Figure 7.1 illustrates the results of the program.

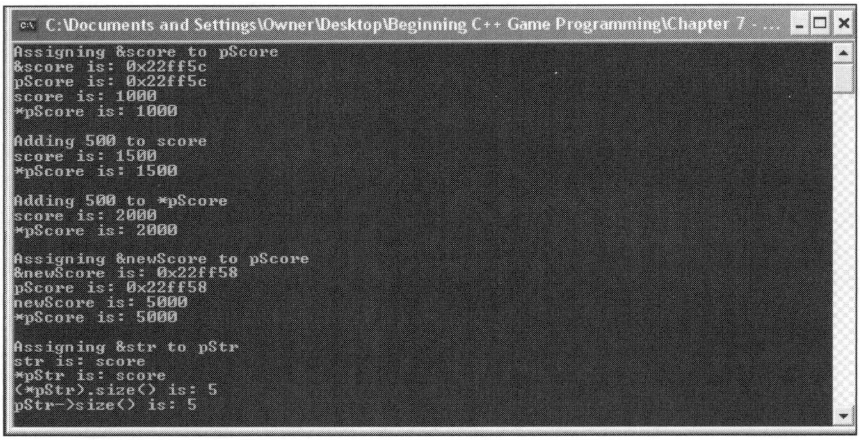

Figure 7.1
The pointer pScore first points to the variable score and then to the variable newScore, while the pointer pStr points to the variable str.

The code for the program is in the Chapter 7 folder on the CD-ROM that came with this book; the file name is pointing.cpp.

```
// Pointing
// Demonstrates using pointers

#include <iostream>
#include <string>

using namespace std;

int main()
{
    int* pAPointer;    //declare a pointer

    int* pScore = 0;   //declare and initialize a pointer
```

```
int score = 1000;
pScore = &score;    //assign pointer pScore address of variable score

cout << "Assigning &score to pScore\n";
cout << "&score is: " << &score << "\n";        //address of score variable
cout << "pScore is: " << pScore << "\n";        //address stored in pointer
cout << "score is: " << score << "\n";
cout << "*pScore is: " << *pScore << "\n\n"; //value pointed to by pointer

cout << "Adding 500 to score\n";
score += 500;
cout << "score is: " << score << "\n";
cout << "*pScore is: " << *pScore << "\n\n";

cout << "Adding 500 to *pScore\n";
*pScore += 500;
cout << "score is: " << score << "\n";
cout << "*pScore is: " << *pScore << "\n\n";

cout << "Assigning &newScore to pScore\n";
int newScore = 5000;
pScore = &newScore;
cout << "&newScore is: " << &newScore << "\n";
cout << "pScore is: " << pScore << "\n";
cout << "newScore is: " << newScore << "\n";
cout << "*pScore is: " << *pScore << "\n\n";

cout << "Assigning &str to pStr\n";
string str = "score";
string* pStr = &str;    //pointer to string object
cout << "str is: " << str << "\n";
cout << "*pStr is: " << *pStr << "\n";
cout << "(*pStr).size() is: " << (*pStr).size() << "\n";
cout << "pStr->size() is: " << pStr->size() << "\n";

return 0;
}
```

Declaring Pointers

With the first statement in main() I declare a pointer named pAPointer.

```
int* pAPointer;    //declare a pointer
```

Because pointers work in such a unique way, programmers often prefix pointer variable names with the letter "p" to remind them that the variable is indeed a pointer.

Just like an iterator, a pointer is declared to point to a specific type of value. pAPointer is a pointer to int, which means that it can only point to an int value. pAPointer can't point to a `float` or a `char`, for example. Another way to say this is that `pAPointer` can only store the address of an `int`.

To declare a pointer of your own, begin with the type of object to which the pointer will point, followed by an asterisk, followed by the pointer name. When you declare a pointer, you can put whitespace on either side of the asterisk. So `int* pAPointer;`, `int *pAPointer;`, and `int * pAPointer;` all declare a pointer named `pAPointer`.

trap

When you declare a pointer, the asterisk only applies to the single variable name that immediately follows it. So the following statement declares `pScore` as a pointer to `int` and score as an `int`.

```
int* pScore, score;
```

`score` is not a pointer! It's a variable of type `int`. One way to make this clearer is to play with the whitespace and rewrite the statement as:

```
int *pScore, score;
```

However, the clearest way to declare a pointer is to declare it in its own statement, as in the following lines.

```
int* pScore;
int score;
```

Initializing Pointers

As with other variables, you can initialize a pointer in the same statement you declare it. That's what I do next with the following line, which assigns 0 to `pScore`.

```
int* pScore = 0;   //declare and initialize a pointer
```

Assigning 0 to a pointer has special meaning. Loosely translated, it means, "Point to nothing." Programmers call a pointer with the value of zero a *null pointer*. You should always initialize a pointer with some value when you declare it, even if that value is zero.

hint

Many programmers assign NULL to a pointer instead of 0 to make the pointer a null pointer. NULL is a constant equal to 0 and is defined in multiple library files, including `iostream`.

Assigning Addresses to Pointers

Because pointers store addresses of objects, you need a way to get addresses into the pointers. One way to do that is to get the memory address of an existing variable and assign it to a pointer. That's what I do in the following line, which gets the address of the variable score and assigns it to pScore.

```
pScore = &score;    //assign pointer address of variable score
```

I get the address of score by preceding the variable name with &, the *address of* operator. (Yes, you've seen the & symbol before, when it was used as the reference operator. However, in this context, the & symbol gets the address of an object.)

As a result of the preceding line of code, pScore contains the address of score. It's as if pScore knows exactly where score is located in the computer's memory. This means you can use pScore to get to score and manipulate the value stored by score. Figure 7.2 serves as a visual illustration of the relationship between pScore and score.

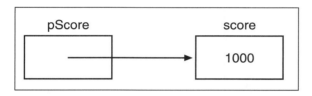

Figure 7.2
The pointer pScore points to score, which stores the value 1000.

To prove that pScore contains the address of score, I display the address of the variable and the value of the pointer with the following lines.

```
cout << "&score is: " << &score << "\n";    //address of score variable
cout << "pScore is: " << pScore << "\n";    //address stored in pointer
```

As you can see from Figure 7.1, pScore contains 0x22ff5c, which is the address of score. (The specific addresses displayed by the Pointing program might be different on your system. The important thing is that the values for pScore and &score are the same.)

Dereferencing Pointers

Just as you dereference an iterator to access the object to which it refers, you dereference a pointer to access the object to which it points. You accomplish the dereferencing the same way—with *, the dereference operator. I put the dereference operator to work with the following line, which displays 1000 because *pScore accesses the value stored in score.

```
cout << "*pScore is: " << *pScore << "\n\n"; //value pointed to by pointer
```

Remember, *pScore means, "the object to which pScore points."

trap

Don't dereference a null pointer because it could lead to disastrous results.

Next, I add 500 to `score` with the following line.

```
score += 500;
```

When I send `score` to `cout`, 1500 is displayed, as you'd expect. When I send `*pScore` to `cout`, the contents of `score` are again sent to `cout`, and 1500 is displayed once more.

Next, I add 500 to the value to which `pScore` points with the following line.

```
*pScore += 500;
```

Because `pScore` points to `score`, the preceding line of code adds 500 to `score`. Therefore, when I next send `score` to `cout`, 2000 is displayed. Then, when I send `*pScore` to `cout`... you guessed it, 2000 is displayed again.

trap

Don't change the value of a pointer when you want to change the value of the object to which the pointer points. For example, if I want to add 500 to the `int` that `pScore` points to, then the following line would be a big mistake.

```
pScore += 500;
```

The preceding code adds 500 to the address stored in `pScore`, not to the value to which `pScore` originally pointed. As a result, `pScore` now points to some address that might contain anything. Dereferencing a pointer like this can lead to disastrous results.

Reassigning Pointers

Unlike references, pointers can point to different objects at different times during the life of a program. Reassigning a pointer works like reassigning any other variable. Next, I reassign `pScore` with the following line.

```
pScore = &newScore;
```

As the result, `pScore` now points to `newScore`. To prove this, I display the address of `newScore` by sending `&newScore` to `cout`, followed by the address stored in `pScore`. Both statements display the same address. Then I send `newScore` and `*pScore` to `cout`. Both display 5000 because they both access the same chunk of memory that stores this value.

trap

Don't change the value to which a pointer points when you want to change the pointer itself. For example, if I want to change pScore to point to newScore, then the following line would be a big mistake.

```
*pScore = newScore;
```

This code simply changes the value to which pScore currently points; it doesn't change pScore itself. If newScore is equal to 5000, then the previous code is equivalent to *pScore = 5000; and pScore still points to the same variable it pointed to before the assignment.

Using Pointers to Objects

So far, the Pointing program has worked only with values of a built-in type, int. But you can use pointers with objects just as easily. I demonstrate this next with the following lines, which create str, a string object equal to "score", and pStr, a pointer that points to that object.

```
string str = "score";
string* pStr = &str;    //pointer to string object
```

pStr is a pointer to string, meaning that it can point to any string object. Another way to say this is to say that pStr can store the address of any string object.

You can access an object through a pointer using the dereference operator. That's what I do next with the following line.

```
cout << "*pStr is: " << *pStr << "\n";
```

By using the dereference operator with *pStr, I send the object to which pStr points (str) to cout. As a result, the text score is displayed.

You can call the member functions of an object through a pointer the same way you can call the member functions of an object through an iterator. One way to do this is by using the dereference operator and the member access operator, which is what I do next with the following lines.

```
cout << "(*pStr).size() is: " << (*pStr).size() << "\n";
```

The code (*pStr).size() says, "Take the result of dereferencing pStr and call that object's size() member function." Because pStr refers to the string object equal to "score", the code returns 5.

hint

> Whenever you dereference a pointer to access a data member or member function, surround the dereferenced pointer by a pair of parentheses. This ensures that the dot operator will be applied to the object to which the pointer points.

Just as with iterators, you can use the `->` operator with pointers for a more readable way to access object members. That's what I demonstrate next with the following line.

```
cout << "pStr->size() is: " << pStr->size() << "\n";
```

The preceding statement again displays the number of characters in the string object equal to "score"; however, I'm able to substitute `pStr->size()` for `(*pStr).size()` this time, making the code more readable.

Understanding Pointers and Constants

There are still some pointer mechanics you need to understand before you can start to use pointers effectively in your game programs. You can use the keyword `const` to restrict the way a pointer works. These restrictions can act as safeguards and can make your programming intentions clearer. Since pointers are quite versatile, restricting how a pointer can be used is in line with the programming mantra of asking only for what you need.

Using a Constant Pointer

As you've seen, pointers can point to different objects at different times in a program. However, by using the `const` keyword when you declare and initialize a pointer, you can restrict the pointer so it can only point to the object it was initialized to point to. A pointer like this is called a *constant pointer*. Another way to say this is to say that the address stored in a constant pointer can never change—it's constant. Here's an example of creating a constant pointer:

```
int score = 100;
int* const pScore = &score;   //a constant pointer
```

The preceding code creates a constant pointer, `pScore`, which points to `score`. You create a constant pointer by putting `const` right before the name of the pointer when you declare it.

Like all constants, you must initialize a constant pointer when you first declare it. The following line is illegal and will produce a big, fat compile error.

```
int* const pScore;   //illegal -- you must initialize a constant pointer
```

Because `pScore` is a constant pointer, it can't ever point to any other memory location. The following code is also quite illegal.

```
pScore = &anotherScore;   //illegal -- pScore can't point to a different object
```

Although you can't change pScore itself, you can use pScore to change the value to which it points. The following line is completely legal.

```
*pScore = 500;
```

Confused? Don't be. It's perfectly fine to use a constant pointer to change the value to which it points. Remember, the restriction on a constant pointer is that its value—the address that the pointer stores—can't change.

The way a constant pointer works should remind you of something—a reference. Like a reference, a constant pointer can refer only to the object it was initialized to refer to.

hint

Although you can use a constant pointer instead of a reference in your programs, you should stick with references whenever possible. References have a cleaner syntax than pointers and can make your code easier to read.

Using a Pointer to a Constant

As you've seen, you can use pointers to change the values to which they point. However, by using the const keyword when you declare a pointer, you can restrict a pointer so it can't be used to change the value to which it points. A pointer like this is called a *pointer to a constant*. Here's an example of declaring such a pointer:

```
const int* pNumber;   //a pointer to a constant
```

The preceding code declares a pointer to a constant, pNumber. You declare a pointer to a constant by putting const right before the type of value to which the pointer will point.

You assign an address to a pointer to a constant as you did before.

```
int lives = 3;
pNumber = &lives;
```

However, you can't use the pointer to change the value to which it points. The following line is illegal.

```
*pNumber -= 1;   //illegal -- can't use pointer to a constant to change value
                 //that pointer points to
```

Although you can't use a pointer to a constant to change the value to which it points, the pointer itself can change. This means that a pointer to a constant can point to different objects in a program. The following code is perfectly legal.

```
const int MAX_LIVES = 5;
pNumber = &MAX_LIVES;   //pointer itself can change
```

Using a Constant Pointer to a Constant

A *constant pointer to a constant* combines the restrictions of a constant pointer and a pointer to a constant. This means that a constant pointer to a constant can only point to the object that it was initialized to point to. In addition, it can't be used to change the value of the object to which it points. Here's the declaration and initialization of such a pointer:

```
const int* const pBONUS = &BONUS;   //a constant pointer to a constant
```

The preceding code creates a constant pointer to a constant named pBONUS that points to the constant BONUS.

hint

Like a pointer to a constant, a constant pointer to a constant can point to either a non-constant or constant value.

You can't reassign a constant pointer to a constant. The following line is not legal.

```
pBONUS = &MAX_LIVES;   //illegal -- pBONUS can't point to another object
```

You can't use a constant pointer to a constant to change the value to which it points. This means that the following line is illegal.

```
*pBONUS = MAX_LIVES;   //illegal -- can't change value through pointer
```

In many ways, a constant pointer to a constant acts like a constant reference, which can only refer to the value it was initialized to refer to and which can't be used to change that value.

hint

Although you can use a constant pointer to a constant instead of a constant reference in your programs, you should stick with constant references whenever possible. References have a cleaner syntax than pointers and can make your code easier to read.

Summarizing Constants and Pointers

I've presented a lot of information on constants and pointers, so I want to provide a summary to help crystallize the new concepts. Here are three examples of the different ways in which you can use the keyword const when you are declaring pointers:

- ■ `int* const p = &i;`
- ■ `const int* p;`
- ■ `const int* const p = &I;`

The first example declares and initializes a constant pointer. A constant pointer can only point to the object to which it was initialized to point. The value—the memory address—stored in the pointer itself is constant and can't change. A constant pointer can only point to a non-constant value; it can't point to a constant.

The second example declares a pointer to a constant. A pointer to a constant can't be used to change the value to which it points. A pointer to a constant can point to different objects during the life of a program. A pointer to a constant can point to a constant or non-constant value.

The third example declares a constant pointer to a constant. A constant pointer to a constant can only point to the value to which it was initialized to point. In addition, it can't be used to change the value to which it points. A constant pointer to a constant can be initialized to point to a constant or a non-constant value.

Passing Pointers

Even though references are the preferred way to pass arguments because of their cleaner syntax, you still might need to pass objects through pointers. For example, suppose you're using a graphics engine that returns a pointer to a 3D object. If you want another function to use this object, you'll probably want to pass the pointer to the object for efficiency. Therefore, it's important to know how to pass pointers as well as references.

Introducing the Swap Pointer Version Program

The Swap Pointer Version program works just like the Swap program from Chapter 6, except that the Swap Pointer Version program uses pointers instead of references. The Swap Pointer Version program defines two variables—one that holds my pitifully low score and another that holds your impressively high score. After displaying the scores, the program calls a function meant to swap the scores. Because only copies of the score values are sent to the function, the original variables are unaltered. Next, the program calls another swap function. This time, through the use of constant pointers, the original variables' values are successfully exchanged (giving me the great big score and leaving you with the small one). Figure 7.3 shows the program in action.

Figure 7.3
Passing pointers allows a function to alter variables outside of the function's
scope.

The code for the program is in the Chapter 7 folder on the CD-ROM that came with this
book; the file name is swap_pointer_ver.cpp.

```cpp
// Swap Pointer
// Demonstrates passing constant pointers to alter argument variables

#include <iostream>

using namespace std;

void badSwap(int x, int y);
void goodSwap(int* const pX, int* const pY);

int main()
{
    int myScore = 150;
    int yourScore = 1000;
    cout << "Original values\n";
    cout << "myScore: " << myScore << "\n";
    cout << "yourScore: " << yourScore << "\n\n";

    cout << "Calling badSwap()\n";
    badSwap(myScore, yourScore);
    cout << "myScore: " << myScore << "\n";
    cout << "yourScore: " << yourScore << "\n\n";

    cout << "Calling goodSwap()\n";
    goodSwap(&myScore, &yourScore);
    cout << "myScore: " << myScore << "\n";
    cout << "yourScore: " << yourScore << "\n";
```

```
        return 0;
}

void badSwap(int x, int y)
{
        int temp = x;
        x = y;
        y = temp;
}

void goodSwap(int* const pX, int* const pY)
{
        //store value pointed to by pX in temp
        int temp = *pX;
        //store value pointed to by pY in address pointed to by pX
        *pX = *pY;
        //store value originally pointed to by pX in address pointed to by pY
        *pY = temp;
}
```

Passing by Value

After I declare and initialize myScore and yourScore, I send them to cout. As you'd expect, 150 and 1000 are displayed. Next I call badSwap(), which passes both arguments by value. This means that when I call the function with the following line, copies of myScore and yourScore are sent to the parameters, x and y.

```
        badSwap(myScore, yourScore);
```

Specifically, x is assigned 150 and y is assigned 1000. As a result, nothing I do with x and y in badSwap() will have any effect on myScore and yourScore.

When badSwap() executes, x and y *do* exchange values—x becomes 1000 and y becomes 150. However, when the function ends, both x and y go out of scope. Control then returns to main(), in which myScore and yourScore haven't changed. When I then send myScore and yourScore to cout, 150 and 1000 are displayed again. Sadly, I still have the tiny score and you still have the large one.

Passing a Constant Pointer

You've seen that it's possible to give a function access to variables by passing references. It's also possible to accomplish this using pointers. When you pass a pointer, you pass only the address of an object. This can be quite efficient, especially if you're working with large objects. Passing a pointer is like e-mailing a friend the URL of a Web site instead of trying to send him the entire site.

Before you can pass a pointer to a function, you need to specify function parameters as pointers. That's what I do in the goodSwap() header.

```
void goodSwap(int* const pX, int* const pY)
```

This means that pX and pY are constant pointers and will each accept a memory address. I made the parameters constant pointers because, although I plan to change the values they point to, I don't plan to change the pointers themselves. Remember, this is just how references work. You can change the value to which a reference refers, but not the reference itself.

In main(), I pass the addresses of myScore and yourScore when I call goodSwap() with the following line.

```
goodSwap(&myScore, &yourScore);
```

Notice that I send the addresses of the variables to goodSwap() by using the address of operator. When you pass an object to a pointer, you need to send the address of the object.

In goodSwap(), pX stores the address of myScore and pY stores the address of yourScore. Anything done to *pX will be done to myScore; anything done to *pY will be done to yourScore.

The first line of goodSwap() takes the value that pX points to and assigns it to temp.

```
int temp = *pX;
```

Because pX points to myScore, temp becomes 150.

The next line assigns the value pointed to by pY to the object to which pX points.

```
*pX = *pY;
```

This statement copies the value stored in yourScore, 1000, and assigns it to the memory location of myScore. As a result, myScore becomes 1000.

The last statement in the function stores the value of temp, 150, in the address pointed to by pY.

```
*pY = temp;
```

Because pY points to yourScore, yourScore becomes 150.

After the function ends, control returns to main(), where I send myScore and yourScore to cout. This time, 1000 and 150 are displayed. The variables have exchanged values. Success at last!

hint

You can also pass a constant pointer to a constant. This works much like passing a constant reference, which is done to efficiently pass an object that you don't need to change. I've adapted the Inventory Displayer program from Chapter 6, which demonstrates passing constant references, to pass a constant pointer to a constant. The program is in the Chapter 7 folder on the CD-ROM that came with this book; the file name is inventory_displayer_pointer_ver.cpp.

Returning Pointers

Before references, the only option game programmers had for returning objects efficiently from functions was using pointers. And even though using references provides a cleaner syntax than using pointers, you might still need to return objects through pointers.

Introducing the Inventory Pointer Program

The Inventory Pointer program demonstrates returning pointers. Through returned pointers, the program displays and even alters the values of a vector that holds a hero's inventory. Figure 7.4 shows the results of the program.

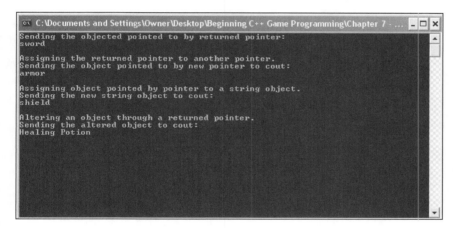

Figure 7.4
A function returns a pointer (not a `string` object) to each item in the hero's inventory.

The code for the program is in the Chapter 7 folder on the CD-ROM that came with this book; the file name is inventory_pointer.cpp.

```
// Inventory Pointer
// Demonstrates returning a pointer

#include <iostream>
#include <string>
#include <vector>

using namespace std;

//returns a pointer to a string element
string* ptrToElement(vector<string>* const pVec, int i);
```

```
int main()
{
    vector<string> inventory;
    inventory.push_back("sword");
    inventory.push_back("armor");
    inventory.push_back("shield");

    //displays string object that the returned pointer points to
    cout << "Sending the objected pointed to by returned pointer:\n";
    cout << *(ptrToElement(&inventory, 0)) << "\n\n";

    //assigns one pointer to another -- inexpensive assignment
    cout << "Assigning the returned pointer to another pointer.\n";
    string* pStr = ptrToElement(&inventory, 1);
    cout << "Sending the object pointed to by new pointer to cout:\n";
    cout << *pStr << "\n\n";

    //copies a string object -- expensive assignment
    cout << "Assigning object pointed by pointer to a string object.\n";
    string str = *(ptrToElement(&inventory, 2));
    cout << "Sending the new string object to cout:\n";
    cout << str << "\n\n";

    //altering the string object through a returned pointer
    cout << "Altering an object through a returned pointer.\n";
    *pStr = "Healing Potion";
    cout << "Sending the altered object to cout:\n";
    cout << inventory[1] << endl;

    return 0;
}

string* ptrToElement(vector<string>* const pVec, int i)
{
    //returns address of the string in position i of vector that pVec points to
    return &((*pVec)[i]);
}
```

Returning a Pointer

Before you can return a pointer from a function, you must specify that you're returning one. That's what I do in the refToElement() header.

```
string* ptrToElement(vector<string>* const pVec, int i)
```

By starting the header with string*, I'm saying that the function will return a pointer to a string object (and not a string object itself). To specify that a function returns a pointer to an object of a particular type, put an asterisk after the type name of the return type.

The body of the function `ptrToElement()` contains only one statement, which returns a pointer to the element at position i in the vector pointed to by pVec.

```
return &((*pVec)[i]);
```

The `return` statement might look a little cryptic, so I'll step through it. Whenever you come upon a complex expression, evaluate it like the computer does—by starting with the innermost part. I'll start with `(*pVec)[i]`, which means the element in position i of the vector pointed to by pVec. By applying the address of operator (`&`) to the expression, it becomes the address of the element in position i of the vector pointed to by pVec.

trap

Although returning a pointer can be an efficient way to send information back to a calling function, you have to be careful not to return a pointer that points to an out-of-scope object. For example, the following function returns a pointer that, if used, will most likely crash the program.

```
string* badPointer()
{
    string local = "This string will cease to exist once the function ends.";
    string* pLocal = &local;
    return pLocal;
}
```

That's because `badPointer()` returns a pointer to a string that no longer exists after the function ends. A pointer to a non-existent object is called a *dangling pointer*. Attempting to dereference a dangling pointer can lead to disastrous results. One way to avoid dangling pointers is to never return a pointer to a local variable.

Using a Returned Pointer to Display a Value

After I create `inventory`, a vector of items, I display a value with a returned pointer.

```
cout << *(ptrToElement(&inventory, 0)) << "\n\n";
```

The preceding code calls `ptrToElement()`, which returns a pointer to `inventory[0]`. (Remember, `ptrToElement()` doesn't return a copy of one of the elements of `inventory`; it returns a pointer to one of them.) The line then sends the `string` object pointed to by the pointer to `cout`. As a result, `sword` is displayed.

Assigning a Returned Pointer to a Pointer

Next I assign a returned pointer to another pointer with the following line.

```
string* pStr = ptrToElement(&inventory, 1);
```

The call to `prtToElement()` returns a pointer to `inventory[1]`. The statement assigns that pointer to `pStr`. This is an efficient assignment because assigning a pointer to a pointer does not involve copying the `string` object.

To help you understand the results of this line of code, take a look at Figure 7.5, which shows a representation of `pStr` after the assignment. (Note that the figure is abstract because the vector `inventory` doesn't contain the string literals `"sword"`, `"armor"`, and `"shield"`; instead, it contains `string` objects.)

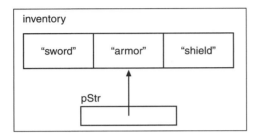

Figure 7.5
`pStr` points to the element at position 1 of `inventory`.

Next I send `*pStr` to `cout` and `armor` is displayed.

Assigning to a Variable the Value Pointed to by a Returned Pointer

Next I assign the value pointed to by a returned pointer to a variable.

```
string str = *(ptrToElement(&inventory, 2));
```

The call to `prtToElement()` returns a pointer to `inventory[2]`. However, the preceding statement doesn't assign this pointer to `str`—it can't because `str` is a `string` object. Instead, the computer quietly makes a copy of the `string` object to which the pointer points and assigns that object to `str`. To help drive this point home, check out Figure 7.6, which provides an abstract representation of the results of this assignment.

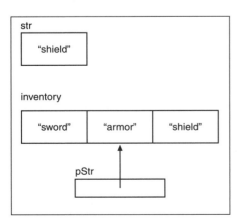

Figure 7.6
`str` is a new `string` object, totally independent from `inventory`.

An assignment like this one, where an object is copied, is more expensive than the assignment of one pointer to another. Sometimes the cost of copying an object is perfectly acceptable, but you should be aware of the extra overhead associated with this kind of assignment and avoid it when necessary.

Altering an Object through a Returned Pointer

You can also alter the object to which a returned pointer points. This means that I can change the hero's inventory through pStr.

```
*pStr = "Healing Potion";
```

Because pStr points to the element in position 1 of inventory, this code changes inventory[1] so it's equal to "Healing Potion". To prove this, I display the element with the following line, which does indeed show Healing Potion.

```
cout << inventory[1] << endl;
```

For an abstract representation, check out Figure 7.7, which shows the status of the variables after the assignment.

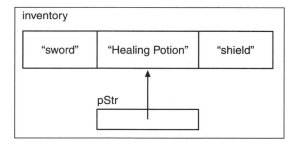

Figure 7.7
inventory[1] is changed through the returned pointer stored in pStr.

---

hint

If you want to protect an object pointed to by a returned pointer, make sure to restrict the pointer. Return either a pointer to a constant or a constant pointer to a constant.

Understanding the Relationship between Pointers and Arrays

Pointers have an intimate relationship with arrays. In fact, an array name is really a constant pointer to the first element of the array. Because the elements of an array are stored in a contiguous block of memory, you can use the array name as a pointer for random access to elements. This relationship also has important implications for how you can pass and return arrays, as you'll soon see.

Introducing the Array Passer Program

The Array Passer program creates an array of high scores and then displays them, using the array name as a constant pointer. Next, the program passes the array name as a constant pointer to a function that increases the scores. Finally, the program passes the array name to a function as a constant pointer to a constant to display the new high scores. Figure 7.8 shows the results of the program.

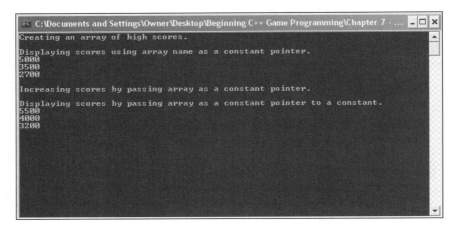

Figure 7.8
Using an array name as a pointer, the high scores are displayed, altered, and passed to functions.

The code for the program is in the Chapter 7 folder on the CD-ROM that came with this book; the file name is array_passer.cpp.

```
//Array Passer
//Demonstrates relationship between pointers and arrays

#include <iostream>

using namespace std;

void increase(int* const array, const int NUM_ELEMENTS);
void display(const int* const array, const int NUM_ELEMENTS);

int main()
{
```

```
    cout << "Creating an array of high scores.\n\n";
    const int NUM_SCORES = 3;
    int highScores[NUM_SCORES] = {5000, 3500, 2700};

    cout << "Displaying scores using array name as a constant pointer.\n";
    cout << *highScores << endl;
    cout << *(highScores + 1) << endl;
    cout << *(highScores + 2) << "\n\n";

    cout << "Increasing scores by passing array as a constant pointer.\n\n";
    increase(highScores, NUM_SCORES);

    cout << "Displaying scores by passing array as a constant pointer to a
            constant.\n";
    display(highScores, NUM_SCORES);

    return 0;
}

void increase(int* const array, const int NUM_ELEMENTS)
{
    for (int i = 0; i < NUM_ELEMENTS; ++i)
        array[i] += 500;
}

void display(const int* const array, const int NUM_ELEMENTS)
{
    for (int i = 0; i < NUM_ELEMENTS; ++i)
        cout << array[i] << endl;
}
```

Using an Array Name as a Constant Pointer

Because an array name is a constant pointer to the first element of the array, you can dereference the name to get at the first element. That's what I do after I create an array of high scores, called highScores.

```
    cout << *highScores << endl;
```

I dereference highScores to access the first element in the array and send it to cout. As a result, 5000 is displayed.

You can randomly access array elements using an array name as a pointer through simple addition. All you have to do is add the position number of the element you want to access to the pointer before you dereference it. This is simpler than it sounds. For example, I next access the score at position 1 in highScores with the following line, which displays 3500.

```
    cout << *(highScores + 1) << endl;
```

In the preceding code, `*(highScores + 1)` is equivalent to `highScores[1]`. Both return the element in position 1 of `highScores`.

Next, I access the score at position 2 in `highScores` with the following line, which displays 2700.

```
cout << *(highScores + 2) << endl;
```

In the preceding code, `*(highScores + 2)` is equivalent to `highScores[2]`. Both return the element in position 2 of `highScores`. In general, you can write `arrayName[i]` as `*(arrayName + i)`, where `arrayName` is the name of an array.

Passing and Returning Arrays

Because an array name is a constant pointer, you can use it to efficiently pass an array to a function. That's what I do next with the following line, which passes to `increase()` a constant pointer to the first element of the array and the number of elements in the array.

```
increase(highScores, NUM_SCORES);
```

hint

When you pass an array to a function, it's usually a good idea to also pass the number of elements in the array so the function can use this to avoid attempting to access an element that doesn't exist.

As you can see from the function header of `increase()`, the array name is accepted as a constant pointer.

```
void increase(int* const array, const int NUM_ELEMENTS)
```

The function body adds 500 to each score.

```
for (int i = 0; i < NUM_ELEMENTS; ++i)
    array[i] += 500;
```

I treat `array` just like any array and use the subscripting operator to access each of its elements. Alternatively, I could have treated `array` as a pointer and substituted `*(array + i) += 500` for the expression `array[i] += 500`, but I opted for the more readable version.

After `increase()` ends, control returns to `main()`. To prove that `increase()` did in fact increase the high scores, I call a function to show the scores.

```
display(highScores, NUM_SCORES);
```

The function `display()` also accepts `highScore` as a pointer. However, as you can see from the function's header, the function accepts it as a constant pointer to a constant.

```
void display(const int* const array, const int NUM_ELEMENTS)
```

By passing the array in this way, I keep it safe from changes. Because all I want to do is display each element, it's the perfect way to go.

Finally, the body of `display()` runs and all of the scores are listed, showing that they've each increased by 500.

hint

You can pass a C-style string to a function, just like any other array. In addition, you can pass a string literal to a function as a constant pointer to a constant.

Because an array name is a pointer, you can return an array using the array name, just as you would any other pointer to an object.

Introducing the Tic-Tac-Toe 2.0 Game

The project for this chapter is a modified version of the project from Chapter 6, the Tic-Tac-Toe game. From the player's perspective, the Tic-Tac-Toe 2.0 game looks exactly the same as the original because the changes are under the hood—I've replaced all of the references with pointers. This means that objects such as the Tic-Tac-Toe board are passed as constant pointers instead of as references. This has other implications, including the fact that the address of a Tic-Tac-Toe board must be passed instead of the board itself.

The new version of the program is in the Chapter 7 folder on the CD-ROM that came with this book; the file name is tic-tac-toe2.cpp. I won't go over the code because much of it remains the same. But even though the number of changes isn't great, the changes are critical. This is a good program to study because, although you should use references whenever you can, you should be equally comfortable passing pointers.

Summary

In this chapter, you should have learned the following concepts:

- Computer memory is organized in an ordered way, where each chunk of memory has its own unique address.
- A pointer is a variable that contains a memory address.
- In many ways, pointers act like iterators from the STL. For example, just as with iterators, you use pointers to indirectly access an object.
- To declare a pointer, you list a type, followed by an asterisk, followed by a name.
- Programmers often prefix pointer variable names with the letter "p" to remind them that the variable is indeed a pointer.

- Just like an iterator, a pointer is declared to refer to a value of a specific type.

- It's good programming practice to initialize a pointer when you declare it.

- If you assign 0 to a pointer, the pointer is called a null pointer.

- To get the address of a variable, put the address of operator (&) before the variable name.

- When a pointer contains the address of an object, it's said to point to the object.

- Unlike references, you can reassign pointers. That is, a pointer can point to different objects at different times during the life of a program.

- Just as with iterators, you dereference a pointer to access the object it points to with *, the dereference operator.

- Just as with iterators, you can use the -> operator with pointers for a more readable way to access object data members and member functions.

- A constant pointer can only point to the object it was initialized to point to. You declare a constant pointer by putting the keyword const right before the pointer name, as in int* const p = &i;.

- You can't use a pointer to a constant to change the value to which it points. You declare a pointer to a constant by putting the keyword const before the type name, as in const int* p;.

- A constant pointer to a constant can only point to the value it was initialized to point to, and it can't be used to change that value. You declare a constant pointer to a constant by putting the keyword const before the type name and right before the pointer name, as in const int* const p = &I;.

- You can pass pointers for efficiency or to provide direct access to an object.

- If you want to pass a pointer for efficiency, you should pass a pointer to a constant or a constant pointer to a constant so the object you're passing access to can't be changed through the pointer.

- A dangling pointer is a pointer to an invalid memory address. Dangling pointers are often caused by deleting an object to which a pointer pointed. Dereferencing such a pointer can lead to disastrous results.

- You can return a pointer from a function, but be careful not to return a dangling pointer.

Questions and Answers

Q: How is a pointer different from the variable to which it points?

A: A pointer stores a memory address. If a pointer points to a variable, it stores the address of that variable.

Q: What good is it to store the address of a variable that already exists?

A: One big advantage of storing the address of an existing variable is that you can pass a pointer to the variable for efficiency instead of passing the variable by value.

Q: Does a pointer always have to point to an existing variable?

A: No. You can create a pointer that points to an unnamed chunk of computer memory as you need it. You'll learn more about allocating memory in this dynamic fashion in Chapter 9, "Advanced Classes and Dynamic Memory: Game Lobby."

Q: Why should I pass variables using references instead of pointers whenever possible?

A: Because of the sweet, syntactic sugar that references provide. Passing a reference or a pointer is an efficient way to provide access to objects, but pointers require extra syntax (like the dereference operator) to access the object itself.

Q: Why should I initialize a pointer when I declare it or soon thereafter?

A: Because dereferencing an uninitialized pointer can lead to disastrous results, including a program crash.

Q: What's a dangling pointer?

A: A pointer that points to an invalid memory location, where any data could exist.

Q: What's so dangerous about a dangling pointer?

A: Like using an uninitialized pointer, using a dangling pointer can lead to disastrous results, including a program crash.

Q: Why should I initialize a pointer to 0?

A: By initializing a pointer to 0, you create a null pointer, which is understood as a pointer to nothing.

Q: So then it's safe to dereference a null pointer, right?

A: No! Although it's good programming practice to assign 0 to a pointer that doesn't point to an object, dereferencing a null pointer is as dangerous as dereferencing a dangling pointer.

Q: What will happen if I dereference a null pointer?

A: Just like dereferencing a dangling pointer or an uninitialized pointer, the results are unpredictable. Most likely, you'll crash your program.

Q: What good are null pointers?

A: They're often returned by functions as a sign of failure. For example, if a function is supposed to return a pointer to an object that represents the graphics screen, but that function couldn't initialize the screen, it might return a null pointer.

Q: How does using the keyword const when declaring a pointer affect the pointer?

A: It depends on how you use it. Generally, you use const when you are declaring a pointer to restrict what the pointer can do.

Q: What kinds of restrictions can I impose on a pointer by declaring it with const?

A: You can restrict a pointer so it can only point to the object it was initialized to point to, or you can restrict a pointer so it can't change the value of the object it points to, or both.

Q: Why would I want to restrict what a pointer can do?

A: For safety. For example, you might be working with an object that you know you don't want to change.

Q: To what type of pointers can I assign a constant value?

A: A pointer to a constant or a constant pointer to a constant.

Q: How can I safely return a pointer from a function?

A: One way is by returning a pointer to an object that you received from the calling function. This way, you're returning a pointer to an object that exists back in the calling code. (In Chapter 9, you'll discover another important way when you learn about dynamic memory.)

Discussion Questions

1. What are the advantages and disadvantages of passing a pointer?
2. What kinds of situations call for a constant pointer?
3. What kinds of situations call for a pointer to a constant?
4. What kinds of situations call for a constant pointer to a constant?
5. What kinds of situations call for a non-constant pointer to a non-constant object?

Exercises

1. Write a program with a pointer to a pointer to a string object. Use the pointer to the pointer to call the size() member function of the string object.

2. Rewrite the final project from Chapter 5, the Mad Lib game, so that no string objects are passed to the function that tells the story. Instead, the function should accept pointers to string objects.

3. Will the three memory addresses displayed by the following program all be the same? Explain what's going on in the code.

```
#include <iostream>
using namespace std;

int main()
{
    int a = 10;
    int& b = a;
    int* c = &b;

    cout << &a << endl;
    cout << &b << endl;
    cout << &(*c) << endl;

    return 0;
}
```

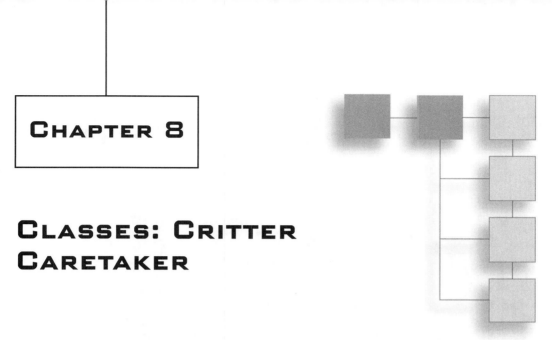

CHAPTER 8

CLASSES: CRITTER CARETAKER

*O*bject-oriented programming (OOP) is a different way of thinking about programming. It's a modern methodology that's used in the creation of the vast majority of games (and other commercial software, too). In OOP, you define different types of objects with relationships to each other that allow the objects to interact. You've already worked with objects from types defined in libraries, but one of the key characteristics of OOP is the ability to make your own types from which you can create objects. In this chapter, you'll see how to define your own types and create objects from them. Specifically, you'll learn to:

- Create new types by defining classes
- Declare class data members and member functions
- Instantiate objects from classes
- Set member access levels
- Declare static data members and member functions

Defining New Types

Whether you're talking about alien spacecrafts, poisonous arrows, or angry mutant chickens, games are full of objects. Fortunately, C++ lets you represent game entities as software objects, complete with member functions and data members. These objects work just like the others you've already seen, such as `string` and `vector` objects. But to use a new kind of object (say, an angry mutant chicken object), you must first define a type for it.

Introducing the Simple Critter Program

The Simple Critter program defines a brand-new type called Critter for creating virtual pet objects. The program uses this new type to create two Critter objects. Then, it gives each critter a hunger level. Finally, each critter offers a greeting and announces its hunger level to the world. Figure 8.1 shows the results of the program.

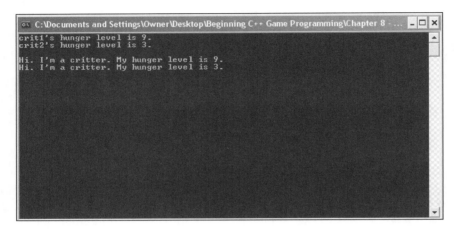

Figure 8.1
Each critter says hi and announces how hungry it is.

The code for the program is in the Chapter 8 folder on the CD-ROM that came with this book; the file name is simple_critter.cpp.

```
//Simple Critter
//Demonstrates creating a new type

#include <iostream>

using namespace std;

class Critter              // class definition -- defines a new type, Critter
{
public:
    int m_Hunger;          // data member
    void Greet();          // member function prototype
};

void Critter::Greet()      // member function definition
{
    cout << "Hi. I'm a critter. My hunger level is " << m_Hunger << ".\n";
}
```

```
int main()
{
    Critter crit1;
    Critter crit2;

    crit1.m_Hunger = 9;
    cout << "crit1's hunger level is " << crit1.m_Hunger << ".\n";

    crit2.m_Hunger = 3;
    cout << "crit2's hunger level is " << crit2.m_Hunger << ".\n\n";

    crit1.Greet();
    crit2.Greet();

    return 0;
}
```

Defining a Class

To create a new type, you can define a *class*—code that groups data members and member functions. From a class, you create individual objects that have their own copies of each data member and access to all of the member functions. A class is like a blueprint. Just as a blueprint defines the structure of a building, a class defines the structure of an object. And just as a foreman can create many houses from the same blueprint, a game programmer can create many objects from the same class. Some real code will help solidify this theory. I begin a class definition in the Simple Critter program with

```
class Critter           // class definition -- defines a new type, Critter
```

for a class named Critter. To define a class, start with the keyword class, followed by the class name. By convention, class names begin with an uppercase letter. You surround the class body with curly braces and end it with a semicolon.

Declaring Data Members

In a class definition, you can declare class data members to represent object qualities. I give the critters just one quality, hunger. I see hunger as a range that could be represented by an integer, so I declare an int data member m_Hunger.

```
    int m_Hunger;          // data member
```

This means that every Critter object will have its own hunger level, represented by its own data member named m_Hunger. Notice that I prefix the data member name with m_. Some game programmers follow this naming convention so that data members are instantly recognizable.

Declaring Member Functions

In a class definition, you can also declare member functions to represent object abilities. I give a critter just one—the ability to greet the world and announce its hunger level—by declaring the member function `Greet()`.

```
void Greet();        // member function prototype
```

This means that every `Critter` object will have the ability to say hi and announce its own hunger level through its member function, `Greet()`. By convention, member function names begin with an uppercase letter. At this point, I've only declared the member function `Greet()`. Don't worry, though, I'll define it outside of the class.

h i n t

You might have noticed the keyword `public` in the class definition. You can ignore it for now. You'll learn more about it a bit later in this chapter, in the section, "Specifying Public and Private Access Levels."

Defining Member Functions

You can define member functions outside of a class definition. Outside of the `Critter` class definition, I define the `Critter` member function `Greet()`, which says hi and displays the critter's hunger level.

```
void Critter::Greet()      // member function definition
{
    cout << "Hi. I'm a critter. My hunger level is " << m_Hunger << ".\n";
}
```

The definition looks like any other function definition you've seen, except for one thing—I prefix the function name with `Critter::`. When you define a member function outside of its class, you need to qualify it with the class name and scope resolution operator so the compiler knows that the definition belongs to the class.

In the member function, I send `m_Hunger` to `cout`. This means that `Greet()` displays the value of `m_Hunger` for the specific object through which the function is called. This simply means that the member function displays the critter's hunger level. You can access the data members and member functions of an object in any member function simply by using the member's name.

Instantiating Objects

When you create an object, you *instantiate* it from a class. In fact, specific objects are called *instances* of the class. In `main()`, I instantiate two instances of `Critter`.

```
Critter crit1;
Critter crit2;
```

As a result, I have two `Critter` objects—crit1 and crit2.

Accessing Data Members

It's time to put these critters to work. Next, I give my first critter a hunger level.

```
crit1.m_Hunger = 9;
```

The preceding code assigns 9 to crit1's data member m_Hunger. Just like when you are accessing an available member function of an object, you can access an available data member of an object using the member selection operator.

To prove that the assignment worked, I display the critter's hunger level.

```
cout << "crit1's hunger level is " << crit1.m_Hunger << ".\n";
```

The preceding code displays crit1's data member m_Hunger and correctly shows 9. Just like when you are assigning a value to an available data member, you can get the value of an available data member through the member selection operator.

Next, I show that the same process works for another `Critter` object.

```
crit2.m_Hunger = 3;
cout << "crit2's hunger level is " << crit2.m_Hunger << ".\n\n";
```

This time, I assign 3 to crit2's data member m_Hunger and display it.

So, crit1 and crit2 are both instances of `Critter`, and yet each exists independently and each has its own identity. Also, each has its own m_Hunger data member with its own value.

Calling Member Functions

Next, I again put the critters through their paces. I get the first critter to give a greeting.

```
crit1.Greet();
```

The preceding code calls crit1's Greet() member function. The function accesses the calling object's m_Hunger data member to form the greeting it displays. Because crit1's m_Hunger data member is 9, the function displays the text: Hi. I'm a critter. My hunger level is 9.

Finally, I get the second critter to speak up.

```
crit2.Greet();
```

The preceding code calls crit2's Greet() member function. This function accesses the calling object's m_Hunger data member to form the greeting it displays. Because crit2's m_Hunger data member is 3, the function displays the text: Hi. I'm a critter. My hunger level is 3.

Using Constructors

When you instantiate objects, you often want to do some initialization—usually assigning values to data members. Luckily, a class has a special member function known as a *constructor* that is automatically called every time a new object is instantiated. This is a big convenience because you can use a constructor to perform initialization of the new object.

Introducing the Constructor Critter Program

The Constructor Critter program demonstrates constructors. The program instantiates a new `Critter` object, which automatically invokes its constructor. First, the constructor announces that a new critter has been born. Then, it assigns the value passed to it to the critter's hunger level. Finally, the program calls the critter's greeting member function, which displays the critter's hunger level, proving that the constructor did in fact initialize the critter. Figure 8.2 shows the results of the program.

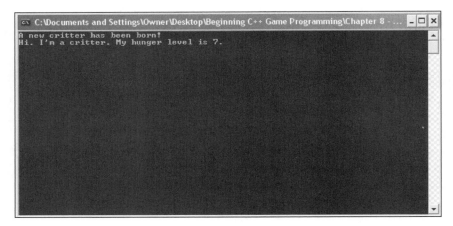

Figure 8.2
The `Critter` constructor initializes a new object's hunger level automatically.

The code for the program is in the Chapter 8 folder on the CD-ROM that came with this book; the file name is `constructor_critter.cpp`.

```
//Constructor Critter
//Demonstrates constructors

#include <iostream>

using namespace std;
```

```
class Critter
{
public:
    int m_Hunger;

    Critter(int hunger = 0);         // constructor prototype
    void Greet();
};

Critter::Critter(int hunger)         // constructor definition
{
    cout << "A new critter has been born!" << endl;
    m_Hunger = hunger;
}

void Critter::Greet()
{
    cout << "Hi. I'm a critter. My hunger level is " << m_Hunger << ".\n\n";
}

int main()
{
    Critter crit(7);
    crit.Greet();

    return 0;
}
```

Declaring and Defining a Constructor

I declare a constructor in `Critter` with the following code:

```
Critter(int hunger = 0);         // constructor prototype
```

As you can see from the declaration, the constructor has no return type. It can't—it's illegal to specify a return type for a constructor. Also, you have no flexibility when naming a constructor. You have to give it the same name as the class itself.

hint

A *default constructor* requires no arguments. If you don't define a default constructor, the compiler defines a minimal one for you that simply calls the default constructors of any data members of the class. If you write your own constructor, then the compiler won't provide a default constructor for you. It's usually a good idea to have a default constructor, so you should make sure to supply your own when necessary. One way to accomplish this is to supply default arguments for all parameters in a constructor definition.

I define the constructor outside of the class with the following code:

```
Critter::Critter(int hunger)          // constructor definition
{
    cout << "A new critter has been born!" << endl;
    m_Hunger = hunger;
}
```

The constructor displays a message saying that a new critter has been born and initializes the object's m_Hunger data member with the argument value passed to the constructor. If no value is passed, then the constructor uses the default argument value of 0.

---

trick

You can use *member initializers* as a shorthand way to assign values to data members in a constructor. To write a member initializer, start with a colon after the constructor's parameter list. Then type the name of the data member you want to initialize, followed by the expression you want to assign to the data member, surrounded by parentheses. If you have multiple initializers, separate them with commas. This is much simpler than it sounds (and it's really useful, too). Here's an example that assigns hunger to m_Hunger and boredom to m_Boredom. Member initializers are especially useful when you have many data members to initialize.

```
Critter::Critter(int hunger, int boredom):
    m_Hunger(hunger),
    m_Boredom(boredom)
    {}  // empty constructor body
```

Calling a Constructor Automatically

You don't explicitly call a constructor; however, whenever you instantiate a new object, its constructor is automatically called. In main(), I put my constructor into action with the following code:

```
    Critter crit(7);
```

When crit is instantiated, its constructor is automatically called and the message A new critter has been born! is displayed. Then, the constructor assigns 7 to the object's m_Hunger data member.

To prove that the constructor worked, back in main() I call the object's Greet() member function and sure enough, it displays Hi. I'm a critter. My hunger level is 7.

Setting Member Access Levels

Like functions, you should treat objects as encapsulated entities. This means that, in general, you should avoid directly altering or accessing an object's data members. Instead, you should call an object's member functions, allowing the object to maintain its own data members and ensure their integrity. Fortunately, you can enforce data member restrictions when you define a class by setting member access levels.

Introducing the Private Critter Program

The Private Critter program demonstrates class member access levels by declaring a class for critters that restricts direct access to an object's data member for its hunger level. The class provides two member functions—one that allows access to the data member and one that allows changes to the data member. The program creates a new critter and indirectly accesses and changes the critter's hunger level through these member functions. However, when the program attempts to change the critter's hunger level to an illegal value, the member function that allows the changes catches the illegal value and doesn't make the change. Finally, the program uses the hunger-level-setting member function with a legal value, which works like a charm. Figure 8.3 shows the results of the program.

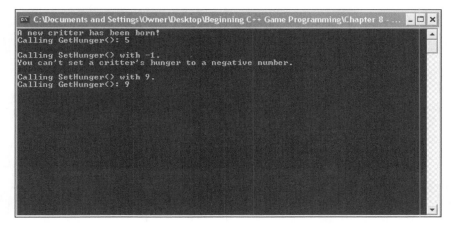

Figure 8.3
By using a `Critter` object's `GetHunger()` and `SetHunger()` member functions, the program indirectly accesses an object's private `m_Hunger` data member.

The code for the program is in the Chapter 8 folder on the CD-ROM that came with this book; the file name is private_critter.cpp.

```
//Private Critter
//Demonstrates setting member access levels

#include <iostream>

using namespace std;
```

```
class Critter
{
public:              // begin public section
    Critter(int hunger = 0);
    int GetHunger() const;
    void SetHunger(int hunger);

private:             // begin private section
    int m_Hunger;
};

Critter::Critter(int hunger): m_Hunger(hunger)
{
    cout << "A new critter has been born!" << endl;
}

int Critter::GetHunger() const
{
    return m_Hunger;
}

void Critter::SetHunger(int hunger)
{
    if (hunger < 0)
        cout << "You can't set a critter's hunger to a negative number.\n\n";
    else
        m_Hunger = hunger;
}

int main()
{
    Critter crit(5);
    //cout << crit.m_Hunger;   //illegal, m_Hunger is private!
    cout << "Calling GetHunger(): " << crit.GetHunger() << "\n\n";

    cout << "Calling SetHunger() with -1.\n";
    crit.SetHunger(-1);

    cout << "Calling SetHunger() with 9.\n";
    crit.SetHunger(9);
    cout << "Calling GetHunger(): " << crit.GetHunger() << "\n\n";

    return 0;
}
```

Specifying Public and Private Access Levels

Every class data member and member function has an access level, which determines from where in your program you can access it. So far, I've always specified class members to have public access levels using the keyword `public`. Again in `Critter`, I start a public section with the following line:

```
public:             // begin public section
```

By using `public:`, I'm saying that any data member or member function that follows (until another access level specifier) will be public. This means that any part of the program can access them. Because I declare all of the member functions in this section, it means that any part of my code can call any member function through a `Critter` object.

Next, I specify a private section with the following line:

```
private:            // begin private section
```

By using `private:`, I'm saying that any data member or member function that follows (until another access level specifier) will be private. This means that only code in the `Critter` class can directly access it. Since I declare `m_Hunger` in this section, it means that only the code in `Critter` can directly access an object's `m_Hunger` data member. Therefore, I can't directly access an object's `m_Hunger` data member through the object in `main()` as I've done in previous programs. So the following line in `main()`, if uncommented, would be an illegal statement:

```
//cout << crit.m_Hunger;   //illegal, m_Hunger is private!
```

Because `m_Hunger` is private, I can't access it outside of the `Critter` class. Again, only code in `Critter` can directly access the data member.

I've only shown you how to make data members private, but you can make member functions private, too. Also, you can repeat access modifiers. So if you want, you could have a private section, followed by a public section, followed by another private section in a class. Finally, member access is private by default. Until you specify an access modifier, any class members you declare will be private.

Defining Accessor Member Functions

An *accessor member function* allows indirect access to a data member. Because `m_Hunger` is private, I wrote an accessor member function, `GetHunger()`, to return the value of the data member. (For now, you can ignore the keyword `const`.)

```
int Critter::GetHunger() const
{
    return m_Hunger;
}
```

I put the member function to work in `main()` with the following line:

```
cout << "Calling GetHunger(): " << crit.GetHunger() << "\n\n";
```

In the preceding code, crit.GetHunger() simply returns the value of crit's m_Hunger data member, which is 5.

trick

Just as you can with regular functions, you can inline member functions. One way to inline a member function is to define it right inside of the class definition, where you'd normally only declare the member function. If you include a member function definition in a class, then of course you don't need to define it outside of the class.

The one exception to this rule is that when you define a member function in a class definition using the keyword virtual, the member function is not automatically inlined. You'll learn about virtual functions in Chapter 10, "Inheritance and Polymorphism: Blackjack."

At this point, you might be wondering why you'd go to the trouble of making a data member private only to grant full access to it through accessor functions. The answer is that you don't generally grant full access. For example, take a look at the accessor member function I defined for setting an object's m_Hunger data member, SetHunger():

```
void Critter::SetHunger(int hunger)
{
    if (hunger < 0)
        cout << "You can't set a critter's hunger to a negative number.\n\n";
    else
        m_Hunger = hunger;
}
```

In this accessor member function, I first check to make sure that the value passed to the member function is greater than zero. If it's not, it's an illegal value and I display a message, leaving the data member unchanged. If the value is greater than zero, then I make the change. This way, SetHunger() protects the integrity of m_Hunger, ensuring that it can't be set to a negative number. Just as I've done here, most game programmers begin their accessor member function names with Get or Set.

Defining Constant Member Functions

A *constant member function* can't modify a data member of its class or call a non-constant member function of its class. Why restrict what a member function can do? Again, it goes back to the tenet of asking only for what you need. If you don't need to change any data members in a member function, then it's a good idea to declare that member function to be constant. It protects you from accidentally altering a data member in the member function, and it makes your intentions clear to other programmers.

trap

Okay, I lied a little. A constant member function can alter a static data member. You'll learn about static data members a bit later in this chapter, in the "Declaring and Initializing Static Data Members" section. Also, if you qualify a data member with the `mutable` keyword, then even a constant member function can modify it. For now, though, don't worry about either of these exceptions.

You can declare a constant member function by putting the keyword `const` at the end of the function header. That's what I do in `Critter` with the following line, which declares `GetHunger()` to be a constant member function.

```
int GetHunger() const;
```

This means that `GetHunger()` can't change the value of any non-static data member declared in the `Critter` class, nor can it call any non-constant `Critter` member function. I made `GetHunger()` constant because it only returns a value and doesn't need to modify any data member. Generally, `Get` member functions can be defined as constant.

Using Static Data Members and Member Functions

Objects are great because each instance stores its own set of data, giving it a unique identity. But what if you want to store some information about an entire class, such as the total number of instances that exist? You might want to do this if you've created a bunch of enemies and you want them to fight the player based on their total number. For example, if their total number is below a certain threshold, you might want the enemies to run away. You could store the total number of instances in each object, but that would be a waste of storage space. Plus, it would be cumbersome to update all of the objects as the total changes. Instead, what you really want is a way to store a single value for an entire class. You can do this with a static data member. Usually the best way to access this kind of variable is through static member functions.

Introducing the Static Critter Program

The Static Critter program declares a new kind of critter with a static data member that stores the total number of critters that have been created. It also defines a static member function that displays the total. Before the program instantiates any new critter objects, it displays the total number of critters by directly accessing the static data member that holds the total. Next, the program instantiates three new critters. Then, it displays the total number of critters by calling a static member function that accesses the static data member. Figure 8.4 shows the results of the program.

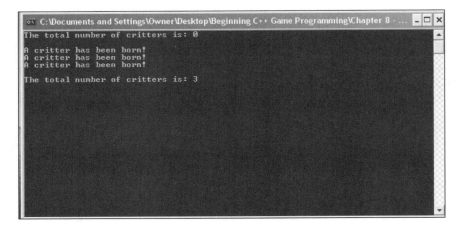

Figure 8.4
The program stores the total number of Critter objects in the static data
member s_Total and accesses that data member in two different ways.

The code for the program is in the Chapter 8 folder on the CD-ROM that came with this
book; the file name is static_critter.cpp.

```
//Static Critter
//Demonstrates static data members and functions

#include <iostream>

using namespace std;

class Critter
{
public:
    static int s_Total;  //static data member
                         //total number of Critter objects in existence

    Critter(int hunger = 0): m_Hunger(hunger)
    {
        cout << "A critter has been born!" << endl;
        ++s_Total;
    }

    static int GetTotal()  //static member function
    {
        return s_Total;
    }

private:
    int m_Hunger;
};
```

```
int Critter::s_Total = 0;  // initialize static data member

int main()
{
    cout << "The total number of critters is: ";
    cout << Critter::s_Total << "\n\n";

    Critter crit1, crit2, crit3;

    cout << "\nThe total number of critters is: ";
    cout << Critter::GetTotal() << "\n";

    return 0;
}
```

Declaring and Initializing Static Data Members

A *static data member* is a single data member that exists for the entire class. In the class definition, I define a static data member to store the number of Critter objects that have been instantiated with the following line, which declares a static data member s_Total.

```
static int s_Total;  // static data member
```

You can declare your own static data members just like I did, by starting the declaration with the static keyword. I prefixed the variable name with s_ so it would be instantly recognizable as a static data member.

Outside of the class definition, I initialize the static data member, which assigns 0 to it.

```
int Critter::s_Total = 0;  // initialize static data member
```

Notice that I qualified the data member name with Critter::. Outside of its class definition, you must qualify a static data member with its class name. After the previous line of code executes, there is a single value associated with the Critter class, stored in its static data member s_Total with a value of 0.

hint

You can declare a static variable in non-class functions, too. The static variable maintains its value between function calls.

Accessing Static Data Members

You can access a public static data member anywhere in your program. In main(), I access s_Total with the following line, which displays 0, the value of the static data member and the total number of Critter objects that have been instantiated.

```
cout << Critter::s_Total << "\n\n";
```

Notice that I had to qualify s_Total with Critter::. Outside of its class, you have to qualify a static data member with its class name.

I also access this static data member in the Critter constructor with the following line, which increments s_Total.

```
++s_Total;
```

This means that every time a new object is instantiated, s_Total is incremented. Notice that I didn't qualify s_Total with Critter::. Just as with non-static data members, you don't have to qualify a static data member with its class name inside a class.

Although I made my static data member public, you can make a static data member private—but then, like any other data member, you can only access it in a class member function.

Defining Static Member Functions

A *static member function* exists for the entire class. I define a static member in Critter with the following line, which defines a static member function GetTotal() that returns the value of the static data member s_Total.

```
static int GetTotal()  //static member function
{
    return s_Total;
}
```

You can define your own static member function like I did, by starting the definition with the keyword static.

Calling Static Member Functions

After I instantiate three Critter objects in main(), I reveal the total number of critters again with the following line, which displays 3.

```
cout << Critter::GetTotal() << "\n\n";
```

To properly identify the static member function, I had to qualify it with Critter::. To call a static member function from outside of its class, you must qualify it with its class name.

> You can also access a static member through any object of the class. Assuming that `crit1` is a `Critter` object, I could display the total number of critters with the following line:
>
> ```
> cout << crit1.GetTotal() << "\n\n";
> ```

Because static member functions don't have to be called through a class instance, they don't have direct access to any class data members or member functions. As a result, static member functions can only directly access other static class members. This also means that it makes no sense to declare a static member function as constant. Just as with a private static data member, a private static member function can only be accessed by other member functions of its class.

Introducing the Critter Caretaker Game

The Critter Caretaker game puts the player in charge of his own virtual pet. The player is completely responsible for keeping the critter happy, which is no small task. He can feed and play with the critter to keep it in a good mood. He can also listen to the critter to learn how the critter is feeling, which can range from happy to mad. Figure 8.5 shows off the game.

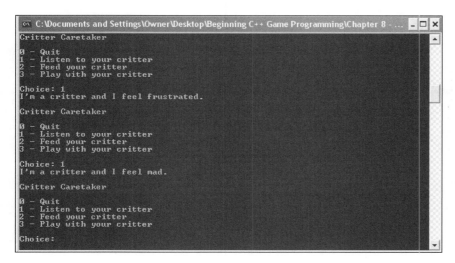

Figure 8.5
If you fail to feed or entertain your critter, it will have a mood change for the worse.
(But don't worry—with the proper care, your critter can return to a sunny mood.)

The code for the program is in the Chapter 8 folder on the CD-ROM that came with this book; the file name is critter_caretaker.cpp.

Planning the Game

The core of the game is the critter itself. Therefore, I first plan my `Critter` class. Because I want the critter to have independent hunger and boredom levels, I know that the class will have private data members for those.

- ▪ `m_Hunger`
- ▪ `m_Boredom`

The critter should also have a mood, directly based on its hunger and boredom levels. My first thought was to have a private data member, but a critter's mood is really a calculated value based on its hunger and boredom. Instead, I decided to have a private member function that calculates a critter's mood on the fly, based on its current hunger and boredom levels.

- ▪ `GetMood()`

Next, I think about public member functions. I want the critter to be able to tell the player how it's feeling. I also want the player to be able to feed and play with the critter to reduce its hunger and boredom levels. I need three public member functions to accomplish each of these tasks.

- ▪ `Talk()`
- ▪ `Eat()`
- ▪ `Play()`

Finally, I want another member function that simulates the passage of time, to make the critter a little more hungry and bored:

- ▪ `PassTime()`

I see this member function as private because it will only be called by other member functions, such as `Talk()`, `Eat()`, or `Play()`.

The class will also have a constructor to initialize data members. Take a look at Figure 8.6, which models the `Critter` class. I preface each data member and member function with a symbol to indicate its access level; I use + for public and - for private.

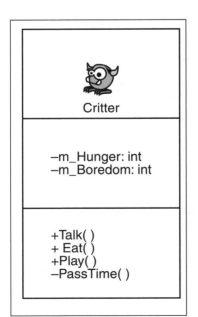

Figure 8.6
Model for the `Critter` class

Planning the Pseudocode

The rest of the program will be pretty simple. It'll basically be a game loop that asks the player whether he wants to listen to, feed, or play with the critter, or quit the game. Here's the pseudocode I came up with:

```
Create a critter
While the player doesn't want to quit the game
    Present a menu of choices to the player
    If the player wants to listen to the critter
        Make the critter talk
    If the player wants to feed the critter
        Make the critter eat
    If the player wants to play with the critter
        Make the critter play
```

The Critter Class

The Critter class is the blueprint for the object that represents the player's critter. The class isn't complicated, and most of it should look familiar, but it's long enough that it makes sense to attack it in pieces.

The Class Definition

After some initial comments and statements, I begin the Critter class.

```
//Critter Caretaker
//Simulates caring for a virtual pet

#include <iostream>

using namespace std;

class Critter
{
public:
    Critter(int hunger = 0, int boredom = 0);
    void Talk();
    void Eat(int food = 4);
    void Play(int fun = 4);

private:
    int m_Hunger;
    int m_Boredom;

    int GetMood() const;
    void PassTime(int time = 1);
};
```

m_Hunger is a private data member that represents the critter's hunger level, while m_Boredom is a private data member that represents its boredom level. I'll go through each member function in its own section.

The Class Constructor

The constructor takes two arguments, hunger and boredom. The arguments each have a default value of zero, which I specified in the constructor prototype back in the class definition. I use hunger to initialize m_Hunger and boredom to initialize m_Boredom.

```
Critter::Critter(int hunger, int boredom):
    m_Hunger(hunger),
    m_Boredom(boredom)
{}
```

The GetMood() Member Function

Next I define GetMood().

```
inline int Critter::GetMood() const
{
    return (m_Hunger + m_Boredom);
}
```

The return value of this inlined member function represents a critter's mood. As the sum of a critter's hunger and boredom levels, a critter's mood gets worse as the number increases. I made this member function private because it should only be invoked by another member function of the class. I made it constant since it won't result in any changes to data members.

The PassTime() Member Function

PassTime() is a private member function that increases a critter's hunger and boredom levels. It's invoked at the end of each member function where the critter does something (eats, plays, or talks) to simulate the passage of time. I made this member function private because it should only be invoked by another member function of the class.

```
void Critter::PassTime(int time)
{
    m_Hunger += time;
    m_Boredom += time;
}
```

You can pass the member function the amount of time that has passed; otherwise, time gets the default argument value of 1, which I specify in the member function prototype in the Critter class definition. .

The Talk() Member Function

The Talk() member function announces the critter's mood, which can be happy, okay, frustrated, or mad. Talk() calls GetMood() and, based on the return value, displays the appropriate message to indicate the critter's mood. Finally, Talk() calls PassTime() to simulate the passage of time.

```
void Critter::Talk()
{
    cout << "I'm a critter and I feel ";
    int mood = GetMood();
    if (mood > 15)
        cout << "mad.\n";
    else if (mood > 10)
        cout << "frustrated.\n";
    else if (mood > 5)
        cout << "okay.\n";
    else
        cout << "happy.\n";
    PassTime();
}
```

The Eat() Member Function

Eat() reduces a critter's hunger level by the amount passed to the parameter food. If no value is passed, food gets the default argument value of 4. The critter's hunger level is kept in check and is not allowed to go below zero. Finally, PassTime() is called to simulate the passage of time.

```
void Critter::Eat(int food)
{
    cout << "Brruppp.\n";
    m_Hunger -= food;
    if (m_Hunger < 0)
        m_Hunger = 0;
    PassTime();
}
```

The Play() Member Function

Play() reduces a critter's boredom level by the amount passed to the parameter fun. If no value is passed, fun gets the default argument value of 4. The critter's boredom level is kept in check and is not allowed to go below zero. Finally, PassTime() is called to simulate the passage of time.

```
void Critter::Play(int fun)
{
    cout << "Wheee!\n";
    m_Boredom -= fun;
```

```
    if (m_Boredom < 0)
        m_Boredom = 0;
    PassTime();
}
```

The main() Function

In main(), I instantiate a new Critter object. Because I don't supply values for m_Hunger or m_Boredom, the data members start out at 0, and the critter begins life happy and content. Next, I create a menu system. If the player enters 0, the program ends. If the player enters 1, the program calls the object's Talk() member function. If the player enters 2, the program calls the object's Eat() member function. If the player enters 3, the program calls the object's Play() member function. If the player enters anything else, he is told that the choice is invalid.

```
int main()
{
    Critter crit;
    crit.Talk();

    int choice;
    do
    {
        cout << "\nCritter Caretaker\n\n";
        cout << "0 - Quit\n";
        cout << "1 - Listen to your critter\n";
        cout << "2 - Feed your critter\n";
        cout << "3 - Play with your critter\n\n";

        cout << "Choice: ";
        cin >> choice;

        switch (choice)
        {
        case 0:
            cout << "Good-bye.\n";
            break;
        case 1:
            crit.Talk();
            break;
        case 2:
            crit.Eat();
            break;
        case 3:
            crit.Play();
            break;
        default:
            cout << "\nSorry, but " << choice << " isn't a valid choice.\n";
```

```
        }
    } while (choice != 0);

    return 0;
}
```

Summary

In this chapter, you should have learned the following concepts:

- Object-oriented programming (OOP) is a way of thinking about programming in which you define different types of objects with relationships that interact with each other.
- You can create a new type by defining a class.
- A class is a blueprint for an object.
- In a class, you can declare data members and member functions.
- When you define a member function outside of a class definition, you need to qualify it with the class name and scope resolution operator (::).
- You can inline a member function by defining it directly in the class definition.
- You can access data members and member functions of objects through the member selection operator (.).
- Every class has a constructor—a special member function that's automatically called every time a new object is instantiated. Constructors are often used to initialize data members.
- A default constructor requires no arguments. If you don't provide a constructor definition in your class, the compiler will create a default constructor for you.
- Member initializers provide shorthand to assign values to data members in a constructor.
- You can set member access levels in a class by using the keywords public, private, and protected. (You'll learn about protected in Chapter 9, "Advanced Classes and Dynamic Memory: Game Lobby.")
- A public member can be accessed by any part of your code through an object.
- A private member can only be accessed by a member function of that class.
- An accessor member function allows indirect access to a data member.
- A static data member exists for the entire class.
- A static member function exists for the entire class.

- Some game programmers prefix private data member names with m_ and static data member names with s_ so that they're instantly recognizable.
- A constant member function can't modify non-static data members or call non-constant member functions of its class.

Questions and Answers

Q: What is procedural programming?

A: A paradigm where tasks are broken down into a series of smaller tasks and implemented in manageable chunks of code, such as functions. In procedural programming, functions and data are separate.

Q: What is an object?

A: An entity that combines data and functions.

Q: Why create objects?

A: Because the world—and especially a game world—is full of objects. By creating your own types, you can represent objects and their relationships to other objects more directly and intuitively than you might be able to otherwise.

Q: What is object-oriented programming?

A: A paradigm where work is accomplished through objects. It allows programmers to define their own types of objects. The objects usually have relationships to each other and can interact.

Q: Is C++ an object-oriented programming language or a procedural programming language?

A: C++ is a multi-paradigm programming language. It allows a game programmer to write games in a procedural way or an object-oriented way—or through a combination of both (to name just a few options).

Q: Should I always try to write object-oriented game programs?

A: Although object-oriented programming is used in almost every commercial game on the market, you don't have to write games using this paradigm. C++ lets you use one of several programming paradigms. In general, though, large game projects will almost surely benefit from an object-oriented approach.

Q: Why not make all class members public?

A: Because it goes against the idea of encapsulation.

Q: What is encapsulation?

A: The quality of being self-contained. In the world of OOP, encapsulation prevents client code from directly accessing the internals of an object. Instead, it encourages client code to use a defined interface to the object.

Q: What are the benefits of encapsulation?

A: In the world of OOP, encapsulation protects the integrity of an object. For example, you might have a `spaceship` object with a `fuel` data member. By preventing direct access to this data member, you can guarantee that it never becomes an illegal value (such as a negative number).

Q: Should I provide access to data members through accessor member functions?

A: Some game programmers say you should never provide access to data members through accessor member functions because even though this kind of access is indirect, it goes against the idea of encapsulation. Instead, they say you should write classes with member functions that provide the client with all of the functionality it could need, eliminating the client's need to access a specific data member.

Q: What are mutable data members?

A: Data members that can be modified even by constant member functions. You create a mutable data member using the keyword `mutable`. You can also modify a mutable data member of a constant object.

Q: Why is it useful to have a default constructor?

A: Because there might be times when objects are automatically created without any argument values passed to a constructor—for example, when you create an array of objects.

Q: What is a structure?

A: A structure is very similar to a class. The only real difference is that the default access level for structures is public. You define a structure by using the keyword `struct`.

Q: Why does C++ have both structures and classes?

A: So that C++ retains backward compatibility with C.

Q: When should I use structures?

A: Some game programmers use structures to group only data together, without functions (because that's how C structures work). But it's probably best to avoid structures whenever possible and use classes instead.

Discussion Questions

1. What are the advantages and disadvantages of procedural programming?
2. What are the advantages and disadvantages of object-oriented programming?
3. Are accessor member functions a sign of poor class design? Explain.
4. How are constant member functions helpful to a game programmer?

5. When is it a good idea to calculate an object's attribute on the fly rather than storing it as a data member?

Exercises

1. Improve the Critter Caretaker program so that you can enter an unlisted menu choice that reveals the exact values of the critter's hunger and boredom levels.

2. Change the Critter Caretaker program so that the critter is more expressive about its needs by hinting at how hungry and bored it is.

3. What design problem does the following program have?

```cpp
#include <iostream>
using namespace std;

class Critter
{
public:
    int GetHunger() const {return m_Hunger;}
private:
    int m_Hunger;
};

int main()
{
    Critter crit;
    cout << crit.GetHunger() << endl;
    return 0;
}
```

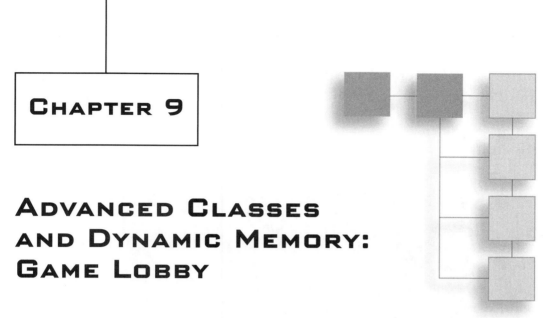

CHAPTER 9

ADVANCED CLASSES AND DYNAMIC MEMORY: GAME LOBBY

C++ gives a game programmer a high degree of control over the computer. One of the most fundamental abilities is direct control over memory. In this chapter, you'll learn about *dynamic memory*—memory that you manage yourself. But with great power comes great responsibility, so you'll also see the pitfalls of dynamic memory and how to avoid them. You'll learn a few more things about classes, too. Specifically, you'll learn to:

- Combine objects
- Use friend functions
- Overload operators
- Dynamically allocate and free memory
- Avoid memory leaks
- Produce deep copies of objects

Using Aggregation

Game objects are often composed of other objects. For example, in a racing game, a drag racer could be seen as a single object composed of other individual objects, such as a body, four tires, and an engine. Other times, you might see an object as a collection of related objects. In a zookeeper simulation, you might see the zoo as a collection of an arbitrary number of animals. You can mimic these kinds of relationships among objects in OOP using *aggregation*—the combining of objects so that one is part of another. For example, you could write a Drag_Racer class that has an engine data member that's an Engine object. Or, you could write a Zoo class that has an animals data member that is a collection of Animal objects.

Introducing the Critter Farm Program

The Critter Farm program defines a new kind of critter with a name. After the program announces a new critter's name, it creates a critter farm—a collection of critters. Finally, the program calls roll on the farm and each critter announces its name. Figure 9.1 shows the results of the program.

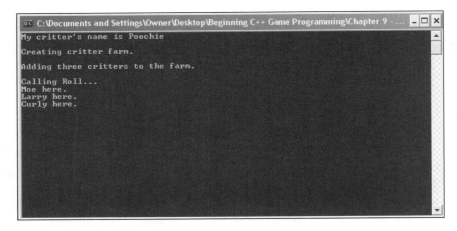

Figure 9.1
The critter farm is a collection of critters, each with a name.

The code for the program is in the Chapter 9 folder on the CD-ROM that came with this book; the file name is critter_farm.cpp.

```
//Critter Farm
//Demonstrates object containment

#include <iostream>
#include <string>
#include <vector>

using namespace std;

class Critter
{
public:
    Critter(const string& name = ""): m_Name(name) {}
    string GetName() const { return m_Name; }
private:
    string m_Name;
};

class Farm
{
public:
```

```
    Farm(int spaces = 1) { m_Critters.reserve(spaces); }
    void Add(const Critter& aCritter) { m_Critters.push_back(aCritter); }
    void RollCall() const
    {
        for (vector<Critter>::const_iterator iter = m_Critters.begin();
            iter != m_Critters.end(); ++iter)
            cout << iter->GetName() << " here.\n";
    }
private:
    vector<Critter> m_Critters;
};

int main()
{
    Critter crit("Poochie");
    cout << "My critter's name is " << crit.GetName() << endl;

    cout << "\nCreating critter farm.\n";
    Farm myFarm(3);

    cout << "\nAdding three critters to the farm.\n";
    myFarm.Add(Critter("Moe"));
    myFarm.Add(Critter("Larry"));
    myFarm.Add(Critter("Curly"));

    cout << "\nCalling Roll...\n";
    myFarm.RollCall();

    return 0;
}
```

Using Object Data Members

One way to use aggregation when you're defining a class is to declare a data member that can hold another object. That's what I did in `Critter` with the following line, which declares the data member `m_Name` to hold a `string` object.

```
    string m_Name;
```

Generally, you use aggregation when an object has another object. In this case, a critter has a name. These kinds of relationships are called *has-a* relationships.

I put the declaration for the critter's name to use when I instantiate a new object with:

```
    Critter crit("Poochie");
```

which calls the `Critter` constructor:

```
    Critter(const string& name = ""): m_Name(name) {}
```

By passing the string literal "Poochie", the constructor is called and a string object for the name is instantiated, which the constructor assigns to m_Name. A new critter named Poochie is born.

Next, I display the critter's name with the following line:

```
cout << "My critter's name is " << crit.GetName() << endl;
```

The code crit.GetName() returns a copy of the string object for the name of the critter, which is then sent to cout and displayed on the screen.

Using Container Data Members

You can also use containers as data members for your objects. That's what I do when I define Farm. The single data member I declare for the class is simply a vector that holds Critter objects called m_Critter.

```
vector<Critter> m_Critters;
```

When I instantiate a new Farm object with:

```
Farm myFarm(3);
```

it calls the constructor:

```
Farm(int spaces = 1) { m_Critters.reserve(spaces); }
```

which allocates memory for three Critter objects in the Farm object's m_Critter vector.

Next, I add three critters to the farm by calling the Farm object's Add() member function.

```
myFarm.Add(Critter("Moe"));
myFarm.Add(Critter("Larry"));
myFarm.Add(Critter("Curly"));
```

The following member function accepts a constant reference to a Critter object and adds a copy of the object to the m_Critters vector.

```
void Add(const Critter& aCritter) { m_Critters.push_back(aCritter); }
```

trap

Because push_back() adds a copy of an object to a vector, this means that I create an extra copy of each Critter object every time I call Add(). This is no big deal in the Critter Farm program, but if I were adding many large objects, it could become a performance issue. You can reduce this overhead by using, say, a vector of pointers to objects. You'll see how to work with pointers to objects later in this chapter.

Finally, I take roll through the `Farm` object's `RollCall()` member function.

```
myFarm.RollCall();
```

This iterates through the vector, calling each `Critter` object's `GetName()` member function and getting each critter to speak up and say its name.

Using Friend Functions and Operator Overloading

Friend functions and operator overloading are two advanced concepts related to classes. *Friend functions* have complete access to any member of a class. *Operator overloading* allows you to define new meanings for built-in operators as they relate to objects of your own classes. As you'll see, you can use these two concepts together.

Introducing the Friend Critter Program

The Friend Critter program creates a `Critter` object. It then uses a friend function, which is able to directly access the private data member that stores the critter's name to display the critter's name. Finally, the program displays the `Critter` object by sending the object to the standard output. This is accomplished through a friend function and operator overloading. Figure 9.2 displays the results of the program.

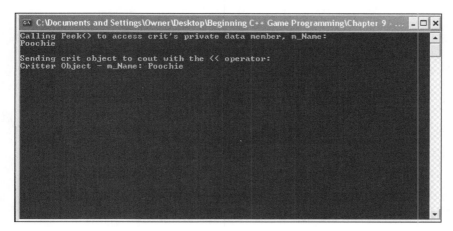

Figure 9.2
The name of the critter is displayed through a friend function, and the `Critter` object is displayed by sending it to the standard output.

The code for the program is in the Chapter 9 folder on the CD-ROM that came with this book; the file name is friend_critter.cpp.

```
//Friend Critter
//Demonstrates friend functions and operator overloading
```

```cpp
#include <iostream>
#include <string>

using namespace std;

class Critter
{
    //make following global functions friends of the Critter class
    friend void Peek(const Critter& aCritter);
    friend ostream& operator<<(ostream& os, const Critter& aCritter);

public:
    Critter(const string& name = ""): m_Name(name) {}

private:
    string m_Name;
};

void Peek(const Critter& aCritter);
ostream& operator<<(ostream& os, const Critter& aCritter);

int main()
{
    Critter crit("Poochie");

    cout << "Calling Peek() to access crit's private data member, m_Name: \n";
    Peek(crit);

    cout << "\nSending crit object to cout with the << operator:\n";
    cout << crit;

    return 0;
}

//global friend function which can access all of a Critter object's members
void Peek(const Critter& aCritter)
{
    cout << aCritter.m_Name << endl;
}

//global friend function which can access all of Critter object's members
//overloads the << operator so you can send a Critter object to cout
ostream& operator<<(ostream& os, const Critter& aCritter)
{
    os << "Critter Object - ";
    os << "m_Name: " << aCritter.m_Name;
    return os;
}
```

Creating Friend Functions

A friend function can access any member of a class of which it's a friend. You specify that a function is a friend of a class by listing the function prototype preceded by the keyword friend inside the class definition. That's what I do inside the Critter definition with the following line, which says that the global function Peek() is a friend of Critter.

```
friend void Peek(const Critter& aCritter);
```

This means Peek() can access any member of Critter even though it's not a member function of the class. Peek() takes advantage of this relationship by accessing the private data member m_Name to display the name of a critter passed to the function.

```
void Peek(const Critter& aCritter)
{
    cout << aCritter.m_Name << endl;
}
```

When I call Peek() in main() with the following line, the private data member m_Name of crit is displayed and Poochie appears on the screen.

```
Peek(crit);
```

Overloading Operators

Overloading operators might sound like something you want to avoid at all costs—as in, "Look out, that operator is overloaded and she's about to blow!"—but it's not. *Operator overloading* lets you give meaning to built-in operators used with new types that you define. For example, you could overload the * operator so that when it is used with two 3D matrices (objects instantiated from some class that you've defined), the result is the multiplication of the matrices.

To overload an operator, define a function called operatorX, where X is the operator you want to overload. That's what I do when I overload the << operator; I define a function named operator<<.

```
ostream& operator<<(ostream& os, const Critter& aCritter)
{
    os << "Critter Object - ";
    os << "m_Name: " << aCritter.m_Name;
    return os;
}
```

The function overloads the << operator so that when I send a Critter object with the << to cout, the data member m_Name is displayed. Essentially, the function allows me to easily display Critter objects. The function can directly access the private data member m_Name of a Critter object because I made the function a friend of the Critter class with the following line in Critter:

```
friend ostream& operator<<(ostream& os, const Critter& aCritter);
```

This means I can simply display a Critter object by sending it to cout with the << operator, which is what I do in main() with the following line, which displays the text Critter Object - m_Name: Poochie.

```
cout << crit;
```

hint

> With all the tools and debugging options available to game programmers, sometimes simply displaying the values of variables is the best way to understand what's happening in your programs. Overloading the << operator can help you do that.

This function works because cout is of the type ostream, which already overloads the << operator so that you can send built-in types to cout.

Dynamically Allocating Memory

So far, whenever you've declared a variable, C++ has allocated the necessary memory for it. When the function that the variable was created in ended, C++ freed the memory. This memory, which is used for local variables, is called the *stack*. But there's another kind of memory that persists independently of the functions in a program. You, the programmer, are in charge of allocating and freeing this memory, collectively called the *heap* (or *free store*).

At this point, you might be thinking, "Why bother with another type of memory? The stack works just fine, thank you." Using the dynamic memory of the heap offers great benefits that can be summed up in one word: efficiency. By using the heap, you can use only the amount of memory you need at any given time. If you have a game with a level that has 100 enemies, you can allocate the memory for the enemies at the beginning of the level and free the memory at the end. The heap also allows you to create an object in one function that you can access even after that function ends (without having to return a copy of the object). You might create a screen object in one function and return access to it. You'll find that dynamic memory is an important tool in writing any significant game.

Introducing the Heap Program

The Heap program demonstrates dynamic memory. The program dynamically allocates memory on the heap for an integer variable, assigns it a value, and then displays it. Next, the program calls a function that dynamically allocates memory on the heap for another integer variable, assigns it a value, and returns a pointer to it. The program takes the returned pointer, uses it to display the value, and then frees the allocated memory on the heap. Finally, the program contains two functions that demonstrate the misuse of dynamic memory. I don't call these functions, but I use them to illustrate what *not* to do with dynamic memory. Figure 9.3 shows the program.

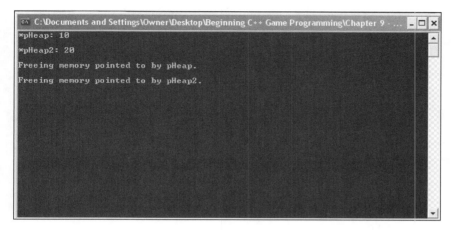

Figure 9.3
The two int values are stored on the heap.

The code for the program is in the Chapter 9 folder on the CD-ROM that came with this book; the file name is heap.cpp.

```cpp
// Heap
// Demonstrates dynamically allocating memory

#include <iostream>

using namespace std;

int* intOnHeap();  //returns an int on the heap
void leak1();  //creates a memory leak
void leak2();  //creates another memory leak

int main()
{
    int* pHeap = new int;
    *pHeap = 10;
    cout << "*pHeap: " << *pHeap << "\n\n";

    int* pHeap2 = intOnHeap();
    cout << "*pHeap2: " << *pHeap2 << "\n\n";

    cout << "Freeing memory pointed to by pHeap.\n\n";
    delete pHeap;

    cout << "Freeing memory pointed to by pHeap2.\n\n";
    delete pHeap2;
```

```
    //get rid of dangling pointers
    pHeap = 0;
    pHeap2 = 0;

    return 0;
}

int* intOnHeap()
{
    int* pTemp = new int(20);
    return pTemp;
}

void leak1()
{
    int* drip1 = new int(30);
}

void leak2()
{
    int* drip2 = new int(50);
    drip2 = new int(100);
    delete drip2;
}
```

Using the new Operator

The new operator allocates memory on the heap and returns its address. You use new followed by the type of value you want to reserve space for. That's what I do in the first line of main().

```
    int* pHeap = new int;
```

The new int part of the statement allocates enough memory on the heap for one int and returns the address on the heap for that chunk of memory. The other part of the statement, int* pHeap, declares a local pointer, pHeap, which points to the newly allocated chunk of memory on the heap.

By using pHeap, I can manipulate the chunk of memory on the heap reserved for an integer. That's what I do next; I assign 10 to the chunk of memory and then I display that value stored on the heap, using pHeap, as I would any other pointer to int. The only difference is that pHeap points to a piece of memory on the heap, not the stack.

hint

You can initialize memory on the heap at the same time you allocate it by placing a value, surrounded by parentheses, after the type. This is even easier than it sounds. For example, the following line allocates a chunk of memory on the heap for an `int` variable and assigns 10 to it. The statement then assigns the address of that chunk of memory to `pHeap`.

```
int* pHeap = new int(10);
```

One of the major advantages of memory on the heap is that it can persist beyond the function in which it was allocated, meaning that you can create an object on the heap in one function and return a pointer or reference to it. That's what I demonstrate with the following line:

```
int* pHeap2 = intOnHeap();
```

The statement calls the function `intOnHeap()`, which allocates a chunk of memory on the heap for an `int` and assigns 20 to it.

```
int* intOnHeap()
{
    int* pTemp = new int(20);
    return pTemp;
}
```

Then, the function returns a pointer to this chunk of memory. Back in `main()`, the assignment statement assigns the address of the chunk of memory on the heap to `pHeap2`. Next, I use the returned pointer to display the value.

```
cout << "*pHeap2: " << *pHeap2 << "\n\n";
```

hint

Up until now, if you wanted to return a value created in a function, you had to return a copy of that value. By using dynamic memory, you can create an object on the heap in one function and simply return a pointer to it to another function.

Using the delete Operator

Unlike storage for local variables on the stack, memory that you've allocated on the heap must be explicitly freed. When you're finished with memory that you've allocated with `new`, you should free it with `delete`. That's what I do with the following line, which frees the memory on the heap that stored 10.

```
delete pHeap;
```

That memory is returned to the heap for future use. The data that was stored in it is no longer available. Next, I use delete to free the memory on the heap that stored 20.

```
delete pHeap2;
```

That memory is returned to the heap for future use, and the data that was stored in it is no longer available. Notice that there's no difference, as far as delete is concerned, regarding where in the program I allocated the memory on the heap that I'm deleting.

trick

Because you need to free memory that you've allocated once you're finished with it, a good rule of thumb is that every new should have a corresponding delete. In fact, some programmers write the delete statement just after writing the new statement whenever possible, so they don't forget it.

An important point to understand here is that the two previous statements free the memory on the heap, but they do not directly affect the local variables pHeap and pHeap2. This creates a potential problem because pHeap and pHeap2 now point to memory that has been returned to the heap, meaning that they point to memory that the computer can use in some other way at any given time. Pointers like this are called *dangling pointers* and they are quite dangerous. You should never attempt to dereference a dangling pointer. One way to deal with dangling pointers is to assign 0 to them, and that's what I do with the following lines, which reassign both dangling pointers so they no longer point to some memory to which they should not point.

```
pHeap = 0;
pHeap2 = 0;
```

Another good way to deal with a dangling pointer is to assign a valid memory address to it.

trap

Using delete on a dangling pointer can cause your program to crash. Be sure to set a dangling pointer to 0 or reassign it to point to a new, valid chunk of memory.

Avoiding Memory Leaks

One problem with allowing a programmer to allocate and free memory is that he might allocate memory and lose any way to get at it, thus losing any way to ever free it. When memory is lost like this, it's called a *memory leak*. Given a large enough leak, a program might run out of memory and crash. As a game programmer, it's your responsibility to avoid memory leaks.

I've written two functions in the Heap program that purposely create memory leaks in order to show you what *not* to do when using dynamic memory. The first function is `leak1()`, which simply allocates a chunk of memory on the heap for an `int` value and then ends.

```
void leak1()
{
    int* drip1 = new int(30);
}
```

If I were to call this function, memory would be lost forever. (Okay, it would be lost until the program ended.) The problem is that `drip1`, which is the only connection to the newly acquired chunk of memory on the heap, is a local variable and ceases to exist when the function `leak1()` ends. So, there's no way to free the allocated memory. Take a look at Figure 9.4 for a visual representation of how the leak occurs.

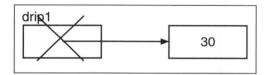

Figure 9.4
The memory that stores 30 can no longer be accessed to be freed, so it has leaked out of the system.

To avoid this memory leak, I could do one of two things. I could use `delete` to free the memory in `leak1()`, or I could return a copy of the pointer `drip1`. If I choose the second option, I have to make sure to free this memory in some other part of the program.

The second function that creates a memory leak is `leak2()`.

```
void leak2()
{
    int* drip2 = new int(50);
    drip2 = new int(100);
    delete drip2;
}
```

The memory leak is a little more subtle, but there is still a leak. The first line in the function body, `int* drip2 = new int(50);`, allocates a new piece of memory on the heap, assigns 50 to it, and has `drip2` point to that piece of memory. So far, so good. The second line, `drip2 = new int(100);`, points `drip2` to a new piece of memory on the heap, which stores 100. The problem is that the memory on the heap that stores 50 now has nothing pointing to it, so there is no way for the program to free that memory. As a result, that piece of memory has essentially leaked out of the system. Check out Figure 9.5 for a visual representation of how the leak occurs.

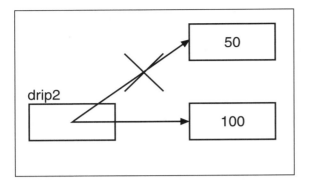

Figure 9.5
By changing drip2 so that it points to the memory that stores 100, the memory that
stores 50 is no longer accessible and has leaked out of the system.

The last statement of the function, delete drip2;, frees the memory that stores 100, so this
won't be the source of another memory leak. But remember, the memory on the heap that
stores 50 has still leaked out of the system. Also, I don't worry about drip2, which technically has become a dangling pointer, because it will cease to exist when the function ends.

Working with Data Members and the Heap

It's possible to declare data members that are pointers to values on the heap. However,
problems can arise when you do this because of the way that some default object behaviors work.

Introducing the Heap Data Member Program

The Heap Data Member program defines a new type of critter with a data member that
is a pointer, which points to an object stored on the heap. The class defines a few new
member functions to handle situations in which an object is destroyed, copied, or
assigned to another object. The program destroys, copies, and assigns objects to show that
the objects behave as you'd expect, even with data members pointing to values on the
heap. Figure 9.6 shows the results of the Heap Data Member program.

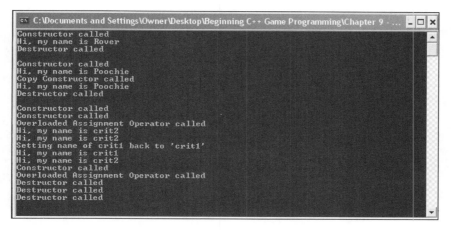

Figure 9.6
Objects, each with a data member that points to a value on the heap, are
instantiated, destroyed, and copied.

The code for the program is in the Chapter 9 folder on the CD-ROM that came with this
book; the file name is heap_data_member.cpp.

```cpp
//Heap Data Member
//Demonstrates an object with a dynamically allocated data member

#include <iostream>
#include <string>

using namespace std;

class Critter
{
public:
    Critter(const string& name = "")
    {
        cout << "Constructor called\n";
        m_pName = new string(name);
    }

    ~Critter()                    //destructor
    {
        cout << "Destructor called\n";
        delete m_pName;
    }

    Critter(const Critter& c)     //copy constructor
    {
        cout << "Copy Constructor called\n";
```

```cpp
        m_pName = new string;
        *m_pName = c.GetName();
    }

    Critter& operator=(const Critter& c)   //overloaded assignment operator
    {
        cout << "Overloaded Assignment Operator called\n";

        if (this == &c)
        {
            return *this;
        }
        else
        {
            *m_pName = c.GetName();
            return *this;
        }
    }

    string GetName() const { return *m_pName; }
    void SetName(const string& name = "") { *m_pName = name; }
    void SayHi() const { cout << "Hi, my name is " << GetName() << "\n"; }

private:
    string* m_pName;
};

void testDestructor();
void testCopyConstructor(Critter copy);
void testAssignmentOp();

int main()
{
    testDestructor();
    cout << endl;

    Critter crit("Poochie");
    crit.SayHi();
    testCopyConstructor(crit);
    cout << endl;

    testAssignmentOp();

    return 0;
}

void testDestructor()
{
```

```
    Critter crit("Rover");
    crit.SayHi();
}

//passing object by value invokes its copy constructor
void testCopyConstructor(Critter copy)
{
    copy.SayHi();
}

void testAssignmentOp()
{
    Critter crit1("crit1");
    Critter crit2("crit2");
    crit1 = crit2;
    crit1.SayHi();
    crit2.SayHi();

    cout << "Setting name of crit1 back to 'crit1'\n";
    crit1.SetName("crit1");
    crit1.SayHi();
    crit2.SayHi();

    Critter crit("crit");
    crit = crit;
}
```

Declaring Data Members That Point to Values on the Heap

To declare a data member that points to a value on the heap, you first need to declare a data member that's a pointer. That what I do in `Critter` with the following line, which declares `m_pName` as a pointer to a `string` object.

```
    string* m_pName;
```

In the class constructor, you can allocate memory on the heap, assign a value to the memory, and then point the pointer to the memory. That's what I do in the constructor with the following line, which allocates memory for a `string` object, assigns `name` to it, and points `m_pName` to that chunk of memory on the heap.

```
    m_pName = new string(name);
```

When `main()` calls `testDestructor()`, the function instantiates a `Critter` object. The object has an `m_pName` data member that points to a `string` object equal to "Rover" that's stored on the heap. Figure 9.7 provides a visual representation of the `Critter` object. Note that the image is abstract because the name of the critter is actually stored as a `string` object, not a string literal.

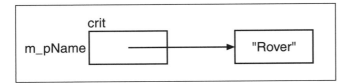

Figure 9.7
A representation of a `Critter` object. The `string` object equal to `"Rover"` is
stored on the heap.

Defining Destructors

A *destructor* is member function that's called just before an object is destroyed.
Destructors are most often used by programmers to perform any necessary cleanup before
an object disappears forever. A destructor must have the name of the class preceded by
~ (the tilde character). A destructor cannot have any parameters and cannot return a
value. If you don't write a destructor of your own, the compiler will supply a default
destructor for you. The behavior of the default destructor is usually fine for simple classes, but when you have a class with data members that point to values on the heap, you
should write your own destructor so you can free the memory on the heap associated with
the object before the object disappears, avoiding a memory leak. That's what I do in the
`Critter` class.

```
~Critter()                              //destructor
{
    cout << "Destructor called.\n";
    delete m_pName;
}
```

The destructor displays a message and then frees the memory pointed to by `m_pName`. Notice
that I don't assign 0 to `m_pName` even though it technically becomes a dangling pointer after
the `delete` operation. That's okay because `m_pName` will cease to exist when the destructor
ends and the object is gone.

hint

When you have a class that allocates memory on the heap, you should write a destructor that
cleans up and frees that memory.

Defining Copy Constructors

Sometimes an object is copied automatically for you. This occurs when an object is

- Passed by value to a function
- Returned from a function

- Initialized to another object through an initializer
- Provided as a single argument to the object's constructor

The copying is done by a special member function called the *copy constructor*. Like constructors and destructors, a default copy constructor is supplied for you if you don't write one of your own. The default copy constructor simply copies the value of each data member to data members of the same name in the new object—a *member-wise copy*.

For simple classes, the default copy constructor is usually fine. However, when you have a class with a data member that points to value on the heap, you usually write your own copy constructor. Why? Imagine a Critter object that has a data member that's a pointer to a string object on the heap. With only a default copy constructor, the automatic copying of the object would result in a new object that points to the same single string on the heap because the pointer of the new object would simply get a copy of the address stored in the pointer of the original object. This member-wise copying produces a *shallow copy*, in which the pointer data members of the copy point to the same chunks of memory as the pointer data members in the original object.

Let me give you a specific example. If I hadn't written my own copy constructor in the Heap Data Member program, when I passed a Critter object by value with the following function call, the program would have automatically made a shallow copy of crit called copy that existed in testCopyConstructor().

```
testCopyConstructor(crit);
```

copy's m_pName data member would point to the exact same string object on the heap as crit's m_pName data member does. Figure 9.8 shows you what I mean. Note that the image is abstract because the name of the critter is actually stored as a string object, not a string literal.

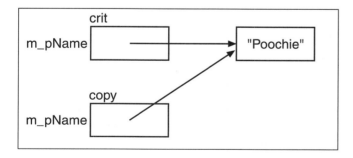

Figure 9.8
If a shallow copy of crit were made, both copy and crit would have a data member that points to the same chunk of memory on the heap.

Why is this a problem? Once testCopyConstructor() ends, copy's destructor is called, freeing the memory on the heap pointed to by copy's m_pName data member. Because of this, crit's m_pName data member would point to memory that has been freed, which would mean that the crits's m_pName data member would be a dangling pointer! Figure 9.9 provides you with a visual representation of this. Note that the image is abstract because the name of the critter is actually stored as a string object, not a string literal.

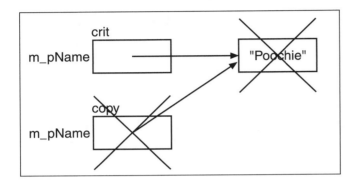

Figure 9.9
When the shallow copy of the Critter object is destroyed, the memory on the heap that it shared with the original object is freed. As result, the original object now has a dangling pointer.

What you really need is a copy constructor that produces a new object with its own chunk of memory on the heap that the object points to—a *deep copy*. That's what I do when I define the following copy constructor, which overloads the default one provided by the compiler.

```
Critter(const Critter& c)        //copy constructor
{
    cout << "Copy Constructor called.\n";
    m_pName = new string;
    *m_pName = c.GetName();
}
```

Just like this one, a copy constructor must have the same name as the class. It returns no value, but accepts a reference to an object of the class—the object that needs to be copied. The reference is almost always made a constant reference to protect the original object from being changed during the copy process.

When I call testCopyConstructor() by passing crit to the function by value, the copy constructor I wrote is called. You know this because the text Copy Constructor called. appears on the screen. The copy constructor creates a new Critter object (the copy) and accepts a reference to the original in c. With the line m_pName = new string;, the copy constructor allocates a new chunk of memory on the heap and points the m_pName data member of the copy to this memory. In the next line, `*m_pName = c.GetName();`, the copy constructor gets a copy of the `string` object equal to `"Poochie"` from the original and copies that to the newly acquired chunk of memory. As a result, a deep copy of `crit` is made, and that's what gets used in `testCopyConstructor()`.

When `testCopyConstructor()` ends, the copy of the `Critter` object used in the function is destroyed. The destructor frees the chunk of memory on the heap associated with the copy, leaving the original `Critter` object and its chunk of memory on the heap unaffected. Figure 9.10 shows the results. Note that the image is abstract because the name of the critter is actually stored as a `string` object, not a string literal.

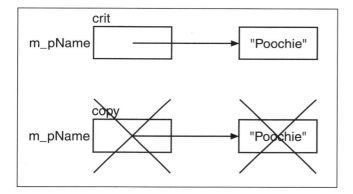

Figure 9.10
With a proper copy constructor, the original and the copy each point to their own chunk of memory on the heap. Then, when the copy is destroyed, the original is unaffected.

hint

When you have a class with data members that point to memory on the heap, you should consider writing a copy constructor that allocates memory for a new object and creates a deep copy.

Overloading the Assignment Operator

When both sides of an assignment statement are objects of the same class, the class' assignment operator member function is called. Like a default copy constructor, a default assignment operator member function is supplied for you if you don't write one of your own. Also like the default copy constructor, the default assignment operator provides only member-wise duplication.

For simple classes, the default assignment operator is usually fine. However, when you have a class with a data member that points to a value on the heap, you usually provide an overloaded assignment operator of your own. If you don't, you'll end up with shallow copies of objects when you assign one object to another. To avoid this problem, I overloaded the assignment operator for Critter.

```
Critter& operator=(const Critter& c)  //overloaded assignment operator
{
    cout << "Overloaded Assignment Operator called.\n";

    if (this == &c)
    {
        return *this;
    }
    else
    {
        *m_pName = c.GetName();
        return *this;
    }
}
```

Notice that the member function returns a reference to a Critter object. For robust assignment operation, return a reference from the overloaded assignment operator member function.

Next in main(), I call a function that tests the overloaded assignment operator for this class.

```
testAssignmentOp();
```

The testAssignmentOp() creates two objects and assigns one to the other.

```
Critter crit1("crit1");
Critter crit2("crit2");
crit1 = crit2;
```

The preceding assignment statement, crit1 = crit2;, calls the assignment operator member function—operator=()—for crit1. In the operator=() function, c is a constant reference to crit2. After operator=() displays a message that the overloaded assignment operator has been called, it uses the this pointer. What's the this pointer? It's a pointer that all non-static member functions automatically have, which points to the object that was used to call the function. In this case, this points to crit1, the object being assigned to. The next line, if (this == &c), checks to see whether the address of crit1 is equal to the address of crit2—that is, it checks whether the object is being assigned to itself. Because it's not, the else clause executes. Next, *m_pName = c.GetName(); assigns the string object equal to "crit2" to the chunk of memory that crit1's m_pName data member points to. Finally, the function returns a copy of the new crit1 by returning *this.

I prove that the assignment worked by calling crit1 and crit2's SayHi() member functions. Both statements display the message Hi, my name is crit2, proving that the assignment worked.

Next, I want to prove that the assignment didn't produce shallow copies and that both crit1 and crit2 have data members that point to two different chunks of memory on the heap. So, I change the value stored in the chunk of memory to which the data member of crit1 points.

```
crit1.SetName("crit1");
```

If all goes well, changing the name of crit1 should have no effect on crit2. To show this, I call crit1 and crit2's SayHi() member functions again. This time, the messages Hi, my name is crit1 and Hi, my name is crit2 are displayed, proving that both objects have their own chunks of memory on the heap to store their names.

Finally, I want to show you what happens when you assign an object to itself. That's what I do next in the function with the following lines:

```
Critter crit("crit");
crit = crit;
```

The preceding assignment statement, crit = crit;, calls the assignment operator member function—operator=()—for crit. The statement if (this == &c) checks to see whether crit is being assigned to itself. Because it is, the member function simply returns a copy of crit by returning *this.

hint

When you have a class with a data member that points to memory on the heap, you should consider overloading the assignment operator for the class.

Introducing the Game Lobby Program

The Game Lobby program simulates a game lobby—a waiting area for players, usually in an online game. The program doesn't actually involve an online component. It creates a single line in which players can wait. The user of the program runs the simulation and has four choices. He can add a person to the lobby, remove a person from the lobby (the first person in line is the first to leave), clear out the lobby, or quit the simulation. Figure 9.11 shows the program in action.

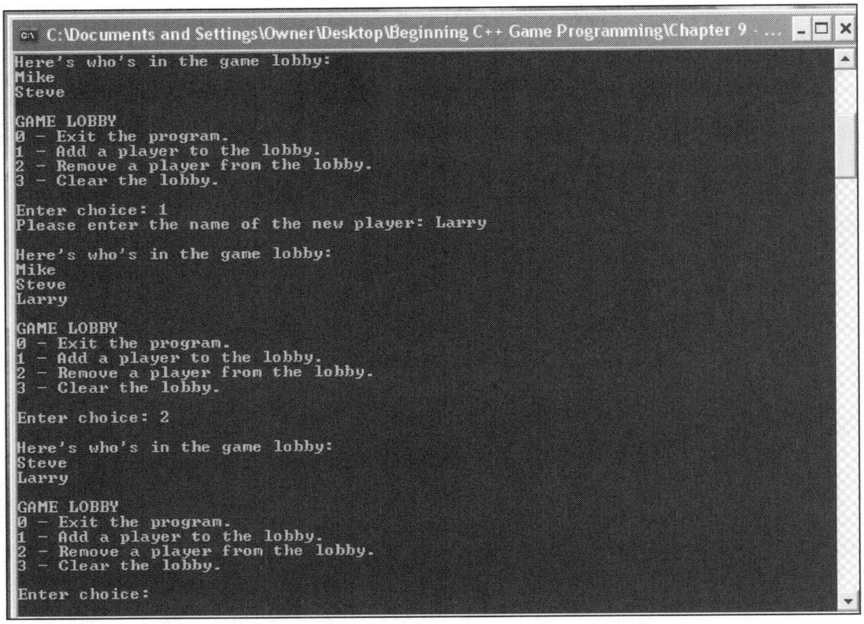

Figure 9.11
The lobby holds players who are removed in the order in which they were added.

The Player Class

The first thing I do is create a `Player` class to represent the players who are waiting in the game lobby. Because I don't know how many players I'll have in my lobby at one time, it makes sense to use a dynamic data structure. Normally, I'd go to my toolbox of containers from the STL. But I decided to take a different approach in this program and create my own kind of container using dynamically allocated memory that I manage. I didn't do this because it's a better programming choice—always see whether you can leverage good work done by other programmers, like the STL—but because it makes for a better game programming example. It's a great way to really see dynamic memory in action.

The code for the program is in the Chapter 9 folder on the CD-ROM that came with this book; the file name is game_lobby.cpp. Here's the beginning of the program, which includes the `Player` class:

```
//Game Lobby
//Simulates a game lobby where players wait
```

```
#include <iostream>
#include <string>

using namespace std;

class Player
{
public:
    Player(const string& name = ""): m_Name(name), m_pNext(0) {}
    string GetName() const { return m_Name; }
    Player* GetNext() const { return m_pNext; }
    void SetNext(Player* next) { m_pNext = next; }
private:
    string m_Name;
    Player* m_pNext;   //Pointer to next player in list
};
```

The m_Name data member holds the name of a player. That's pretty straightforward, but you might be wondering about the other data member, m_pNext. It's a pointer to a Player object, which means that each Player object can hold a name and point to another Player object. You'll get the point of all this when I talk about the Lobby class. Figure 9.12 provides a visual representation of a Player object.

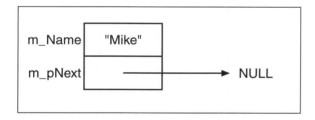

Figure 9.12
A Player object can hold a name and point to another Player object.

The class has a get accessor method for m_Name and get and set accessor member functions for m_pNext. Finally, the constructor is pretty simple. It initializes m_Name to a string object based on what's passed to the constructor. It also sets m_pNext to 0, making it a null pointer.

The Lobby Class

The Lobby class represents the lobby or line in which players wait.

```
class Lobby
{
```

```
        friend ostream& operator<<(ostream& os, const Lobby& aLobby);
public:
    Lobby(): m_pHead(0) {}
    ~Lobby() { Clear(); }
    void AddPlayer();
    void RemovePlayer();
    void Clear();
private:
    Player* m_pHead;
};
```

The data member m_pHead is a pointer that points to a Player object, which represents the first person in line. m_pHead represents the head of the line.

Because each Player object has an m_pNext data member, you can link a bunch of Player objects in a *linked list*. Individual elements of linked lists are often called *nodes*. Figure 9.13 provides a visual representation of a game lobby—a series of player nodes linked with one player at the head of the line.

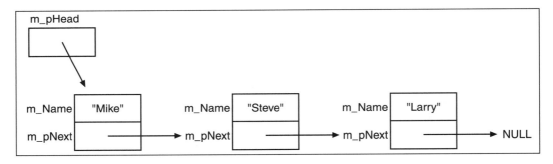

Figure 9.13
Each node holds a name and a pointer to the next player in the list. The first player in line is at the head.

One way to think about the player nodes is as a group of train cars that carry cargo and are connected. In this case, the train cars carry a name as cargo and are linked through a pointer data member, m_pNext. The Lobby class allocates memory on the heap for each Player object in the list. The Lobby data member m_pHead provides access to the first Player object at the head of the list.

The constructor is very simple. It simply initializes the data member m_pHead to 0, making it a null pointer. The destructor simply calls Clear(), which removes all the Player objects from the list, freeing the allocated memory. AddPlayer() instantiates a Player object on the heap and adds it to the end of the list. RemovePlayer() removes the first Player object in the list, freeing the allocated memory.

I declare the function operator<<() a friend of Lobby so that I can send a Lobby object to cout using the << operator.

The Lobby::AddPlayer() Member Function

The Lobby::AddPlayer() member function adds a player to the end of the line in the lobby.

```
void Lobby::AddPlayer()
{
    //create a new player node
    cout << "Please enter the name of the new player: ";
    string name;
    cin >> name;
    Player* pNewPlayer = new Player(name);

    //if list is empty, make head of list this new player
    if (m_pHead == 0)
    {
        m_pHead = pNewPlayer;
    }
    //otherwise find the end of the list and add the player there
    else
    {
        Player* pIter = m_pHead;
        while (pIter->GetNext() != 0)
        {
            pIter = pIter->GetNext();
        }
        pIter->SetNext(pNewPlayer);
    }
}
```

The first thing the function does is gets the new player's name from the user and use it to instantiate a new Player object on the heap. Then it sets the object's pointer data member to the null pointer.

Next, the function checks to see whether the lobby is empty. If the Lobby object's data member m_pHead is 0, then there's no one in line. If so, the new Player object becomes the head of the line and m_pHead is set to point to a new Player object on the heap.

If the lobby isn't empty, the player is added to the end of the line. The function accomplishes this by moving through the list one node at a time, using pIter's GetNext() member function, until it reaches a Player object whose GetNext() returns 0, meaning that it's the last node in the list. Then, the function makes that node point to the new Player object on the heap, which has the effect of adding the new object to the end of the list. Figure 9.14 illustrates this process.

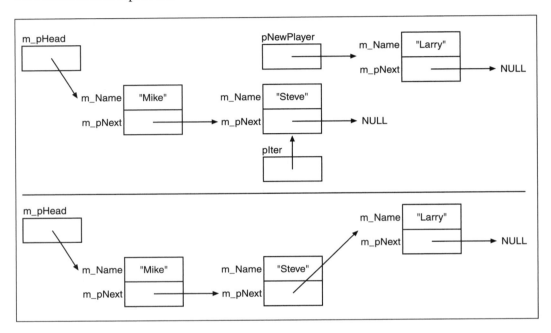

Figure 9.14
The list of players just before and just after a new player node is added.

trap

Lobby::AddPlayer() marches through the entire list of Player objects every time it's called. For small lists this isn't a problem, but with large lists this inefficient process can become unwieldy. There are more efficient ways to do what this function does. In one of the chapter exercises, your job will be to implement one of these more efficient methods.

The Lobby::RemovePlayer() Member Function

The Lobby:: RemovePlayer() member function removes the player at the head of the line.

```
void Lobby::RemovePlayer()
{
```

```
    if (m_pHead == 0)
    {
        cout << "The game lobby is empty.  No one to remove!\n";
    }
    else
    {
        Player* pTemp = m_pHead;
        m_pHead = m_pHead->GetNext();
        delete pTemp;
    }
}
```

The function tests m_pHead. If it's 0, then the lobby is empty and the function displays a message that says so. Otherwise, the first Player object in the list is removed. The function accomplishes this by creating a pointer, pTemp, and pointing it to the first Player object in the list. Then the function sets m_pHead to the next thing in the list—either the next Player object or 0. Finally, the function destroys the Player object pointed to by pTemp. Check out Figure 9.15 for a visual representation of how this works.

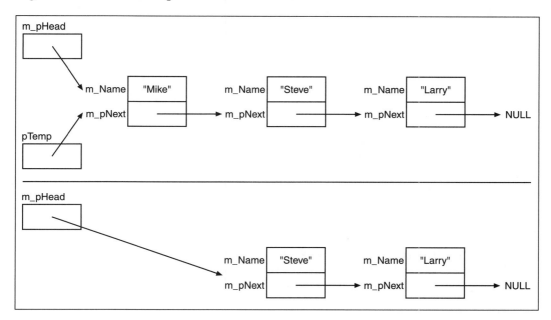

Figure 9.15
The list of players just before and just after a player node is removed.

The Lobby::Clear() Member Function

The Lobby::Clear() member function removes all of the players from the lobby.

```
void Lobby::Clear()
{
```

```
    while (m_pHead != 0)
    {
        RemovePlayer();
    }
}
```

If the list is empty, the loop isn't entered and the function ends. Otherwise, the loop is entered and the function keeps removing the first `Player` object in the list by calling `RemovePlayer()` until there are no more `Player` objects.

The operator<<() Member Function

The `operator<<()` member function overloads the `<<` operator so I can display a `Lobby` object by sending it to `cout`.

```
ostream& operator<<(ostream& os, const Lobby& aLobby)
{
    Player* pIter = aLobby.m_pHead;

    os << "\nHere's who's in the game lobby:\n";
    if (pIter == 0)
    {
        os << "The lobby is empty.\n";
    }
    else
    {
        while (pIter != 0)
        {
            os << pIter->GetName() << endl;
            pIter = pIter->GetNext();
        }
    }

    return os;
}
```

If the lobby is empty, the appropriate message is sent to the output stream. Otherwise, the function cycles through all of the players in the list, sending their names to the output stream, using `pIter` to move through the list.

The main() Function

The `main()` function displays the players in the lobby, presents the user with a menu of choices, and performs the requested action.

```
int main()
{
    Lobby myLobby;
    int choice;
```

```
do
{
    cout << myLobby;
    cout << "\nGAME LOBBY\n";
    cout << "0 - Exit the program.\n";
    cout << "1 - Add a player to the lobby.\n";
    cout << "2 - Remove a player from the lobby.\n";
    cout << "3 - Clear the lobby.\n";
    cout << endl << "Enter choice: ";
    cin >> choice;

    switch (choice)
    {
        case 0: cout << "Good-bye.\n"; break;
        case 1: myLobby.AddPlayer(); break;
        case 2: myLobby.RemovePlayer(); break;
        case 3: myLobby.Clear(); break;
        default: cout << "That was not a valid choice.\n";
    }
}
while (choice != 0);

return 0;
}
```

The function first instantiates a new Lobby object, and then it enters a loop that presents a menu and gets the user's choice. Then it calls the corresponding Lobby object's member function. If the user enters an invalid choice, he or she is told so. The loop continues until the user enters 0.

Summary

In this chapter, you should have learned the following concepts:

- Aggregation is the combining of objects so that one is part of another.
- Friend functions have complete access to any member of a class.
- Operator overloading allows you to define new meanings for built-in operators as they relate to objects of your own classes.
- The stack is an area of memory that is automatically managed for you and is used for local variables.
- The heap (or free store) is an area of memory that you, the programmer, can use to allocate and free memory.
- The new operator allocates memory on the heap and returns its address.
- The delete operator frees memory on the heap that was previously allocated.

- A dangling pointer points to an invalid memory location. Dereferencing or deleting a dangling pointer can cause your program to crash.

- A memory leak is an error in which memory that has been allocated becomes inaccessible and can no longer be freed. Given a large enough leak, a program might run out of memory and crash.

- A destructor is a member function that's called just before an object is destroyed. If you don't write a destructor of your own, the compiler will supply a default destructor for you.

- The copy constructor is a member function that's invoked when an automatic copy of an object is made. A default copy constructor is supplied for a class if you don't write one of your own.

- The default copy constructor simply copies the value of each data member to data members with the same names in the copy, producing a member-wise copy.

- Member-wise copying can produce a shallow copy of an object, in which the pointer data members of the copy point to the same chunks of memory as the pointers in the original object.

- A deep copy is a copy of an object that has no chunks of memory in common with the original.

- A default assignment operator member function, which provides only member-wise duplication, is supplied for you if you don't write one of your own.

- The this pointer is a pointer that all non-static member functions automatically have; it points to the object that was used to call the function.

Questions and Answers

Q: Why should you use aggregation?

A: To create more complex objects from other objects.

Q: What is composition?

A: A form of aggregation in which the composite object is responsible for the creation and destruction of its object parts. Composition is often called a *uses-a* relationship.

Q: When should I use a friend function?

A: When you need a function to have access to the non-public members of a class.

Q: What is a friend member function?

A: A member function of one class that can access all of the members of another class.

Q: What is a friend class?

A: A class that can access all of the members of another class.

Q: Can't operator overloading become confusing?

A: Yes. Giving too many meanings or unintuitive meanings to operators can lead to code that's difficult to understand.

Q: What happens when I instantiate a new object on the heap?

A: All of the data members will occupy memory on the heap and not on the stack.

Q: Can I access an object through a constant pointer?

A: Sure. But you can only access constant member functions through a constant pointer.

Q: What's wrong with shallow copies?

A: Because shallow copies share references to the same chunks of memory, a change to one object will be reflected in another object.

Q: What is a linked list?

A: A dynamic data structure that consists of a sequence of linked nodes.

Q: How is a linked list different from a vector?

A: Linked lists permit insertion and removal of nodes at any point in the list but do not allow random access, like vectors. However, the insertion and deletion of nodes in the middle of the list can be more efficient than the insertion and deletion of elements in the middle of vectors.

Q: Is there a container class from the STL that serves as a linked list?

A: Yes, the list class.

Q: Is the data structure used in the Game Lobby program a linked list?

A: It shares similarities to a linked list, but it is really a queue.

Q: What's a queue?

A: A data structure in which elements are removed in the same order in which they were entered. This process is often called first in, first out (FIFO).

Q: Is there a kind of container from the STL that serves as a queue?

A: Yes, the queue container adaptor.

Discussion Questions

1. What types of game entities could you create with aggregation?
2. Do friend functions undermine encapsulation in OOP?
3. What advantages does dynamic memory offer to game programs?
4. Why are memory leaks difficult errors to track down?
5. Should objects that allocate memory on the heap always be required to free it?

Exercises

1. Improve the Lobby class from the Game Lobby program by writing a copy constructor and an overloaded assignment operator for it.
2. The Lobby::AddPlayer() member function from the Game Lobby program is inefficient because it iterates through all of the player nodes to add a new player to the end of the line. Add an m_pTail pointer data member to the Lobby class that always points to the last player node in the line and use it to more efficiently add a player.
3. What's wrong with the following code?

```cpp
#include <iostream>
using namespace std;

int main()
{
    int* pScore = new int;
    *pScore = 500;
    pScore = new int(1000);
    delete pScore;
    pScore = 0;

    return 0;
}
```

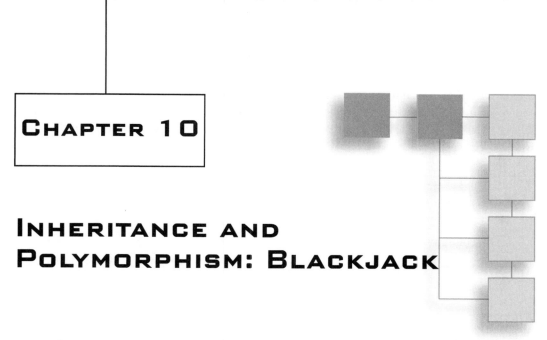

CHAPTER 10

INHERITANCE AND
POLYMORPHISM: BLACKJACK

C lasses give you the perfect way to represent game entities that have attributes and behaviors. But game entities are often related. In this chapter, you'll learn about inheritance and polymorphism, which give you ways to express those connections and can make defining and using game classes even simpler and more intuitive. Specifically, you'll learn to:

- Derive one class from another
- Use inherited data members and member functions
- Override base class member functions
- Define virtual functions to enable polymorphism
- Declare pure virtual functions to define abstract classes
- Split your code up into multiple files

Introducing Inheritance

One of the key elements of OOP is *inheritance*, which allows you to *derive* a new class from an existing one. When you do so, the new class automatically *inherits* (or gets) the data members and member functions of an existing class. It's like getting the work that went into the existing class for free!

Inheritance is especially useful when you want to create a more specialized version of an existing class because you can add data members and member functions to the new class to extend it. For example, imagine you have a class Enemy that defines an enemy in a game with a member function Attack() and a data member m_Damage. You can derive a new class Boss from Enemy for a boss. This means that Boss could automatically have Attack() and m_Damage without you having to write any code for them at all. Then, to make a boss tough, you could add a member function SpecialAttack() and a data member DamageMultiplier to the Boss class. Take a look at Figure 10.1, which shows the relationship between the Enemy and Boss classes.

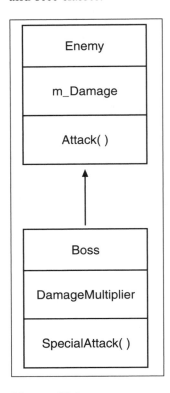

Figure 10.1
Boss inherits Attack() and m_Damage from Enemy while defining SpecialAttack() and m_DamageMultiplier.

One of the many advantages of inheritance is that you can reuse classes you've already written. This reusability produces benefits that include:

- **Less work.** There's no need to redefine functionality you already have. Once you have a class that provides the base functionality for other classes, you don't have to write that code again.

- **Fewer errors.** Once you've got a bug-free class, you can reuse it without errors cropping up in it.

- **Cleaner code**. Because the functionality of base classes exists only once in a program, you don't have to wade through the same code repeatedly, which makes programs easier to understand and modify.

Most related game entities cry out for inheritance. Whether it's the series of enemies that a player faces, squadrons of military vehicles that a player commands, or an inventory of weapons that a player wields, you can use inheritance to define these groups of game entities in terms of each other, which results in faster and easier programming.

Introducing the Simple Boss Program

The Simple Boss program demonstrates inheritance. In it, I define a class for lowly enemies, Enemy. From this class, I derive a new class for tough bosses that the player has to face, Boss. Then, I instantiate an Enemy object and call its Attack() member function. Next, I instantiate a Boss object. I'm able to call Attack() for the Boss object because it inherits the member function from Enemy. Finally, I call the Boss object's SpecialAttack() member function, which I defined in Boss, for a special attack. Since I define SpecialAttack() in Boss, only Boss objects have access to it. Enemy objects don't have this special attack at their disposal. Figure 10.2 shows the results of the program.

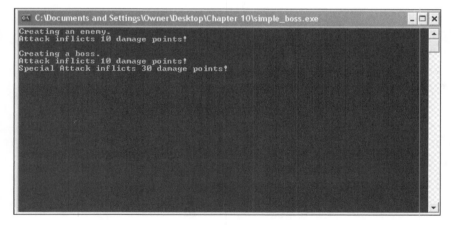

Figure 10.2
The Boss class inherits the Attack() member function and then defines its own SpecialAttack() member function.

The code for the program is in the Chapter 10 folder on the CD-ROM that came with this book; the file name is simple_boss.cpp.

```
//Simple Boss
//Demonstrates inheritance
```

```cpp
#include <iostream>
using namespace std;

class Enemy
{
public:
    int m_Damage;

    Enemy(): m_Damage(10) {}

    void Attack() const
    { cout << "Attack inflicts " << m_Damage << " damage points!\n"; }
};

class Boss : public Enemy
{
public:
    int m_DamageMultiplier;

    Boss(): m_DamageMultiplier(3) {}

    void SpecialAttack() const
    { cout << "Special Attack inflicts " << (m_DamageMultiplier * m_Damage);
      cout << " damage points!\n"; }
};

int main()
{
    cout << "Creating an enemy.\n";
    Enemy enemy1;
    enemy1.Attack();

    cout << "\nCreating a boss.\n";
    Boss boss1;
    boss1.Attack();
    boss1.SpecialAttack();

    return 0;
}
```

Deriving from a Base Class

I derive the Boss class from Enemy when I define Boss with the following line:

```cpp
class Boss : public Enemy
```

Boss is based on Enemy. In fact, Enemy is called the *base class* (or *superclass*) and Boss the *derived class* (or *subclass*). This means that Boss inherits Enemy's data members and member functions, subject to access controls. In this case, Boss inherits and can directly access m_Damage and Attack(). It's as if I defined both m_Damage and Attack() in Boss.

You might have noticed that I made all of the members of the classes public, including their data members. I did this because it makes for the simplest first example of a base and a derived class. You also might have noticed that I used the keyword `public` when deriving `Boss` from `Enemy`. For now, don't worry about this. I'll cover it all in the next example program.

To derive classes of your own, follow my example. After the class name in a class definition, put a colon followed by an access modifier (such as `public`), followed by the name of the base class. It's perfectly acceptable to derive a new class from a derived class, and sometimes it makes perfect sense to do so. However, to keep things simple, I'm only going to deal with one level of inheritance.

There are actually a few base class member functions that are not inherited by derived classes. They are

- Constructors
- Copy constructors
- Destructors
- Overloaded assignment operators

You have to write your own versions of these in the derived class.

Instantiating Objects from a Derived Class

In `main()`, I instantiate an `Enemy` object and then call its `Attack()` member function. This works just as you'd expect. The interesting part of the program begins next, when I instantiate a `Boss` object.

```
Boss boss1;
```

After this line of code, I have a `Boss` object with an `m_Damage` data member equal to 10 and an `m_DamageMultiplier` data member equal to 3. How did this happen? Although constructors and destructors are not inherited from a base class, they are called when an instance is created or destroyed. In fact, a base class constructor is called before the derived class constructor to create its part of the final object.

In this case, when a `Boss` object is instantiated, the default `Enemy` constructor is automatically called and the object gets an `m_Damage` data member with a value of 10 (just like any `Enemy` object would). Then, the `Boss` constructor is called and finishes off the object by giving it an `m_DamageMultiplier` data member with a value of 3. The reverse happens when a `Boss` object is destroyed at the end of the program. First, the `Boss` class destructor is called for the object, and then the `Enemy` class destructor is called. Because I didn't define destructors in this program, nothing special happens before the `Boss` object ceases to exist.

hint

The fact that base class destructors are called for objects of derived classes ensures that each class gets its chance to clean up any part of the object that needs to be taken care of, such as memory on the heap.

Using Inherited Members

Next I call an inherited member function of the Boss object, which displays the exact same message as enemy1.Attack() did.

```
boss1.Attack();
```

That makes perfect sense because the same code is being executed and both objects have an m_Damage data member equal to 10. Notice that the function call looks the same as it did for enemy1. The fact that Boss inherited the member function from Enemy makes no difference in how the function is called.

Next I get Boss to pull out its special attack, which displays the message Special Attack inflicts 30 damage points!

```
boss1.SpecialAttack();
```

The thing to notice about this is that SpecialAttack(), defined in Enemy, uses the data member m_Damage. That's perfectly fine. Boss inherits m_Damage, and it works like any other data member in the Boss class.

Controlling Access under Inheritance

When you derive one class from another, you can control how much access the derived class has to the base class' members. For the same reasons that you want to provide only as much access as is necessary to a class' members to the rest of your program, you want to provide only as much access as is necessary to a class' members to a derived class. Not coincidentally, you use the same access modifiers that you've seen before—public, protected, and private. (Okay, you haven't seen protected before, but I'll explain that modifier in the "Using Access Modifiers with Class Members" section.)

Introducing the Simple Boss 2.0 Program

The Simple Boss 2.0 program is another version of the Simple Boss program from earlier in this chapter. The new version, Simple Boss 2.0, looks exactly the same to the user, but the code is a little different because I put some restrictions on base class members. If you want to see what the program does, take a look back at Figure 10.2.

The code for the program is in the Chapter 10 folder on the CD-ROM that came with this book; the file name is simple_boss2.cpp.

```
//Simple Boss 2.0
//Demonstrates access control under inheritance

#include <iostream>
using namespace std;

class Enemy
{
public:
    Enemy(): m_Damage(10) {}

    void Attack() const
    { cout << "Attack inflicts " << m_Damage << " damage points!\n"; }

protected:
    int m_Damage;
};

class Boss : public Enemy
{
public:
    Boss(): m_DamageMultiplier(3) {}

    void SpecialAttack() const
    { cout << "Special Attack inflicts " << (m_DamageMultiplier * m_Damage);
      cout << " damage points!\n"; }

private:
    int m_DamageMultiplier;
};

int main()
{
    cout << "Creating an enemy.\n";
    Enemy enemy1;
    enemy1.Attack();

    cout << "\nCreating a boss.\n";
    Boss boss1;
    boss1.Attack();
    boss1.SpecialAttack();

    return 0;
}
```

Using Access Modifiers with Class Members

You've seen the access modifiers public and private used with class members before, but there's a third modifier you can use with members of a class—protected. That's what I use with the data member of Enemy.

```
protected:
    int m_Damage;
```

Members that are specified as `protected` are not accessible outside of the class, except in some cases of inheritance. As a refresher, here are the three levels of member access:

- `public` members are accessible to all code in a program.
- `protected` members are accessible only in their own class and certain derived classes, depending upon the access level used in inheritance.
- `private` members are only accessible in their own class, which means they are not directly accessible in any kind of derived class.

Using Access Modifiers when Deriving Classes

When you derive a class from an existing one, you can use an access modifier, such as `public`, which I used in deriving `Boss`.

```
class Boss : public Enemy
```

Using public derivation means that public members in the base class become public members in the derived class, protected members in the base class become protected members in the derived class, and private members are inaccessible.

trick

Even if base data members are private, you can still use them indirectly through base class member functions. You can even get and set their values if the base class has accessor member functions.

This means that `Boss` inherits all of `Enemy`'s public member functions as public member functions. It also means that `Boss` inherits `m_Damage` as a protected data member. The upshot is that the `Boss` class can access `Attack()` and `m_Damage()`. The class essentially acts as if I simply copied and pasted the code for these two `Enemy` class members right into the `Boss` definition. But through the beauty of inheritance, I didn't have to do this.

hint

You can derive a new class with the `protected` and `private` keywords, but they're rarely used.

Calling and Overriding Base Class Member Functions

You're not stuck with every base class member function you inherit in a derived class as is. You have options that allow you to customize how those inherited member functions work in your derived class. You can override them by giving them new definitions in your derived class. You can also explicitly call a base class member function from any member function of your derived class.

Introducing the Overriding Boss Program

The Overriding Boss program demonstrates calling and overriding base class member functions in a derived class. The program creates an enemy that taunts the player and then attacks him. Next, the program creates a boss from a derived class. The boss also taunts the player and attacks him, but the interesting thing is that the inherited behaviors of taunting and attacking are changed for the boss (who is a bit cockier than the enemy). These changes are accomplished through function overriding and calling a base class member function. Figure 10.3 shows the results of the program.

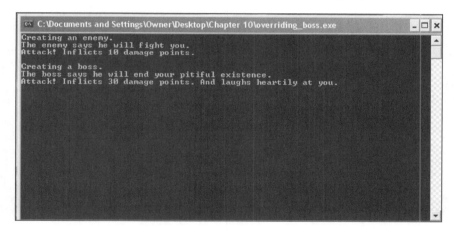

Figure 10.3
The Boss class inherits and overrides the base class member functions
Taunt() and Attack(), creating new behaviors for the functions in Boss.

The code for the program is in the Chapter 10 folder on the CD-ROM that came with this book; the file name is simple_boss2.cpp.

```cpp
//Overriding Boss
//Demonstrates calling and overriding base member functions

#include <iostream>
using namespace std;

class Enemy
{
public:
    Enemy(int damage = 10): m_Damage(damage)
    {}
```

```
        void Taunt() const
        { cout << "The enemy says he will fight you.\n"; }

        void Attack() const
        { cout << "Attack! Inflicts " << m_Damage << " damage points."; }
private:
    int m_Damage;
};

class Boss : public Enemy
{
public:
    Boss(int damage = 30): Enemy(damage) //call base constructor with argument
    {}

    void Taunt() const
    { cout << "The boss says he will end your pitiful existence.\n"; }

    void Attack() const
    {
        Enemy::Attack();
        cout << " And laughs heartily at you.\n";
    }
};

int main()
{
    cout << "Creating an enemy.\n";
    Enemy enemy1;
    enemy1.Taunt();
    enemy1.Attack();

    cout << "\n\nCreating a boss.\n";
    Boss boss1;
    boss1.Taunt();
    boss1.Attack();

    return 0;
}
```

Calling Base Class Constructors

As you've seen, the constructor for a base class is automatically called when an object of a
derived class is instantiated, but you can also explicitly call a base class constructor from
a derived class constructor. The syntax for this is a lot like the syntax for a member initialization list. To call a base class constructor from a derived class constructor, after the
derived constructor's parameter list, type a colon followed by the name of the base class,

followed by a set of parentheses containing whatever parameters the base class constructor you're calling needs. I do this in the `Boss` constructor, which says to explicitly call the `Enemy` constructor and pass it `damage`.

```
Boss(int damage = 30): Enemy(damage) //call base constructor with argument
```

This allows me to pass the `Enemy` constructor the value that gets assigned to `m_Damage`, rather than just accepting its default value.

When I first instantiate `boss1` in `main()`, the `Enemy` constructor is called and passed the value 30, which gets assigned to `m_Damage`. Then, the `Boss` constructor is called (which doesn't do much of anything) and the object is completed.

hint

Being able to call a base class constructor is useful when you want to pass specific values to it.

Overriding Base Class Member Functions

You can override a base class member function in a derived class and give it a new definition simply by defining the function in the derived class. That's what I do with the `Taunt()` member function in `Boss`.

```
void Taunt() const
{ cout << "The boss says he will end your pitiful existence.\n"; }
```

trap

Don't confuse override with overload. When you override a member function, you provide a new definition of it in a derived class. When you overload a function, you create multiple versions of it with different signatures.

This new definition is executed when I call the member function through any `Boss` object. It replaces the definition of `Taunt()` inherited from `Enemy` for all `Boss` objects. When I call the member function in `main()` with the following line, the message `The boss says he will end your pitiful existence.` is displayed.

```
boss1.Taunt();
```

Overriding member functions is useful when you want to change or extend the behavior of base class member functions in derived classes.

trap

When you override an overloaded base class member function, you hide all of the other overloaded versions of the base class member function—meaning that the only way to access the other versions of the member function is to explicitly call the base class member function. So if you override an overloaded member function, it's a good idea to override every version of the overloaded function.

Calling Base Class Member Functions

You can directly call a base class member function from any function in a derived class. All you have to do is prefix the class name to the member function name with the scope resolution operator. That's what I do in the `Attack()` definition of the `Boss` class.

```
void Attack() const
{
    Enemy::Attack();
    cout << " And laughs heartily at you.\n";
}
```

The line `Enemy::Attack();` explicitly calls the `Attack()` member function of `Enemy`. Because the `Attack()` definition in `Boss` overrides the class' inherited version, it's as if I've extended the definition of what it means for a boss to attack. What I'm essentially saying is that when a boss attacks, the boss does exactly what an enemy does and then adds a laughs. When I call the member function for a `Boss` object in `main()` with the following line, `Boss`' `Attack()` member function is called because I've overloaded `Attack()`.

```
boss1.Attack();
```

The first thing that `Boss`' `Attack()` member function does is explicitly call `Enemy`'s `Attack()` member function, which displays the message `Attack! Inflicts 30 damage points`. Then, `Boss`' `Attack()` member function finishes by displaying the message `And laughs heartily at you`.

trick

You can extend the way a member function of a base class works in a derived class by overriding the base class method and then explicitly calling the base class member function from this new definition in the derived class and adding some functionality.

Using Overloaded Assignment Operators and Copy Constructors in Derived Classes

You already know how to write an overloaded assignment operator and a copy constructor for a class. However, writing them for a derived class requires a little bit more work because they aren't inherited from a base class.

When you overload the assignment operator in a derived class, you usually want to call the assignment operator member function from the base class, which you can explicitly call using the base class name as a prefix. If Boss is derived from Enemy, the overloaded assignment operator member function defined in Boss could start:

```
Boss& operator=(const Boss& b)
{
    Enemy::operator=(b);     //handles the data members inherited from Enemy
    //now take care of data members defined in Boss
```

The explicit call to Enemy's assignment operator member function handles the data members inherited from Enemy. The rest of the member function would take care of the data members defined in Boss.

For the copy constructor, you also usually want to call the copy constructor from a base class, which you can call just like any base class constructor. If Boss is derived from Enemy, the copy constructor defined in Boss could start:

```
Boss (const Boss& b): Enemy(b)  //handles the data members inherited from Enemy
{
    //now take care of data members defined in Boss
```

By calling Enemy's copy constructor with Enemy(b), you copy that Enemy's data members into the new Boss object. In the remainder of Boss' copy constructor, you can take care of copying the data members declared in Boss into the new object.

Introducing Polymorphism

One of the pillars of OOP is *polymorphism*, which means that a member function will produce different results depending on the type of object for which it is being called. For example, suppose you have a group of bad guys that the player is facing, and the group is made of objects of different types that are related through inheritance, such as enemies and bosses. Through the magic of polymorphism, you could call the same member function for each bad guy in the group, say to attack the player, and the type of each object would determine the exact effects. The call for the enemy objects could produce one result, such as a weak attack, while the call for bosses could produce a different result, such as a powerful attack. This might sound a lot like overriding, but polymorphism is different because the effect of the function call is dynamic and is determined at run time, depending on the object type. But the best way to understand this isn't through theoretical discussion; it is through concrete examples.

Introducing the Virtual Boss Program

The Virtual Boss program demonstrates how to use virtual member functions to achieve polymorphic behavior. It shows what happens when you use a pointer to a base class to call virtual and non-virtual member functions. It also shows how using vertical destructors ensures that the correct distructors are called for objects pointed to by pointers to a base class. Figure 10.4 shows the results of the program.

Figure 10.4
Using virtual member functions ensures that the correct member functions
and destructors are called for objects pointed to by pointers to a base class.

The code for the program is in the Chapter 10 folder on the CD-ROM that came with this book; the file name is virtual_boss2.cpp.

```cpp
//Virtual Boss
//Demonstrates virtual functions

#include <iostream>

using namespace std;

class Enemy
{
public:
    Enemy(int damage = 10)
    { m_pDamage = new int(damage); }

    virtual ~Enemy()
    {
        cout << "m_pDamage deleted\n";
        delete m_pDamage;
    }

    void Taunt() const
    { cout << "The enemy says he will fight you.\n"; }
```

```
    void virtual VTaunt() const
    { cout << "The enemy says he will fight you.\n"; }

protected:
    int* m_pDamage;
};

class Boss : public Enemy
{
public:
    Boss(int multiplier = 3)
    { m_pDamageMultiplier = new int(multiplier); }

    virtual ~Boss()
    {
        cout << "m_pDamageMultiplier deleted\n";
        delete m_pDamageMultiplier;
    }

    void Taunt() const
    { cout << "The boss says he will end your pitiful existence.\n"; }

    void virtual VTaunt() const
    { cout << "The boss says he will end your pitiful existence.\n";}

protected:
    int* m_pDamageMultiplier;
};

int main()
{
    cout << "Pointer to Enemy that points to a Boss object:\n";
    Enemy* pBadGuy = new Boss();
    pBadGuy->Taunt();
    pBadGuy->VTaunt();

    cout << "\nDeleting pointer to Enemy:\n";
    delete pBadGuy;
    pBadGuy = 0;

    return 0;
}
```

Defining Virtual Member Functions

An object of a derived class is also a member of the base class. For example, in the Virtual Boss program, a Boss object is an Enemy object, too. That makes sense because a boss is really only a specialized kind of enemy. It also makes sense because a Boss object has all of the members of an Enemy object. Okay, so what? Well, because an object of a derived class is also a member of the base class, you can use a pointer to the base class to point to an object of the derived class. That's what I do in main() with the following line, which instantiates a Boss object on the heap and creates a pointer to Enemy that points to the Boss object.

```
Enemy* pBadGuy = new Boss();
```

Why in the world would you want to do this? It's useful because it allows you to deal with objects without requiring that you know their exact type. For example, you could have a function that accepts a pointer to Enemy that could work with either an Enemy or a Boss object. The function wouldn't have to know the exact type of object being passed to it; it could work with the object to produce different results depending on the object's type. But that's not what happens as the result of the next line of code.

```
pBadGuy->Taunt();
```

Instead, the line displays the text The enemy says he will fight you. Yikes! I called the Taunt() member function for a Boss object and got the results of Enemy's Taunt() member function, even though I overrode Taunt() in Boss. This happened as a result of *early binding*, in which the exact member function is bound based on the pointer type—in this case, Enemy. What I need is to have the member function called based on the type of object being pointed to, not fixed by pointer type. I can achieve this flexibility of *late binding* through *virtual functions*, which allow for polymorphic behavior.

To create a virtual member function, simply add the keyword virtual before the name of the function when you declare it. That's what I do in Enemy with the following line:

```
void virtual VTaunt() const
{ cout << "The enemy says he will fight you.\n"; }
```

This means that VTaunt() is a virtual function. It's virtual in Enemy and it's inherited as a virtual function in Boss. This means that when I override VTaunt() in Boss with the following line, the correct version of VTaunt() will be called (based on the type of object) and will not be fixed by the type of pointer.

```
void virtual VTaunt() const
{ cout << "The boss says he will end your pitiful existence.\n";}
```

hint

Once a member function is defined as virtual, it's virtual in any derived class. This means you don't have to use the keyword virtual when you override a virtual member function in a derived class, but you should use it anyway because it will remind you that the function is indeed virtual.

I prove that the behavior will be polymorphic in main() with the following line, which results in the VTaunt() function defined in Boss being called and the text The boss says he will end your pitiful existence. being displayed on the screen.

```
pBadGuy->VTaunt();
```

hint

Virtual functions produce polymorphic behavior through references as well.

trap

The benefits of virtual functions aren't free; there is a performance cost associated with the overhead. Therefore, you should use virtual functions only when you need them. The good news is that once you've defined one virtual member function in a class, defining another doesn't cost you much more.

trap

Slicing is essentially the act of cutting off part of an object. Assigning an object of a derived class to a variable of a base class is legal, but you slice the object, losing the data members declared in the derived class and losing access to member functions of the derived class. Therefore, you should avoid slicing objects.

Defining Virtual Destructors

When you use a pointer to a base class to point to an object of a derived class, you have a potential problem. When you delete the pointer, only the base class' destructor will be called for the object. This could lead to disastrous results because the derived class' destructor might need to free memory (as the destructor for Boss does). The solution, as you might have guessed, is to make the base class' destructor virtual. That way, the derived class' destructor is called, which (as always) leads to the calling of the base class' destructor, giving every class the chance to clean up after itself.

I put this theory into action when I make Enemy's destructor virtual.

```
virtual ~Enemy()
```

When I delete the pointer pointing to the Boss object with the following line, the Boss object's destructor is called, which frees the memory on the heap that m_pDamageMultiplier points to and displays the message m_pDamageMultiplier deleted.

```
delete pBadGuy;
```

Then, Enemy's destructor is called, which frees the memory on the heap that m_pDamage points to and displays the message m_pDamage deleted. The object is destroyed, and all memory associated with the object is freed.

trick

A good rule of thumb is that if you have any virtual member functions in a class, you should make the destructor virtual, too.

Using Abstract Classes

At times you might want to define a class to act as a base for other classes, but it doesn't make sense to instantiate objects from this class because it's so generic. For example, suppose you have a game with a bunch of types of creatures running around in it. Although you have a wide variety of creatures, they all have two things in common: They have a health value and they can offer a greeting. So, you could define a class, Creature, as a base from which to derive other classes, such as Pixie, Dragon, Orc, and so on. Although Creature is helpful, it doesn't really make sense to instantiate a Creature object. It would be great if there were a way to indicate that Creature is a base class only, and not meant for instantiating objects. Well, C++ lets you define a kind of class just like this, called an *abstract class*.

Introducing the Abstract Creature Program

The Abstract Creature program demonstrates abstract classes. In the program, I define an abstract class, Creature, which can be used as a base class for specific creature classes. I define one such class, Orc. Then, I instantiate an Orc object and call a member function to get the orc to grunt hello and another member function to display the orc's health. Figure 10.5 shows the results of the program.

Figure 10.5
The orc is an object of a class derived from an abstract class for all creatures.

The code for the program is in the Chapter 10 folder on the CD-ROM that came with this book; the file name is abstract_creature.cpp.

```cpp
//Abstract Creature
//Demonstrates abstract classes

#include <iostream>
using namespace std;

class Creature   //abstract class
{
public:
    Creature(int health = 100): m_Health(health)
    {}

    virtual void Greet() const = 0;    //a pure virtual member function

    virtual void DisplayHealth() const
    { cout << "Health: " << m_Health << endl; }

protected:
    int m_Health;
};

class Orc : public Creature
{
public:
    Orc(int health = 120): Creature(health)
    {}

    virtual void Greet() const
    { cout << "The orc grunts hello.\n"; }
};

int main()
{
    Creature* pCreature = new Orc();
    pCreature->Greet();
    pCreature->DisplayHealth();

    return 0;
}
```

Declaring Pure Virtual Functions

A *pure virtual function* is one to which you don't need to give a definition. The logic behind this is that there might not be a good definition in the class for the member function. For example, I don't think it makes sense to define the Greet() function in my

Creature class because a greeting really depends on the specific type of creature—a pixie twinkles, a dragon blows a puff of smoke, and an orc grunts.

You specify a pure virtual function by placing an equal sign and a zero at the end of the function header. That's what I did in Creature with the following line:

```
virtual void Greet() const = 0;    //a pure virtual member function
```

When a class contains at least one pure virtual function, it's an abstract class. Therefore, Creature is an abstract class. I can use it as the base class for other classes, but I can't instantiate objects from it.

An abstract class can have data members and virtual functions that are not pure virtual. In Creature, I declare a data member m_Health and a virtual member function DisplayHealth().

Deriving a Class from an Abstract Class

When you derive a new class from an abstract class, you can override its pure virtual functions. If you override all of its pure virtual functions, then the new class is not abstract and you can instantiate objects from it. When I derive Orc from Creature, I override Creature's one virtual function with the following lines:

```
virtual void Greet() const
{ cout << "The orc grunts hello.\n"; }
```

This means I can instantiate an object from Orc, which is what I do in main() with the following line:

```
Creature* pCreature = new Orc();
```

The code instantiates a new Orc object on the heap and assigns the memory location of the object to pCreature, a pointer to Creature. Even though I can't instantiate an object from Creature, it's perfectly fine to declare a pointer using the class. Like all base class pointers, a pointer to Creature can point to any object of a class derived from Creature, such as Orc.

Next, I call Greet(), the pure virtual function that I override in Orc with the following line:

```
pCreature->Greet();
```

The correct greeting, The orc grunts hello., is displayed.

Finally, I call DisplayHealth(), which I define in Creature.

```
pCreature->DisplayHealth();
```

It also displays the proper message, Health: 120.

Organizing Your Code

When your game programs are filled with many functions and classes, they become unwieldy as a single file. In addition, it might be nice to reuse parts of one program, such as some functions or classes, in your next program. C++ lets your break up your code into manageable and useful pieces in multiple files. Generally, you separate related functions or single classes into their own files.

The Critter Project

The Critter project is not just one program file; it is a collection of three files that work together to create a single application. The results of the project are simple. In it, I instantiate a simple critter and have it say hello. This is something you could have done way back in Chapter 8. The interesting thing here is that the project demonstrates how you can break a program into multiple files. Figure 10.6 shows the results of the project.

Figure 10.6
The simple application is the result of three separate C++ files.

Using One File

You could create the results shown in Figure 10.6 with a single C++ file. In fact, the one file of code would be pretty short, as you can see here.

```cpp
#include <iostream>
using namespace std;

class Critter
{
public:
    void Greet();
```

```
};

void Critter::Greet()
{
    cout << "Hi. I'm a critter.\n";
}

int main()
{
    cout << "Instantiating a Critter object.\n\n";

    Critter crit;
    crit.Greet();

    return 0;
}
```

However, you can break up this file into multiple files that work together as a project, as I do. In the project, I create three files.

- **Header file.** This contains only the `Critter` class definition.

- **Implementation file.** This contains the implementation of the `Critter` class member function.

- **Application file.** This contains a program with a `main()` function that uses the `Critter` class from the header and implementation files. This is the file you execute.

hint

──

The exact details of how you get a project contained in multiple files to run depend on your compiler, so check out its documentation.

──

Creating Header Files

Header files are meant to be included in other files. You've already seen header files. In fact, every program in this book includes at least one header file from the standard library, `<iostream>`.

When you break up your program into multiple files, you generally write your own header files—usually one for each class. The files include only the class definition, not its implementation. Following is the header file for the Critter project. It is included in the Chapter 10 folder on the CD-ROM that came with this book; the file name is critter.h. (By convention, header file names end in .h.)

```
//critter.h
//header file
```

```
#ifndef CRITTER_H
#define CRITTER_H

class Critter
{
public:
    void Greet();
};

#endif
```

The class definition for Critter is very simple; it declares only one public member function—Greet().

There are some new ideas in the code. The three lines that begin with # are *preprocessor directives*—basically instructions to your compiler. Together, they tell your compiler not to include the Critter definition in your project if it was already included. I take this precaution because defining the same class more than once in a project will result in an error.

What specifically is going on? The first directive says that if the symbol CRITTER_H is not defined (on a list of symbols that the compiler keeps while it compiles your code), the program should go ahead and process all of the code that follows, up to an end marker.

```
#ifndef CRITTER_H
```

If the symbol is on the list, then the program should skip all of the code that follows, up to the end marker. The end marker is the last directive in the file.

```
#endif
```

The first time the critter.h header file is included in a project that gets compiled, CRITTER_H isn't on the list of symbols, and the Critter class definition is included. In addition, the compiler processes the directive, which says to include the symbol CRITTER_H on its list of symbols.

```
#define CRITTER_H
```

This means that if an attempt were made to include this header file again in a project, the compiler would see CRITTER_H on its list, skip the Critter class definition, and not attempt to define Critter again.

By the way, I chose the symbol CRITTER_H for this header file, critter.h. I could have chosen many other symbols, but the convention is to use the name of the header file in all caps, followed by _H. Following this convention saves you a unique symbol for each header file. Plus, it's what other programmers expect.

Creating Implementation Files

Because header files for classes only contain the class definition, you need to store the class implementation in another file. You do this in a file with the same name as the header file, but with the familiar .cpp extension. The implementation file that corresponds to critter.h is named critter.cpp and contains the implementation of the Critter class. Here's the code, which is in the Chapter 10 folder on the CD-ROM that came with this book. (The file name is critter.cpp.)

```
//critter.cpp
//implementation file

#include <iostream>
#include "critter.h"

using namespace std;

void Critter::Greet()
{
    cout << "Hi. I'm a critter.\n";
}
```

The file contains the implementation of Critter::Greet(). You also include definitions for variables and static members in an implementation file. Notice that I include the header file with the following line:

```
#include "critter.h"
```

When you include a file, it's as if you copy and paste it right where the include statement is. By including critter.h, I have the complete class definition.

hint
_____
When you include a header file that you wrote, you surround the file name with quotation marks.
_____

These two files taken together constitute a tidy way of storing a single class. The next step is to use the class in an actual program.

Creating Application Files

You can include your own header files in an application using an include statement. I include the critter.h file in a simple application. Here's the code, which is in the Chapter 10 folder on the CD-ROM that came with this book. (The file name is critter_app.cpp.)

```
//critter_app.cpp
//application file
```

```
#include <iostream>
#include "critter.h"

using namespace std;

int main()
{
    cout << "Instantiating a Critter object.\n\n";

    Critter crit;
    crit.Greet();

    return 0;
}
```

When I compile this program, the compiler sees the following line and uses the full Critter class definition stored in the files critter.h and critter.cpp.

```
#include "critter.h"
```

It's as if I simply dropped the class definition into the program.

When this simple program runs, it instantiates a Critter object and gets it to say hello.

Introducing the Blackjack Game

The final project for this chapter is a simplified version of the casino card game Blackjack (tacky green felt not included). The game works like this: Players are dealt cards with point values. Each player tries to reach a total of 21 without exceeding that amount. Numbered cards count as their face value. An ace counts as either one or 11 (whichever is best for the player), and any jack, queen, or king counts as 10.

The computer is the house (the casino) and it competes against one to seven players. At the beginning of the round, all participants (including the house) are dealt two cards. Players can see all of their cards, along with their total. However, one of house's cards is hidden for the time being.

Next, each player gets the chance to take one additional card at a time for as long as he likes. If a player's total exceeds 21 (known as *busting*), the player loses. After all players have had the chance to take additional cards, the house reveals its hidden card. The house must then take additional cards as long as its total is 16 or less. If the house busts, all players who have not busted win. Otherwise, each remaining player's total is compared to the house's total. If the player's total is greater than the house's, he wins. If the player's total is less than the house's, he loses. If the two totals are the same, the player ties the house (also known as *pushing*). Figure 10.7 shows the game.

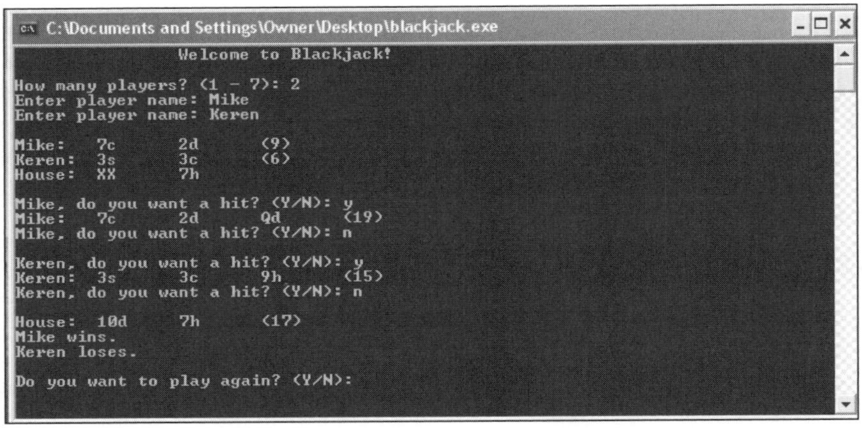

Figure 10.7
One player wins; the other is not so lucky.

Designing the Classes

Before you start coding a project with multiple classes, it is helpful to map them out on paper. You might make a list and include a brief description of each class. Table 10.1 shows my first pass at such a list for the Blackjack game.

Table 10.1 Blackjack Classes

Class	Base Class	Description
Card	None	A Blackjack playing card.
Hand	None	A Blackjack hand. A collection of Card objects.
Deck	Hand	A Blackjack deck. Has extra functionality that Hand doesn't, such as shuffling and dealing.
GenericPlayer	Hand	A generic Blackjack player. Not a full player, but the common elements of a human player and the computer player.
Player	GenericPlayer	A human Blackjack player.
House	GenericPlayer	The computer player, the house.
Game	None	A Blackjack game.

To keep things simple, all member functions will be public and all data members will be protected. Also, I'll use only public inheritance, which means that each derived class will inherit all of its base class members.

In addition to describing your classes in words, it helps to draw a family tree of sorts to visualize how your classes are related. That's what I did in Figure 10.8.

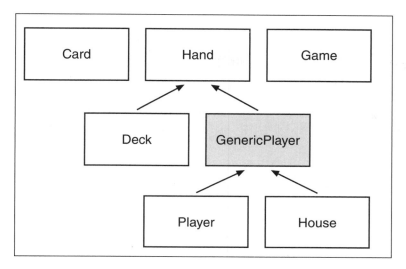

Figure 10.8
Inheritance hierarchy of classes for the Blackjack game. `GenericPlayer` is
shaded because it turns out to be an abstract class.

Next, it's a good idea to get more specific. Ask yourself about the classes. What exactly will they represent? What will they be able to do? How will they work with the other classes?

I see `Card` objects as real-life cards. You don't copy a card when you deal it from the deck to a hand; you move it. For me, that means `Hand` will have a data member that is a vector of pointers to `Card` objects, which will exist on the heap. When a card moves from one `Hand` to another, it's really pointers that are being copied and destroyed.

I see players (the human players and the computer) as Blackjack hands with names. That's why I derive `Player` and `House` (indirectly) from `Hand`. (Another equally valid view is that players have a hand. If I had gone this route, `Player` and `House` would have had `Hand` data members, instead of being derived from `Hand`.)

I define `GenericPlayer` to house the functionality that `Player` and `House` share, as opposed to duplicating this functionality in both classes.

Also, I see the deck as separate from the house. The deck will deal cards to the human players and the computer-controlled house in the same way. This means that `Deck` will have a member function to deal cards that is polymorphic and will work with either a `Player` or a `House` object.

To really flesh things out, you can list the data members and member functions that you think the classes will have, along with a brief description of each. That's what I do next in Tables 10.2 through 10.8. For each class, I list only the members I define in it. Several classes will, of course, be inherited members from base classes.

Table 10.2 Card Class

Member	Description
rank m_Rank	Rank of the card (ace, 2, 3, and so on). rank is an enumeration for all 13 ranks.
suit m_Suit	Suit of the card (clubs, diamonds, hearts, or spades). suit is an enumeration for the four possible suits.
bool m_IsFaceUp	Indicates whether the card is face up. Affects how the card is displayed and the value it has.
int GetValue()	Returns the value of the card.
void Flip()	Flips a card. Face up becomes face down, and face down becomes face up.

Table 10.3 Hand Class

Member	Description
vector<Card*> m_Cards	Collection of cards. Stores pointers to Card objects.
void Add(Card* pCard)	Adds a card to the hand. Adds a pointer to Card to the vector m_Cards.
void Clear()	Clears all cards from the hand. Removes all pointers in the vector m_Cards, deleting all associated Card objects on the heap.
int GetTotal() const	Returns the total value of the hand.

Table 10.4 GenericPlayer Class (Abstract)

Member	Description
string m_Name	Generic player's name.
virtual bool IsHitting() const = 0	Indicates whether the generic player wants another hit. Pure virtual function.
bool IsBusted() const	Indicates whether the generic player is busted.
void Bust() const	Announces that the generic player busts.

Table 10.5 Player Class

Member	Description
`virtual bool IsHitting() const`	Indicates whether the player wants another hit.
`void Win() const`	Announces that the player wins.
`void Lose() const`	Announces that the player loses.
`void Push() const`	Announces that the player pushes.

Table 10.6 House Class

Member	Description
`virtual bool IsHitting() const`	Indicates whether the house is taking another hit.
`void FlipFirstCard()`	Flips over the first card.

Table 10.7 Deck Class

Member	Description
`void Populate()`	Creates a standard deck of 52 cards.
`void Shuffle()`	Shuffles cards.
`void Deal(Hand& aHand)`	Deals one card to a hand.
`void AdditionalCards (GenericPlayer& aGenericPlayer)`	Gives additional cards to a generic player for as long as the generic player can and wants to hit.

Table 10.8 Game Class

Member	Description
`Deck m_Deck`	A deck of cards.
`House m_House`	The casino's hand, the house.
`vector<Player> m_Players`	Collection of human players. A vector of `Player` objects.
`void Play()`	Plays a round of Blackjack.

Planning the Game Logic

The last part of my planning is to map out the basic flow of one round of the game. I wrote some pseudocode for the `Game` class' `Play()` member function. Here's what I came up with:

```
Deal players and the house two initial cards
Hide the house's first card
Display players' and house's hands
Deal additional cards to players
Reveal house's first card
Deal additional cards to house
If house is busted
  Everyone who is not busted wins
Otherwise
  For each player
    If player isn't busted
      If player's total is greater than the house's total
        Player wins
      Otherwise if player's total is less than house's total
        Player loses
      Otherwise
        Player pushes
Remove everyone's cards
```

At this point you know a lot about the Blackjack program and you haven't even seen a single line of code yet! But that's a good thing. Planning can be as important as coding (if not more so). Because I've spent so much time describing the classes, I won't describe every part of the code. I'll just point out significant or new ideas. The code for the program is in the Chapter 10 folder on the CD-ROM that came with this book; the file name is blackjack.cpp.

The Card Class

After some initial statements, I define the `Card` class for an individual playing card.

```cpp
//Blackjack
//Plays a simple version of the casino game of blackjack; for 1 - 7 players

#include <iostream>
#include <string>
#include <vector>
#include <algorithm>
#include <ctime>

using namespace std;

class Card
{
public:
    enum rank {ACE = 1, TWO, THREE, FOUR, FIVE, SIX, SEVEN, EIGHT, NINE, TEN,
               JACK, QUEEN, KING};
    enum suit {CLUBS, DIAMONDS, HEARTS, SPADES};
```

```
        //overloading << operator so can send Card object to standard output
        friend ostream& operator<<(ostream& os, const Card& aCard);

        Card(rank r = ACE, suit s = SPADES, bool ifu = true);

        //returns the value of a card, 1 - 11
        int GetValue() const;

        //flips a card; if face up, becomes face down and vice versa
        void Flip();
private:
        rank m_Rank;
        suit m_Suit;
        bool m_IsFaceUp;
};

Card::Card(rank r, suit s, bool ifu):  m_Rank(r), m_Suit(s), m_IsFaceUp(ifu)
{}

int Card::GetValue() const
{
        //if a cards is face down, its value is 0
        int value = 0;
        if (m_IsFaceUp)
        {
            //value is number showing on card
            value = m_Rank;
            //value is 10 for face cards
            if (value > 10)
                value = 10;
        }
        return value;
}

void Card::Flip()
{
        m_IsFaceUp = !(m_IsFaceUp);
}
```

I define two enumerations, rank and suit, to use as the types for the rank and suit data members of the class, m_Rank and m_Suit. This has two benefits. First, it makes the code more readable. A suit data member will have a value such as CLUBS or HEARTS instead of 0 or 2. Second, it limits the values that these two data members can have. m_Suit can only store a value from suit, and m_Rank can only store a value from rank.

Next, I make the overloaded operator<<() function a friend of the class so I can display a Card object on the screen.

GetValue() returns a value for a Card object, which can be between 0 and 11. Aces are valued at 11. (I deal with potentially counting them as 1 in the Hand class, based on the other cards in the hand.) A face-down card has a value of 0.

The Hand Class

I define the Hand class for a collection of cards.

```
class Hand
{
public:
    Hand();

    virtual ~Hand();

    //adds a card to the hand
    void Add(Card* pCard);

    //clears hand of all cards
    void Clear();

    //gets hand total value, intelligently treats aces as 1 or 11
    int GetTotal() const;

protected:
    vector<Card*> m_Cards;
};

Hand::Hand()
{
    m_Cards.reserve(7);
}

Hand::~Hand()   //don't use the keyword virtual outside of class definition
{
    Clear();
}

void Hand::Add(Card* pCard)
{
    m_Cards.push_back(pCard);
}

void Hand::Clear()
{
    //iterate through vector, freeing all memory on the heap
    vector<Card*>::iterator iter = m_Cards.begin();
    for (iter = m_Cards.begin(); iter != m_Cards.end(); ++iter)
    {
```

```
        delete *iter;
        *iter = 0;
    }
    //clear vector of pointers
    m_Cards.clear();
}

int Hand::GetTotal() const
{
    //if no cards in hand, return 0
    if (m_Cards.empty())
        return 0;

    //if a first card has value of 0, then card is face down; return 0
    if (m_Cards[0]->GetValue() == 0)
        return 0;

    //add up card values, treat each ace as 1
    int total = 0;
    vector<Card*>::const_iterator iter;
    for (iter = m_Cards.begin(); iter != m_Cards.end(); ++iter)
        total += (*iter)->GetValue();

    //determine if hand contains an ace
    bool containsAce = false;
    for (iter = m_Cards.begin(); iter != m_Cards.end(); ++iter)
        if ((*iter)->GetValue() == Card::ACE)
            containsAce = true;

    //if hand contains ace and total is low enough, treat ace as 11
    if (containsAce && total <= 11)
        //add only 10 since we've already added 1 for the ace
        total += 10;

    return total;
}
```

trap

The destructor of the class is virtual, but notice that I don't use the keyword `virtual` outside of the class when I actually define the destructor. You only use the keyword inside the class definition. Don't worry; the destructor is still virtual.

Although I've already covered this, I want to point it out again. All of the Card objects will exist on the heap. Any collection of cards, such as a Hand object, will have a vector of pointers to a group of those objects on the heap.

The Clear() member function has an important responsibility. It not only removes all of the pointers from the vector m_Cards, but it destroys the associated Card objects and frees the memory on the heap that they occupied. This is just like a real-world Blackjack game in which cards are discarded when a round is over. The virtual class destructor calls Clear().

The GetTotal() member function returns the point total of the hand. If a hand contains an ace, it counts it as a 1 or an 11, whichever is best for the player. The program accomplishes this by checking to see whether the hand has at least one ace. If it does, the program checks to see whether treating the ace as 11 will put the hand's point total over 21. If it won't, then the ace is treated as an 11. Otherwise, it's treated as a 1.

The GenericPlayer Class

I define the GenericPlayer class for a generic Blackjack player. It doesn't represent a full player. Instead, it represents the common element of a human player and the computer player.

```
class GenericPlayer : public Hand
{
    friend ostream& operator<<(ostream& os,
                               const GenericPlayer& aGenericPlayer);

public:
    GenericPlayer(const string& name = "");

    virtual ~GenericPlayer();

    //indicates whether or not generic player wants to keep hitting
    virtual bool IsHitting() const = 0;

    //returns whether generic player has busted - has a total greater than 21
    bool IsBusted() const;

    //announces that the generic player busts
    void Bust() const;

protected:
    string m_Name;
};

GenericPlayer::GenericPlayer(const string& name): m_Name(name)
{}

GenericPlayer::~GenericPlayer()
{}

bool GenericPlayer::IsBusted() const
{
```

```
        return (GetTotal() > 21);
}

void GenericPlayer::Bust() const
{
        cout << m_Name << " busts.\n";
}
```

I make the overloaded operator<<() function a friend of the class so I can display GenericPlayer objects on the screen. It accepts a reference to a GenericPlayer object, which means that it can accept a reference to a Player or House object, too.

The constructor accepts a string object for the name of the generic player. The destructor is automatically virtual because it inherits this trait from Hand.

The IsHitting() member function indicates whether a generic player wants another card. Because this member function doesn't have a real meaning for a generic player, I made it a pure virtual function. Therefore, GenericPlayer becomes an abstract class. This also means that both Player and House need to implement their own versions of this member function.

The IsBusted() member function indicates whether a generic player has busted. Because players and the house bust the same way—by having a total greater than 21—I put the definition in this class.

The Bust() member function announces that the generic player busts. Because busting is announced the same way for players and the house, I put the definition of the member function in this class.

The Player Class

The Player class represents a human player. It's derived from GenericPlayer.

```
class Player : public GenericPlayer
{
public:
        Player(const string& name = "");

        virtual ~Player();

        //returns whether or not the player wants another hit
        virtual bool IsHitting() const;

        //announces that the player wins
        void Win() const;

        //announces that the player loses
        void Lose() const;
```

```
        //announces that the player pushes
        void Push() const;
};

Player::Player(const string& name): GenericPlayer(name)
{}

Player::~Player()
{}

bool Player::IsHitting() const
{
    cout << m_Name << ", do you want a hit? (Y/N): ";
    char response;
    cin >> response;
    return (response == 'y' || response == 'Y');
}

void Player::Win() const
{
    cout << m_Name <<  " wins.\n";
}

void Player::Lose() const
{
    cout << m_Name <<  " loses.\n";
}

void Player::Push() const
{
    cout << m_Name <<  " pushes.\n";
}
```

The class implements the IsHitting() member function that it inherits from GenericPlayer.
Therefore, Player isn't abstract. The class implements the member function by asking the
human whether he wants to keep hitting. If the human enters y or Y in response to the
question, the member function returns true, indicating that the player is still hitting. If the
human enters a different character, the member function returns false, indicating that the
player is no longer hitting.

The Win(), Lose(), and Push() member functions simply announce that a player has won,
lost, or pushed, respectively.

The House Class

The House class represents the house. It's derived from GenericPlayer.

```
class House : public GenericPlayer
{
```

```
public:
    House(const string& name = "House");

    virtual ~House();

    //indicates whether house is hitting - will always hit on 16 or less
    virtual bool IsHitting() const;

    //flips over first card
    void FlipFirstCard();
};

House::House(const string& name): GenericPlayer(name)
{}

House::~House()
{}

bool House::IsHitting() const
{
    return (GetTotal() <= 16);
}

void House::FlipFirstCard()
{
    if (!(m_Cards.empty()))
        m_Cards[0]->Flip();
    else cout << "No card to flip!\n";
}
```

The class implements the IsHitting() member function that it inherits from GenericPlayer. Therefore, House isn't abstract. The class implements the member function by calling GetTotal(). If the returned total value is less than or equal to 16, the member function returns true, indicating that the house is still hitting. Otherwise, it returns false, indicating that the house is no longer hitting.

FlipFirstCard() flips the house's first card. This member function is necessary because the house hides its first card at the beginning of the round and then reveals it after all of the players have taken all of their additional cards.

The Deck Class

The Deck class represents a deck of cards. It's derived from Hand.

```
class Deck : public Hand
{
public:
    Deck();
```

```cpp
        virtual ~Deck();

        //create a standard deck of 52 cards
        void Populate();

        //shuffle cards
        void Shuffle();

        //deal one card to a hand
        void Deal(Hand& aHand);

        //give additional cards to a generic player
        void AdditionalCards(GenericPlayer& aGenericPlayer);
};

Deck::Deck()
{
    m_Cards.reserve(52);
    Populate();
}

Deck::~Deck()
{}

void Deck::Populate()
{
    Clear();
    //create standard deck
    for (int s = Card::CLUBS; s <= Card::SPADES; ++s)
            for (int r = Card::ACE; r <= Card::KING; ++r)
                Add(new Card(static_cast<Card::rank>(r),
                            static_cast<Card::suit>(s)));
}

void Deck::Shuffle()
{
    random_shuffle(m_Cards.begin(), m_Cards.end());
}

void Deck::Deal(Hand& aHand)
{
    if (!m_Cards.empty())
    {
        aHand.Add(m_Cards.back());
        m_Cards.pop_back();
    }
    else
    {
        cout << "Out of cards. Unable to deal.";
    }
}
```

```
void Deck::AdditionalCards(GenericPlayer& aGenericPlayer)
{
    cout << endl;
    //continue to deal a card as long as generic player isn't busted and
    //wants another hit
    while ( !(aGenericPlayer.IsBusted()) && aGenericPlayer.IsHitting() )
    {
        Deal(aGenericPlayer);
        cout << aGenericPlayer << endl;

        if (aGenericPlayer.IsBusted())
            aGenericPlayer.Bust();
    }
}
```

hint

Type casting is a way of converting a value of one type to a value of another type. One way to do type casting is to use `static_cast`. You use `static_cast` to return a value of a new type from a value of another type by specifying the new type you want between < and >, followed by the value from which you want to get a new value between parentheses. Here's an example that returns the double value 5.0.

```
static_cast<double>(5);
```

`Populate()` creates a standard deck of 52 cards. The member function loops through all of the possible combinations of `Card::suit` and `Card::rank` values. It uses `static_cast` to cast the `int` loop variables to the proper enumerated types defined in `Card`.

`Shuffle()` shuffles the cards in the deck. It randomly rearranges the pointers in `m_Cards` with `random_shuffle()` from the Standard Template Library. This is the reason I include the `<algorithm>` header file.

`Deal()` deals one card from the deck to a hand. It adds a copy of the pointer stored in the last element of the `Deck` object's `m_Cards` vector to the `Hand` object's `m_Cards` vector. Then it removes the pointer from the `Deck` object's `m_Cards` vector, effectively transferring the card. The powerful thing about `Deal()` is that it accepts a reference to a `Hand` object, which means it can work equally well with a `Player` or a `House` object. And through the magic of polymorphism, `Deal()` can call the object's `Add()` member function without knowing the exact object type.

`AdditionalCards()` gives additional cards to a generic player until the generic player either stops hitting or busts. The member function accepts reference to a `GenericPlayer` object so you can pass a `Player` or `House` object to it. Again, through the magic of polymorphism, `AdditionalCards()` doesn't have to know whether it's working with a `Player` or a `House` object. It can call the `IsBusted()` and `IsHitting()` member functions for the object without knowing the object's type, and the correct code will be executed.

The Game Class

The Game class represents a game of Blackjack.

```
class Game
{
public:
    Game(const vector<string>& names);

    ~Game();

    //plays the game of blackjack
    void Play();

private:
    Deck m_Deck;
    House m_House;
    vector<Player> m_Players;
};

Game::Game(const vector<string>& names)
{
    //create a vector of players from a vector of names
    vector<string>::const_iterator pName;
    for (pName = names.begin(); pName != names.end(); ++pName)
        m_Players.push_back(Player(*pName));

    srand(time(0));      //seed the random number generator
    m_Deck.Populate();
    m_Deck.Shuffle();
}

Game::~Game()
{}

void Game::Play()
{
    //deal initial 2 cards to everyone
    vector<Player>::iterator pPlayer;
    for (int i = 0; i < 2; ++i)
    {
        for (pPlayer = m_Players.begin(); pPlayer != m_Players.end();
             ++pPlayer)
            m_Deck.Deal(*pPlayer);
        m_Deck.Deal(m_House);
    }

    //hide house's first card
    m_House.FlipFirstCard();
```

```
//display everyone's hand
for (pPlayer = m_Players.begin(); pPlayer != m_Players.end(); ++pPlayer)
    cout << *pPlayer << endl;
cout << m_House << endl;

//deal additional cards to players
for (pPlayer = m_Players.begin(); pPlayer != m_Players.end(); ++pPlayer)
    m_Deck.AdditionalCards(*pPlayer);

//reveal house's first card
m_House.FlipFirstCard();
cout << endl << m_House;

//deal additional cards to house
m_Deck.AdditionalCards(m_House);

if (m_House.IsBusted())
{
    //everyone still playing wins
    for (pPlayer = m_Players.begin(); pPlayer != m_Players.end();
        ++pPlayer)
        if ( !(pPlayer->IsBusted()) )
            pPlayer->Win();
}
else
{
    //compare each player still playing to house
    for (pPlayer = m_Players.begin(); pPlayer != m_Players.end();
        ++pPlayer)
        if ( !(pPlayer->IsBusted()) )
        {
            if (pPlayer->GetTotal() > m_House.GetTotal())
                pPlayer->Win();
            else if (pPlayer->GetTotal() < m_House.GetTotal())
                pPlayer->Lose();
            else
                pPlayer->Push();
        }
}

//remove everyone's cards
for (pPlayer = m_Players.begin(); pPlayer != m_Players.end(); ++pPlayer)
    pPlayer->Clear();
m_House.Clear();
}
```

The class constructor accepts a reference to a vector of string objects, which represent the names of the human players. The constructor instantiates a Player object with each name. Next, it seeds the random number generator, and then it populates and shuffles the deck.

The Play() member function faithfully implements the pseudocode I wrote earlier about how a round of play should be implemented.

The main() Function

After declaring the overloaded operator<<() functions, I write the program's main() function.

```
//function prototypes
ostream& operator<<(ostream& os, const Card& aCard);
ostream& operator<<(ostream& os, const GenericPlayer& aGenericPlayer);

int main()
{
    cout << "\t\tWelcome to Blackjack!\n\n";

    int numPlayers = 0;
    while (numPlayers < 1 || numPlayers > 7)
    {
        cout << "How many players? (1 - 7): ";
        cin >> numPlayers;
    }

    vector<string> names;
    string name;
    for (int i = 0; i < numPlayers; ++i)
    {
        cout << "Enter player name: ";
        cin >> name;
        names.push_back(name);
    }
    cout << endl;

    //the game loop
    Game aGame(names);
    char again = 'y';
    while (again != 'n' && again != 'N')
    {
        aGame.Play();
        cout << "\nDo you want to play again? (Y/N): ";
        cin >> again;
    }

    return 0;
}
```

The main() function gets the names of all the players and puts them into a vector of string objects, and then instantiates a Game object, passing a reference to the vector. The main() function keeps calling the Game object's Play() member function until the players indicate that they don't want to play anymore.

Overloading the operator<<() Function

The following function definition overloads the << operator so I can send a Card object to the standard output.

```
//overloads << operator so Card object can be sent to cout
ostream& operator<<(ostream& os, const Card& aCard)
{
    const string RANKS[] = {"0", "A", "2", "3", "4", "5", "6", "7", "8", "9",
                            "10", "J", "Q", "K"};
    const string SUITS[] = {"c", "d", "h", "s"};

    if (aCard.m_IsFaceUp)
        os << RANKS[aCard.m_Rank] << SUITS[aCard.m_Suit];
    else
        os << "XX";

    return os;
}
```

The function uses the rank and suit values of the object as array indices. I begin the array RANKS with "0" to compensate for the fact that the value for the rank enumeration defined in Card begins at 1.

The last function definition overloads the << operator so I can send a GenericPlayer object to the standard output.

```
//overloads << operator so a GenericPlayer object can be sent to cout
ostream& operator<<(ostream& os, const GenericPlayer& aGenericPlayer)
{
    os << aGenericPlayer.m_Name << ":\t";

    vector<Card*>::const_iterator pCard;
    if (!aGenericPlayer.m_Cards.empty())
    {
        for (pCard = aGenericPlayer.m_Cards.begin();
             pCard != aGenericPlayer.m_Cards.end(); ++pCard)
            os << *(*pCard) << "\t";

        if (aGenericPlayer.GetTotal() != 0)
            cout << "(" << aGenericPlayer.GetTotal() << ")";
    }
    else
    {
        os << "<empty>";
    }
    return os;
}
```

The function displays the generic player's name and cards, along with the total value of the cards.

Summary

In this chapter, you should have learned the following concepts:

- One of the key elements of OOP is inheritance, which allows you to derive a new class from an existing one. The new class automatically inherits data members and member functions from the existing class.

- A derived class does not inherit constructors, copy constructors, destructors, or an overloaded assignment operator.

- Base class constructors are automatically called before the derived class constructor when a derived class object is instantiated.

- Base class destructors are automatically called after the derived class destructor when a derived class object is destroyed.

- Protected members are accessible only in their own class and certain derived classes, depending upon the derivation access level.

- Using public derivation means that public members in the base class become public members in the derived class, protected members in the base class become protected members in the derived class, and private members are (as always) inaccessible.

- You can override base class member functions by giving them new definitions in a derived class.

- You can explicitly call a base class member function from a derived class.

- You can explicitly call the base class constructor from a derived class instructor.

- Polymorphism is the quality whereby a member function will produce different results depending on the type of object for which it is called.

- Virtual functions allow for polymorphic behavior.

- Once a member function is defined as virtual, it's virtual in any derived class.

- Slicing is essentially the act of cutting off part of an object.

- A pure virtual function is a function to which you don't need to give a definition. You specify a pure virtual function by placing an equal sign and a zero at the end of the function header.

- An abstract class has at least one pure virtual member function.

- An abstract class can't be used to instantiate an object.

- You can split your programs among multiple files.

Questions and Answers

Q: How many levels of inheritance can you have?

A: Theoretically, as many as you want. But as a beginning programmer, you should keep things simple and try not to go beyond a few levels.

Q: Is friendship inherited? That is, if a function is a friend of a base class, is it automatically a friend of a derived class?

A: No.

Q: Can a class have more than one direct base class?

A: Yes. This is called *multiple inheritance*. It's powerful, but it creates its own set of thorny issues.

Q: Why would you want to call a base class constructor from a derived class constructor?

A: So you can control exactly how the base class constructor is called. For example, you might want to pass specific values to the base class constructor.

Q: Are there any dangers in overriding a base class function?

A: Yes. By overriding a base class member function, you hide all of the overloaded versions of the function in the base class. However, you can still call a hidden base class member function explicitly by using the base class name and the scope resolution operator.

Q: How can I solve this problem of hiding base class functions?

A: One way is to override all of the overloaded version of the base class function.

Q: Why do you usually want to call the assignment operator member function of the base class from the assignment operator member function of a derived class?

A: So that any base class data members can be properly assigned.

Q: Why do you usually want to call the copy constructor of a base class from the copy constructor of a derived class?

A: So that any base class data members can be properly copied.

Q: Why can you lose access to an object's member functions when you point to it with a base class member?

A: Because non-virtual functions are called based on the pointer type and the object type.

Q: Why not make all member functions virtual, just in case you ever need polymorphic behavior from them?

A: Because there's a performance cost associated with making member functions virtual.

Q: When should you make a destructor virtual?

A: If you have any virtual member functions in a class, you should make the destructor virtual, too. However, some programmers say that to be safe, you should always make a destructor virtual.

Q: Can constructors be virtual?

A: No. This also means that copy constructors can't be declared as virtual either.

Q: What good are abstract classes if you can't instantiate any objects from them?

A: Abstract classes can be very useful. They can contain many common class members that other classes will inherit, which saves you the effort of defining those members over and over again.

Q: Why split your programs into multiple files?

A: It might be convenient to put all of the code for small programs into one file, but it becomes unwieldy to work with a single file for large projects.

Q: Is it really necessary to use the #ifndef, #endif, and #define directives in my header files?

A: Yes. Although you might not really need them in some projects, it's not uncommon for fundamental header files to be included across many files. And using the directives can prevent your project from trying to include the same file more than once.

Discussion Questions

1. What benefits does inheritance bring to game programming?
2. How does polymorphism expand the power of inheritance?
3. What kinds of game entities might it make sense to model through inheritance?
4. What kinds of game-related classes would be best implemented as abstract?
5. Why is it advantageous to be able to point to a derived class object with a base class pointer?

Exercises

1. Split the Blackjack game program into multiple files based on individual classes.
2. Improve the Blackjack game program by forcing the deck to repopulate before a round if the number of cards is running low.
3. In the Blackjack game program, define copy constructors and overloaded assignment operator member functions to the Hand class and all of its subclasses.

INDEX

Gamedev.net

The most comprehensive game development resource

- The latest news in game development
- The most active forums and chatrooms anywhere, with insights and tips from experienced game developers
- Links to thousands of additional game development resources
- Thorough book and product reviews
- Over 1000 game development articles!
  Game design
  Graphics
  DirectX
  OpenGL
  AI
  Art
  Music
  Physics
  Source Code
  Sound
  Assembly
  And More!

Gamedev.net

License Agreement/Notice of Limited Warranty